STUDIES IN BIOETHICS

THE END OF LIFE

STUDIES IN BIOETHICS

General Editor *Peter Singer*

Studies in Bioethics is a series aimed at introducing more rigorous argument into the discussion of ethical issues in medicine and the biological sciences.

THE END
OF LIFE

Euthanasia and Morality

JAMES RACHELS

Oxford   New York   Melbourne
OXFORD UNIVERSITY PRESS

Oxford University Press, Walton Street, Oxford OX2 6DP

Oxford New York Toronto
Delhi Bombay Calcutta Madras Karachi
Petaling Jaya Singapore Hong Kong Tokyo
Nairobi Dar es Salaam Cape Town
Melbourne Auckland

and associated companies in
Beirut Berlin Ibadan Nicosia

Oxford is a trade mark of Oxford University Press

First published 1986 as an Oxford University Press
paperback and simultaneously in a hardback edition

Oxford paperback reprinted 1987

British Library Cataloguing in Publication Data

Rachels, James
The end of life: the morality of euthanasia.
—(Studies in bioethics)
1. Euthanasia 2. Medical ethics
I. Title II. Series
174'.24 R 726
ISBN 0-19-217746-X
ISBN 0-19-286070-4 Pbk

Library of Congress Cataloging in Publication Data

Rachels, James, 1941–
The end of life.
(Studies in bioethics)
Includes bibliographical references and index.
1. Euthanasia. I. Title. II. Series.
R726.R33 1986 174'24 85-15561
ISBN 0-19-217746-X
ISBN 0-19-286070-4 (pbk.)

Set by Colset Private Ltd.
Printed in Great Britain by
Richard Clay Ltd.
Bungay, Suffolk

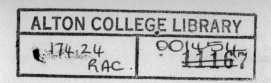
CONTENTS

INTRODUCTION

David Hume, the great Scottish philosopher of the eighteenth century, remarked that the aim of philosophy should be to replace 'superstition and false religion' with reason and understanding. Hume realized that our thinking about even the most common-place matters may be corrupted by false assumptions—and we may take these assumptions so much for granted that we never even think of questioning them. Our moral thinking is especially vulner-able to this sort of corruption. We absorb the prejudices of our culture and the mistakes of our parents, mix in the pronounce-ments of our religion, add the influence of our selfishness, and then regard the resulting beliefs as the merest common sense. We end up, like the Greeks and Callatians in Herodotus' story, with strong convictions but with little to support them:

Darius, after he had got the kingdom, called into his presence certain Greeks who were at hand, and asked—'What he should pay them to eat the bodies of their fathers when they died?' To which they answered, that there was no sum that would tempt them to do such a thing. He then sent for certain Indians, of the race called Callatians, men who eat their fathers, and asked them, while the Greeks stood by, and knew by the help of an interpreter all that was said—'What he should give them to burn the bodies of their fathers at their decease?' The Indians exclaimed aloud, and bade him forbear such language. Such is men's wont herein; and Pindar was right, in my judgement, when he said, 'Custom is the king o'er all.'

Herodotus concluded from this that morality is nothing more than customs and feelings—and indeed, it is easy for morality to degen-erate into that, if we are content with 'superstition and false reli-gion'. But morality should be a matter of reason as well as feeling. Following Hume's admonition, we should ask *why* we accept the rules we do, what interests (if any) they serve, and what values (if any) they protect.

In this essay I shall examine the ideas and assumptions that lie

Finish it

behind one of the most important moral rules, the rule against killing. Killing people is, in general, wrong. But why is it wrong, and when may exceptions be made?

In considering these questions, I will assume that moral philosophy may be revisionary, and not merely descriptive. It is not our business simply to expound what we already happen to believe. What we believe may be naive or mistaken. I shall assume that we may reject received opinion if it goes against reason. Where killing is concerned, I believe that the dominant moral tradition of our culture is, in fact, contrary to reason. The material presented in this essay adds up to a systematic argument against the traditional view and a defence of an alternative account.

The traditional view

Consider the recent case of Hans Florian and his wife. They had been married for thirty-three years when he shot her dead. She was a victim of Alzheimer's disease, which attacks the brain, and for which there is no known cause or cure. The effects of the disease are devastating. The deterioration of the brain can be traced through several stages, as the victim loses all semblance of human personality.

Soon after the onset of the disease, Mrs Florian began to lose the ability to do simple chores and, at the same time, began to develop abnormal fears. She could not drive or write, and would panic when her husband would leave the room. As the disease progressed, he would have to feed her by forcing her mouth open, and he would bathe her and change her clothes several times each day as she soiled them. Then her vocabulary shrank to two words: 'fire' and 'pain', screamed in her native German. Finally, she had to be placed in a nursing home for her own safety. Although her condition was irreversible, it was not 'terminal'—she could have lived on, in this deranged state, indefinitely.

Was it wrong for Hans Florian to have killed his wife? He explained that he killed her because, being seventeen years older, he did not want to die first and leave her alone. Legally, of course, he had no right to do it. Under American law, he could have been found guilty of murder in the first degree—although no charges were brought, because the Florida grand jury refused to indict him. (As we shall see, juries often react this way in such cases.) But, legal questions aside, was his act *immoral*?

We may certainly feel sympathy for Hans Florian; he faced a terrible situation, and acted from honourable motives. Nevertheless, according to the dominant moral tradition of our culture, what he did was indefensible. He intentionally killed an innocent human being, and, according to our tradition, that is always wrong. This tradition is largely the product of Christian teaching. Christianity says, of course, that every human being is made in the image of God, and so all human life is sacred. Killing a person, even one so pitiable as Mrs Florian, is therefore an offence against the Creator.

Most people in the Western world accept some such perspective as this. Even those who imagine themselves to have rejected this way of thinking continue, more often than not, to be influenced by it—it is not easy to shrug off the values of the culture in which one has been raised and educated. Thus, even those who reject the old theological ideas may continue to accept their secular equivalents —if one no longer believes that human life is 'sacred', then one can at least believe that human life is 'intrinsically valuable' or that 'every human life has a special dignity and worth'. And, on the strength of this, one may continue to doubt whether Mr Florian acted correctly.

The traditional view is not, however, a simple view. Through the centuries various thinkers have contributed to its development, and a complex account of the morality of killing has resulted. This account appeals to a series of distinctions that, taken together, define a class of actions said to be absolutely forbidden. In deciding whether a particular killing is permissible, the method is to apply the distinctions to determine whether the act falls into the forbidden class.

Some of these distinctions have to do with the status of the victim: for example, the distinction between human and non-human is held to be crucial. At the heart of the traditional doctrine is the idea that the protection of *human* life—all human life—is immensely important. If one is human, and alive, then according to the traditional view one's life is sacred. At the same time, *non-human* life is given relatively little importance. So, in general, killing people is said to be gravely wrong, while killing other animals requires almost no justification at all.

But this does not mean that killing people can never be justified. Sometimes it is justified, and here it matters a great deal whether the human in question is 'innocent'. Capital punishment and killing in war are traditionally sanctioned, on the grounds that the people who are killed are not innocent. It is the killing of the *innocent*, such as Mrs Florian, that is prohibited.

Other traditional distinctions focus on other qualities of the act; for example, it matters whether the killing would be *intentional*. (Like 'innocent', 'intentional' is something of a technical term, whose meaning we will have occasion to examine later.) It is *the intentional killing of innocent humans* that is absolutely forbidden.

But perhaps the most interesting of the traditional distinctions is between *killing people* and merely *letting people die*. On the traditional view, even though killing innocent people is forbidden, letting them die is sometimes permitted. This is especially important in considering what may or may not be done in medical treatment. The point is that we are not always required to use every available resource to prolong life, even if it is the life of an innocent human. When extraordinary means are required to keep someone alive, those means may be omitted. (The use of *ordinary* treatments is morally mandatory, but *extraordinary* treatments are optional—this is another of the distinctions the traditional view finds so important.)

The traditional theory must be taken seriously; not only has its influence been enormous, but from a philosophical point of view it is the only fully worked-out, systematically elaborated theory of the subject we have. Its development has been one of the great intellectual achievements of Western culture, accomplished by thinkers of great ingenuity and high moral purpose. However, I shall be mainly interested in the question of whether this theory is *true*—granted that it has history and tradition on its side, still we may ask whether there is good reason for a rational person to accept it.

If the traditional theory is not true, then in our society many decisions concerning life and death are being made on unsound grounds, and the law concerning such matters is badly in need of reform. I believe that the traditional view is mistaken at almost every point. The maze of distinctions on which it is based cannot withstand analysis. Much of this essay is a defence of that judgement.

An alternative view

To replace the traditional view, I offer a different way of looking at such matters. The alternative view begins by pointing out that there is a deep difference between *having a life* and merely *being alive*. The point of the moral rule against killing is not to keep 'innocent humans' alive. Being alive, in the biological sense, is relatively unimportant. One's *life*, by contrast, is immensely important; it is the sum of one's aspirations, decisions, activities, projects, and human relationships. The point of the rule against killing is the protection of *lives* and the interests that some beings, including ourselves, have in virtue of the fact that we are subjects of lives. Only by paying careful attention to the concept of a life can we understand the value of life and the evil of death.

The details of this account are strikingly different from the traditional approach. The distinction between human and non-human turns out to be less important than has been assumed. From a moral point of view, it is the protection of lives that is important, and so, because most humans have lives, killing them is objectionable. However, some unfortunate humans, such as Mrs Florian, do not have lives, even though they are alive; and so killing *them* is a morally different matter. Moreover, some non-human animals also have lives, and so consistency requires that they also be protected by the rule against killing.

The other traditional distinctions—between innocence and non-innocence, intentional and non-intentional killing, and ordinary and extraordinary means—also turn out to be not so important. And, I will argue, the distinction between killing and letting die is morally insignificant as well: the fact that one act is an act of killing (for example, 'mercy-killing') while another act is an act of 'merely' letting someone die (for example, 'pulling the plug' of a life-sustaining medical device) is not in itself a reason for thinking one act morally better than the other.

The upshot is that this view is much simpler than the traditional view, in that not nearly so many things are considered important. In deciding questions of life and death, the crucial question is: Is a *life*, in the biographical sense, being destroyed or otherwise adversely affected? If not, the rule against killing offers no objection. The species of the subject of the life, and the means that are used, as well as the intention with which the act is done, are all more or less irrelevant.

As one might suspect, the implication for Mrs Florian is different from the implication of the traditional view. Although this unfortunate woman was still alive, that fact has little significance. The critical fact is that, when her husband shot her, her life was already over. He was not destroying her life; it had already been destroyed by Alzheimer's disease. Thus he was not behaving immorally.

This approach assumes a certain conception of morality. The traditional theory is often presented in theological terms, but its partisans emphasize that the religious trappings are not necessary. It is meant to be a moral view, not a religious dogma, binding on moral agents regardless of their theological convictions or lack of them. My approach is secular in this sense, plus another. It sees being moral, not as a matter of faithfulness to abstract rules or divine laws, but as a matter of doing what is best for those who are affected by our conduct. If we should not kill, it is because in killing we are *harming someone*. That is the reason killing is wrong. The rule against killing has as its point the protection of the victims.

If this seems a truism, remember Mrs Florian. This conception leads directly to the conclusion that her husband did no wrong. She was not harmed by her husband's killing her—indeed, if anything, it seems more likely that she was helped. But on the traditional view, this has little importance: Mrs Florian was an innocent human, and so she could not intentionally be killed. Against the background of the traditional view, the alternative approach emerges not as a truism but as a radical idea.

1 THE WESTERN TRADITION

The origins of the tradition

History is a liberating subject. Because our experience is so limited, we may easily assume that our opinions are the common sense of mankind, natural and unchanging. The smallest acquaintance with history teaches us the fallacy in this. The ideas that seem so self-evident to us are, in fact, the products of long and often irrational development. Far from being universally accepted, our views would seem quite strange to other peoples in other times.

Of course, this does not necessarily mean that our ideas are false. It may be that the process of historical development has finally produced, in us, true opinion. But reflecting upon the sources of our ideas may at least open our minds to other possibilities. This is especially important in ethics, where often people place such excessive faith in their feelings that they are unwilling even to consider that they might be mistaken.

Traditional accounts of Western history begin with ancient Greece, a culture whose philosophy, art, and political institutions we often admire. But the Greeks took an attitude towards human life that is very different from our own. They did not believe that all human life is precious, or that it should be preserved at all costs. In Sparta, for example, it was required by law that deformed infants be put to death—this was considered better than an unhappy life for them and their parents. For modern readers, who take a dim view of infanticide, this may not come as much of a shock: after all, Spartan morality has never enjoyed high esteem. But the approval of infanticide was not limited to Sparta. In Athens, which we consider to have been a more enlightened community, the destruction of deformed or unhealthy babies was also approved. The Athenians did not *require* that they be killed, as did the Spartans, but on the other hand there was no condemnation of the practice. It is worth remembering that we are not talking about a backward society, but about one of the world's great civilizations.

The fact that the Greeks approved infanticide is not a sign that they placed no value on human life. They were not a murderous people; and they took a stern view of some other types of killing. In general, they did not approve of suicide: Pythagoras, Plato, and Aristotle all rejected it as a cowardly way of avoiding life's hardships and one's duties to self and State. However, all three of these philosophers thought it foolish to prohibit suicide in *every* situation. They allowed that in cases of incurable disease accompanied by great pain, a person has the right to choose an earlier death. The difference between suicide and euthanasia in such cases was not thought important—if the dying person needed help to end his life, it was permitted for others to assist him.

The Greek whose views are most often remembered on this subject represented a minority of thinkers. Hippocrates, sometimes counted as the 'father of medicine', was the author of an oath still taken by new doctors; in it, they pledge *not* to practise euthanasia: 'If any shall ask of me a drug to produce death I will not give it, nor will I suggest such counsel.' This part of the Hippocratic Oath would not have been endorsed, without qualification, by the majority of Greek thinkers. Hippocrates also forbade doctors to perform abortions, although Aristotle, to name but one dissenter, thought abortion was acceptable.

The Romans shared many of the Greeks' attitudes. The Stoic philosopher Seneca, for example, wrote without apology, 'We destroy monstrous births, and drown our children if they are born weakly and unnaturally formed.' There was, in the code of Justinian, an attempt to limit abortion, but the reason was to protect the right of the father to his children—the child's interests do not seem to have mattered. If anything, the Romans regarded killing—in special circumstances—even more indifferently than the Greeks. The Stoic and Epicurean philosophers thought suicide an acceptable option *whenever* one no longer cares for life. The most famous statement of this view is by Epictetus: 'If the room is smoky, if only moderately, I will stay; if there is too much smoke I will go. Remember this, keep a firm hold on it, the door is always open.' To those with such a frame of mind, it seemed obvious that a wise person will not avoid death at any cost, but will choose it at the right time. Seneca, again, wrote:

I will not relinquish old age if it leaves my better part intact. But if it begins to shake my mind, if it destroys my faculties one by one, if it leaves me not life but breath, I will depart from the putrid or the tottering edifice. If I know that I must suffer without hope of relief I will depart not through fear of the pain but because it prevents all for which I would live.

There was no controlling doctrine about killing, among either the Greeks or the Romans, that could properly be called 'orthodox'. The nearest thing to an orthodoxy was the idea that life itself, apart from the chance of a meaningful or happy existence, has little value. The approach of most thinkers to moral questions of life and death was decidedly unsystematic: each kind of killing—infanticide, euthanasia, and so on—was treated independently. The result, as we have seen, was a set of attitudes toward killing much less strict than those to which twentieth-century Westerners are accustomed.

The coming of Christianity caused vast changes in these attitudes. In its first three centuries, the Church had no official position on the morality of killing. In fact, it is a little misleading to speak of 'the Church' during this early period; before the conversion of Constantine, there were only the various Christian communities, without central authority. Yet there was a kind of consensus among Christian thinkers even at this early date. They were, by and large, resolutely pacifist, opposing the killing of humans in almost every context. The Church fathers embraced the principle that killing human beings is always wrong, and permitted exceptions only in a few odd cases. For example, a virgin was permitted to commit suicide to avoid being raped. (Among early Christians virginity in women was very highly prized.) But even this permission was withdrawn when St Augustine argued that chastity is a more a matter of the mind than the body, and there is no record of how many women took advantage of it. Some Church thinkers also conceded that homicide would be permitted upon a special direct command from God. Beyond these odd exceptions, however, killing humans was absolutely forbidden. Later, more substantial exceptions were to be admitted, so that the Church's doctrine was not so radical. But in the beginning the strictness of this precept set the Christians very much against the prevailing culture.

Infanticide was prohibited, for it was thought that all who are born of woman, no matter how monstrous or miserable, are made in God's image. Suicide was forbidden because one's life was viewed as a trust from God, and only He had the right to take it. The same was said about euthanasia. Under the influence of the Church, what for the Greek and Roman philosophers had been a compassionate solution to the problem of lingering, degrading death became a mortal sin. Suffering, no matter how horrible or seemingly pointless, came to be viewed as a burden imposed by God himself, for purposes known only to him, which men and women must bear until the 'natural' end.

Considering the non-pacifist views of most modern Christians, it may be surprising to learn that participation in warfare was also condemned by the early Church: even killing sanctioned by the State, or in self-defence, was forbidden. The Latin fathers—Lactantius, Tertullian, Origen—were all in agreement on this. It is not difficult to see why. Jesus himself had taught strict non-violence. He said, according to St Matthew,

Do not resist one who is evil. But if anyone strikes you on the right cheek, turn to him the other also . . . You have heard that it was said, 'You shall love your neighbour and hate your enemy.' But I say to you, Love your enemies and pray for those who persecute you.

Apparently the early Church fathers simply took this teaching at face value. Of war, Tertullian wrote, quoting Jesus again, 'Can it be lawful to handle the sword, when the Lord himself has declared that he who uses the sword shall perish by it?'

The Church continued to denounce infanticide, suicide, and euthanasia, but it soon modified its position on war. One interpretation of this change might be that, despite the teachings of Jesus, Christians came to recognize a valid moral difference between killing in a just war and other forms of homicide. A different view is taken by the sociologist–philosopher Edward Westermarck, who remarked in his classic work *Christianity and Morals*,

A divine law which prohibited all resistance to enemies could certainly not be accepted by the State, especially at a time when the empire was seriously threatened by foreign invaders. Christianity could therefore never become a State religion unless it gave up its attitude towards war. And it gave it up.

The early Church had also condemned capital punishment, which was not surprising considering the number of Church figures, including Jesus himself and St Peter, who had been executed. But this position, too, was soon modified, bringing the Church's stance more into line with political requirements. The imposition of death as punishment was said to be all right, so long as priests took no part in the proceedings.

The doctrine of innocence

These developments forced the Church to face a problem of moral theory. As long as all killing was condemned, it was clear what principle the Church followed. The principle was very simple: all killing of human beings is wrong. But after war and capital punishment were accepted, that principle could no longer be claimed. What, then, was the new principle the Church affirmed? What principle would allow killing both in war and as punishment, while prohibiting it in the other cases?

The key to solving this problem was found in the idea that neither the enemy soldier nor the criminal is 'innocent'. The enemy soldier is not innocent because, assuming his side is not in the right, he unjustly threatens the lives of others. The criminal is not innocent because, assuming the laws of the State are just, he has violated just laws. The principle affirmed by the Church, then, was not the simple rule that killing humans is always wrong. It was the more sophisticated principle: the intentional killing of *innocent* humans is always wrong.

This principle came to dominate the thinking of almost everyone who tried to reason systematically about the morality of killing. For centuries during the Middle Ages it was regarded as a self-evident truth; nothing more was required to clinch the case against a form of homicide than to invoke the principle. 'Infanticide, suicide, and euthanasia are all the direct killing of the innocent; therefore, they are forbidden. Killing in a just war, and the lawful execution of criminals, are not the killing of innocents; therefore, they are not forbidden.'

We find this reasoning repeated time and again. To cite but one example: in arguing that suicide is not permitted, St Thomas Aquinas follows the lead of St Augustine, who emphasized that the rule against killing does not merely prohibit the killing of *other* men, but prohibits killing *men*. Augustine wrote, 'The commandment is, "Thou shalt not kill man"; therefore neither another nor yourself, for he who kills himself still kills nothing else but man.' To this Aquinas added that, in killing oneself, one kills an *innocent* person, and, he reminds us, 'It is in no way lawful to slay the innocent.'

'Innocent', as the word is used here, is something of a technical term. It does not mean 'morally pure'; a person could be morally tainted in all sorts of ways and still be 'innocent' as that word is used in the tradition. In the technical sense, *a person is 'innocent' unless he has by his own misconduct forfeited his right that others should not kill him.* Using this criterion we can understand why criminals, murderers, and enemy soldiers are said not to be innocent. The murderer forfeits his own right to life when he maliciously kills others; and the enemy soldier forfeits his right not to be killed when he himself kills others, or sets himself to kill others, unjustly. Thus they are not protected by the prohibition upon killing the innocent.

There is one other type of killing that should be mentioned here, namely killing by individuals in self-defence. Once the Church had accepted killing in war, it would seem natural also to accept killing in individual self-defence. After all, the violent repelling of an attacker by an individual is obviously analogous to the violent resistance of an unjust aggressor by the State. It seems clear that any reasonable conception of 'innocence' which excludes enemy soldiers from moral protection will also exclude individual aggressors. If by his acts of aggression the enemy soldier loses his claim not to be killed, then surely the individual aggressor, who lacks even the excuse of superior orders, must also lose that claim.

Surprisingly, however, the Church fathers were slow to concede this. St Augustine, who was one of the first to develop the Christian doctrine of the just war, nevertheless continued to deny the legitimacy of individuals killing in self-defence. 'The law is not just which grants to the wayfarer the power to kill a highway robber,' he wrote, 'for the law does not force them to kill.' Only the State has the right to kill. The fact that Augustine insisted on this, at a time so close to the Church's great moral compromise, is further evidence of the essentially political nature of that compromise. Only when we come to Aquinas, some 900 years later, do we finally see a consistent view of the matter. Aquinas held that, like killing in war, the act of self-defence is 'not unlawful, seeing that it is natural for everything to keep itself in being'. Thus, as the Church developed its moral position, the original admonition to 'turn the other cheek' gave way to a more palatable permission to return violence for violence.

The importance of being human

The Western tradition is, of course, a blend of Greek, Jewish, and Christian influences; and all three agree that humans occupy a special place in creation. From ancient times the Jews had taught that man alone is made in God's image; the other animals were made simply for man's use. In the first chapter of Genesis this is made explicit: 'And God said, let us make man in our image, after our own likeness: and let them have dominion over the fish of the sea, and over the fowl of the air, and over the earth, and over every creeping thing that creepeth upon the earth.'

This idea, expressed at first in purely theological terms, was given a non-theological interpretation by later thinkers. Aristotle had held that man is unique among animals because he is rational, and so when Christianity merged with classical culture this teaching was put to use by the doctors of the Church. The divine element in man was said to be his rational nature; and other animals, no matter how clever they might appear to be, lack this nature. Thus it was argued by Aquinas that man has dominion over the other animals because it is natural for the rational beings to prevail over the non-rational: 'Other creatures', he contended, are 'for the sake of the intellectual creatures.'

Aquinas was consciously an apologist for the Church; but the idea he advances has also been defended by many thinkers not so closely identified with Christian orthodoxy. Five centuries after Aquinas, at the height of the Enlightenment, we find Kant reasoning in exactly the same way: humanity, in virtue of its rational nature, is 'an end in itself', never to be used as a mere means. 'But so far as animals are concerned', he says 'we have no direct duties. Animals. . . are there merely as means to an end. That end is man.'

If man's special place in the scheme of things is due to his rationality, we might wonder about the place of non-rational humans. Infants and severely retarded people lack the capacities of thought and intellect which allegedly put man in a special moral category;

so we might expect that they would not qualify for the special standing. When we turn to the writings of those who defend the traditional doctrine, however, this expectation is disappointed. *All* humans, regardless of how non-rational, are assumed to have the same moral protection. The controlling idea is, apparently, that human *nature* is rational, and the extent to which one's life is sacred is determined by the norm for the species, regardless of one's individual characteristics.

As for the other animals, it isn't that their moral status is merely less than that of man—in a strict sense, they have no moral status at all. Traditional thought does not admit that people have *any* moral duties to other animals—not even the duty not to torture them. According to Aquinas, and many others, we should not be cruel to other animals, but the reason has nothing to do with concern for them. The reason is that cruelty to animals might lead eventually to a similar cruelty toward *men*. It is only the interests of men that matter. Aquinas writes:

if any passages of Holy Writ seem to forbid us to be cruel to dumb animals, for instance to kill a bird with its young: this is either to remove man's thoughts from being cruel to other men, and lest through being cruel to animals one becomes cruel to human beings: or because injury to an animal leads to the temporal hurt of man, either the doer of the deed, or of another.

As before, Kant follows Aquinas exactly: although he holds that we have no 'direct duties' to animals, he adds that it may not be advisable to treat them cruelly since 'He who is cruel to animals becomes hard also in his dealings with men.'

Considering that the traditional doctrine will not even allow concern for an animal's pain, it should come as no surprise that it offers no objection to killing them. Again, the official reason is that, unlike us, they are not rational beings, and that in the natural order established by God the non-rational beings are there for our use. To quote Aquinas once more:

Hereby is refuted the error of those who said it is sinful for a man to kill dumb animals: for by divine providence they are intended for man's use in the natural order. Hence it is no wrong for man to make use of them, either by killing or in any other way whatever.

Intentional killing

The principle ultimately developed by the Church was that *The intentional killing of innocent humans is always wrong*. We have seen how emphasis came to be placed on innocence and on humanness. Now let us turn to the other crucial term in the formula—the notion of *intentional* killing.

When the Church compromised its original pacifism in order to allow killing in war, it was the task of theorists like Augustine to explain how this could be consistent. For Augustine, the trick was to realize that moral goodness is not a property of actions, but of the attitude with which one peforms them. 'What is required', he said, 'is not a bodily action, but an inward disposition. The sacred seat of virtue is the heart.' Thus violence may be permitted if it is performed with the right intention. The right intention will be, not to kill other people, but to 'bring under the yoke the unbridled lusts of war, and to abolish vices which ought, under a just government, to be either extirpated or suppressed'. Augustine's original idea was developed by later thinkers into the doctrine that *only non-intentional killing is permitted*.

The word 'intentional' is not being used here in its ordinary meaning. If I say that Cain killed someone intentionally, you may take me to mean that it was not an accident or a mistake; he knew exactly what he was doing. That is not the meaning we are concerned with. Instead, the meaning of 'intentional' here has to do with *what one is trying to accomplish* by an action. The distinction between intentional and non-intentional killing is, roughly, between intending or aiming to kill someone, and killing someone as the foreseen but unintended by-product of an action which is aimed at some other goal.

An example may help to make the idea clearer. Suppose, in time of war, a military commander orders his air force to bomb the homes of a civilian community—he wants to punish the enemy population, or perhaps to damage morale. There is an ammunition factory nearby, and some of the bombs may fall on it, because the bomb-sights are not perfect; but that is not part of the plan. The plan is just to kill the civilians. In this case, the killing of the civilians is intentional; it is an integral part of the commander's plan. On the other hand, suppose the planes are sent to bomb the ammunition factory. The commander may realize that some bombs will fall on nearby houses, because the bomb-sights are not wholly accurate. Nevertheless, the civilian deaths are not part of his plan—they are merely a foreseen but unintended by-product of the plan. In this case the deaths are not intentional.

The traditional view is that the former action is forbidden but the latter may be all right. The same people are killed, by the same bombs, either way; but the commander's intention is different in the two cases, and that, according to the traditional view, makes such a big difference that one may be permissible while the other is not.

The basic idea was refined considerably, and given its most famous expression in the 'doctrine of double effect', anticipated by Aquinas but first formulated fully by the sixteenth-century theologians of Salamance. The doctrine of double effect says that

An action which has two effects, one good and one bad, may be done provided that four conditions are satisfied:

(1) The act itself, considered apart from its consequences, must be of a type that is permitted. [This condition is necessary because, according to the tradition we are considering, there are some types of actions that are absolutely forbidden no matter what the consequences might be.]

(2) The bad effect may not be aimed at or intended—only the good result may be the intended goal of the act. [This condition has to do with the agent's individual approach to the act. He may not do the act for the purpose of bringing about the bad result; that result must be, from his point of view, unwanted. If he could bring about the good result without the bad, he should be eager to do so.]

(3) The bad result must not be used as a *means* of achieving the good result. [The agent may not aim at the bad result even as a means to the good result. The bad result must be genuinely a by-product of the act, not essential to the agent's plan in any way. The military commander who wants to bomb innocent civilians to 'demoralize' the enemy plans to use the innocent deaths as a means to this end— and so that bombing is ruled out by this condition.]

(4) The amount of good accomplished in the good result must be great enough to outweigh the evil of the bad result. [Thus, if it is an *insignificant* armaments factory being bombed, and *many* innocent deaths will be caused, the bombing will not be permitted even though the other conditions are satisfied.]

The doctrine of double effect will permit something similar to euthanasia, in very special circumstances. Suppose a terminal patient is being given a drug to relieve pain, but over time develops a tolerance for the drug so that larger and larger doses are required. Finally, the only effective dose is one so large that it will cause death. This may be justified on the grounds that the death is only the foreseen but unintended by-product of an action intended to relieve suffering. As odd as this may seem, it is a familiar view among defenders of the traditional doctrine.

In the main, however, euthanasia, along with suicide, infanticide, and the like, have been seen as the intentional killing of the innocent; and as such they have been condemned throughout the Christian era.

Other views about euthanasia

Christianity has been the single most powerful influence in shaping Western morals; however, it would be a mistake to think that the prohibition of euthanasia is exclusively a Christian doctrine. Jewish law also forbids it. In fact, we find a rare consensus among rabbinic authorities on this subject. The medieval Jewish theologians were no less emphatic than their Christian counterparts: the great Maimonides, for example, wrote in the twelfth century that 'One who is in a dying condition is regarded as a living person in all respects. . . He who touches him (thereby causing him to expire) is guilty of shedding blood.' The Islamic tradition is also uncompromising, for the Koran explicitly states that the suicide 'shall be excluded from heaven forever', and voluntary euthanasia is regarded simply as a form of assisted suicide. So it is not only Christianity but all these religious traditions that unite against the acceptance of euthanasia.

If we turn for a moment to the experience of other cultures, we find a striking contrast. While these developing Western traditions were opposing euthanasia, most Eastern peoples were comfortably accepting it. In China, Confucian ethics had always allowed voluntary death in the case of hopeless disease, and the great Eastern religions, including Shintoism and Buddhism, took a similar attitude. In *The Dialogues of Buddha* there are described two holy men who commit suicide to escape incurable illness, and this is said to be no obstacle to their attaining 'nirvana', the spiritual goal of all

Buddhist endeavour. Among so-called primitive societies there is a wide range of attitudes towards euthanasia, but it is easy to compile long lists of cultures in which the suicide or killing of those with intolerable illness is approved. In one study, eighteen such societies are mentioned in the space of two pages.

In the West, however, the early Christian view took a firm hold on the minds of almost everyone who bothered to think about the subject, and throughout the Middle Ages the prohibition on these practices was virtually unchallengeable. Not until 1516 do we find an important defence of mercy-killing. In that year Sir Thomas More, later to be made a saint of the Church, wrote in his *Utopia* that in the imaginary perfect community,

When any is taken with a torturing and lingering pain, so that there is no hope either of cure or ease, the priests and magistrates come and exhort them, that, since they are now unable to go on with the business of life, are become a burden to themselves and all about them, and they have really outlived themselves, they should no longer nourish such a rooted distemper, but choose rather to die since they cannot live but in such misery.

Remarkably, More advocates in this passage not only that euthanasia be permitted, but that it be urged on people even when they are reluctant to accept it. I know of no other advocate of euthanasia who would agree with *that*.

Gradually, more and more thinkers came to believe that the prohibition of euthanasia ought to be relaxed. It was, however, a very slow movement, and those who favoured the relaxation remained in a distinct minority. After Thomas More, the next notable proponent of euthanasia was Francis Bacon, who defined the role of the physician as 'not only to restore the health, but to mitigate pain and dolours; and not only when such mitigation may conduce to recovery, but when it may serve to make a fair and easy passage'. Almost exactly a century separated More and Bacon.

During the seventeenth and eighteenth centuries, philosophers moved away from the idea that morality requires a religious foundation. Most remained theists, and God still held a prominent place in their understandings of the universe, but they no longer regarded the Church as the primary moral authority. Instead, human reason and the individual conscience were regarded as the sources of moral knowledge. This did not mean, however, that these thinkers abandoned traditional morality. Although they were revolutionary in their ideas concerning the *sources* of morality, they were often not so radical in their particular moral opinions. Both Kant and Hegel, for example, held that moral truths are known through the use of reason alone; but when they exercised their reason on such matters as suicide and euthanasia, they discovered that the Church had been right all along. David Hume was a notable exception to this way of thinking. Hume argued vigorously that one has the right to end one's life whenever one pleases. A sceptic about religion, he particularly tried to refute the theological arguments to the contrary.

Hume anticipated the nineteenth-century utilitarians, who were the first modern philosophers to provide a principled defence of euthanasia. Their advocacy is largely responsible for giving the position whatever respectability it has today. Bentham argued that the essence of morality is not the service of God, or obedience to abstract rules, but the promotion of the greatest possible happiness for creatures on earth. We ought to calculate how our actions, laws, and social policies will actually affect people (and other animals, too—Bentham denied that the distinction between human and non-human is all that important). Will they result in people being made happier, in people having better lives? Or will they result in people being made more miserable? According to Bentham, our decisions should be made on that basis, and *only* on that basis.

The implications for euthanasia were obvious. For the utilitarians, the question was simply this: Does it increase or decrease happiness to provide a quick, painless death for those who are dying in agony? Clearly, they reasoned, the only consequences of such actions will be to decrease the amount of misery in the world; therefore, euthanasia must be morally acceptable, regardless of what was by then a very long-standing tradition against it. It is said that Bentham himself asked for euthanasia in his last hours.

2 THE SANCTITY OF LIFE

The Eastern tradition

The doctrine of the sanctity of life is associated with two great traditions of thought, one Eastern and the other Western. In the preceding chapter I set out the main tenets of the Western doctrine; here I want to comment briefly on the other principal tradition, and then introduce the alternative view I will defend.

Perhaps the Eastern tradition is most perfectly realized in Jainism, a religion of India said to be older than recorded history. Like the Buddhists, the Jains believe that all life is sacred, with no sharp distinction drawn between animal life and human life. The Jain monk's devotion to this precept is awesome:

The monk must strain his water before drinking; he wears a gauze mask to prevent the unintentional inhalation of innocent insects; the monk is required to sweep the ground before him as he goes, so living beings are not crushed by his footsteps; and always he treads softly, for the very atoms underfoot harbour minute life-monads.

The monk's discipline cannot be matched by the ordinary Jain, who as a practical matter cannot take up the gauze mask and the broom. Nevertheless, the monk's practice stands as an ideal, and the others do what they can.

Plants, too, are treated with respect in the Eastern tradition. In Buddhist writings we find admonitions not to eat seeds, green plants, or shoots. The idea, apparently, is that we should not engage in activities that involve taking life—even plant life—needlessly. On the other hand, fruit, grains, and pods may be consumed without harming the plants; so the recommendation is that we restrict our diets to them.

All this is apt to be a little intimidating to Westerners who like to think that they also believe in the sanctity of life. At least on the surface, the Buddhists and Jains appear to be more consistent. We abhor the killing of humans, but, unlike the Jains, we think nothing of crushing bugs beneath our feet. Yet, if life is sacred, why isn't the life of a bug sacred? A bug is a living thing just as surely as we humans are living things.

A few Westerners have accepted this conclusion and have embraced the Eastern view. The most notable is Albert Schweitzer, the doctor, scholar, musician, and missionary who won the Nobel Peace Prize in 1952. This extraordinary man preached an ethic of 'reverence for life' that would protect not only humans, but other animals and plants as well. The life he recommends is very much like that endorsed by the Jains. Schweitzer writes:

A man is really ethical only when he obeys the constraint laid on him to help all life which he is able to succour, and when he goes out of his way to avoid injuring anything living. He does not ask how far this or that life deserves sympathy as valuable in itself, nor how far it is capable of feeling. To him life as such is sacred. He shatters no ice crystal that sparkles in the sun, tears no leaf from its tree, breaks off no flower, and is careful not to crush any insect as he walks. If he works by lamplight on a summer evening, he prefers to keep his window shut and to breathe stifling air, rather than to see insect after insect fall on his table with singed and sinking wings.

There is something undeniably attractive about this view of moral life, especially when we remember Schweitzer's own example. He devoted many years to working among impoverished people—that is what earned him the Nobel Peace Prize—and it is easy to imagine him breathing the stifling air at his mission in Lambaréné rather than opening his window to the insects. It is tempting to conclude, uncritically, that the moral view he articulates, and which his own life exemplifies, is a higher and nobler ideal than the rest of us are willing to embrace. Yet a more sceptical attitude might be in order. We might wonder whether, from an objective point of view, this moral position is correct. Are there any compelling reasons why a sensible person should accept it?

Schweitzer's reasons were different from the Jains' reasons. The Jains believe that each human soul passes through an immense number of incarnations, all the while striving for release. Upon its liberation, the soul ascends to a level of existence higher than the heavens, where it is at peace for eternity. Morality is viewed by them as a means of progressing toward liberation, and respect for life is a part of the selfless spiritual discipline which leads ultimately to nirvana. Obviously, for those who have grown up within that culture, this will provide a powerful reason for accepting the ethic. But for those who do not share the Jain world-view, all this will seem merely bizarre. The most that can be said for a doctrine like reincarnation is that there is no objective evidence for its truth.

Schweitzer relied on a very different sort of argument. Each of us, he said, has a 'will-to-live'. We recognize in ourselves 'a yearning for more life'; we value our lives and we do not want to die. He thought that if we attend sympathetically to other living things, we will recognize the same will-to-live in them. Apparently this will-to-live does not depend on a conscious desire, for plants are said to have it too. Be that as it may, Schweitzer thought that consistency requires us to show respect for other life, if we wish respect to be shown for our own. He concludes that 'Ethics consists in this, that I experience the necessity of practicing the same reverence for life toward all will-to-live, as toward my own.'

Schweitzer was an admirable man, whose philosophical gifts were not inconsiderable, and I believe he deserves more attention as a philosopher than he has received. (There is not a single reference to him in the entire eight-volume *Encyclopedia of Philosophy*.) The argument he advances for his conception of 'reverence for life' is, however, weak. The overall strategy of reasoning is sound enough: he begins by explaining why it is wrong to kill people, and then suggests that the very same reasons also apply in the case of other animals and even plants. The problem with the argument is the vague and implausible explanation with which he begins.

What, exactly, is a 'will-to-live'? In order for the argument to be convincing, this vague notion would have to be explained in such a way that (1) humans clearly have it, (2) the fact that humans have it is the reason killing them is morally objectionable, and (3) other animals and plants have it too. But it seems unlikely that there is one unequivocal definition of 'will-to-live' under which all three of these propositions could come out true. Perhaps the most straightforward interpretation of the notion is that it refers to the fact that each organism seeks to preserve itself: animals try to avoid harm, and even plants have aspects which serve to defend them against threats and 'keep them going'. Surely, however, this cannot be the full explanation of why the protection of human life is morally important. If it were, then a melancholic—a person suffering from deep clinical depression, who no longer struggles to survive— would have fallen outside the sphere of moral concern. People can lose their 'will-to-live' for lots of reasons, including because they temporarily underestimate their possibilities and their chances for happiness. But their lives do not thereby become less worthy of moral protection. In searching for an explanation of the value of life, this does not seem a promising path.

In his sympathy for the Eastern outlook, Albert Schweitzer was, however, an exception. The dominant tradition in the West is strikingly different from the Eastern way of thinking. As we have seen, the Western tradition does not endorse the idea that all life is sacred; rather, it emphasizes the difference between human and non-human life, and grants serious moral protection only to the former. Whereas the Jains are vegetarians, the Western tradition sees nothing wrong with eating meat, or with killing animals for any number of other purposes. Imagine what a Jain would think upon reading St Augustine:

Christ himself shows that to refrain from the killing of animals and the destroying of plants is the height of superstition, for judging that there are no common rights between us and the beasts and trees, he sent the devils into a herd of swine and with a curse withered the tree on which he found no fruit.

Thus, what is most sacred to the Buddhists and Jains is mere 'superstition' to the Christians.

Preliminary objections to the traditional views

The Eastern tradition, then, gives us a doctrine of the sanctity of *all* life, while the Western tradition endorses a doctrine of the sanctity of *innocent human* life. Despite their great influence, it is easy to find fault with both ways of thinking. Neither is very plausible. Three obvious objections come to mind.

First, with its emphasis on the protection of all life, the Eastern tradition has difficulty distinguishing among various *kinds* of lives. The life of a person and the life of a bug seem to be equally impor- tant, at least in principle. But of course there are many significant differences between persons and bugs. Humans (and, for that matter, many other species of animals as well) have mental and emotional lives far superior to those of insects. Why shouldn't this put them in different moral categories? It is far too simple-minded to say, as Schweitzer does, that 'all life is one'. The differences are important.

Second, if the Eastern tradition pays too much respect to non-humans, the Western tradition pays far too little. St Augustine expressed the Western attitude very well when he said that 'there are no common rights between us and the beasts'; thus, we kill intelligent and sensitive animals, not only for food, but to test cosmetics, for ingredients for perfume, and simply as sport. Surely there ought to be some mean between the extremes represented by the two traditions.

Third, although it may seem a surprising thing to say, the Western tradition places too much value on human life. There are times when the protection of human life has no point, and the Western tradition has had difficulty acknowledging this. The noble ideal of 'protecting human life' is invoked even when the life involved does its subject no good and even when it is not wanted. Babies that are hopelessly deformed, and will never mature into children, may nevertheless be kept alive at great cost. Euthanasia for persons dying of horrible diseases is illegal. St Augustine called respect for animal life 'the height of superstition'; in these cases, it is respect for human life that seems to have degenerated into superstition.

In my opinion, all these objections are sound, and both the Eastern and Western doctrines ought to be rejected. (I shall have more to say about the issues raised by these objections later.) But these objections are also, in a certain sense, superficial. At a deeper level, there is one fundamental mistake that underlies both doctrines. This is somewhat surprising, considering how different they are. Nevertheless, this one basic mistake explains why both are inadequate guides for conduct. I will explain what that mistake is, and at the same time show what a better understanding of the sanctity of life would be like.

A new understanding of the sanctity of life

It is important to realize that we use the word 'life' in two ways. On the one hand, when we speak of 'life', we may be referring to living things, to things that are *alive*. To be alive is to be a functioning biological organism. Here the contrast is with things that are dead, or with things that are neither alive nor dead, such as rocks. Not only people, but chimpanzees and bugs, and even trees and bushes, are living things. A person who asks 'Is there life on other planets?' is using the word in this sense.

On the other hand, when we speak of 'life', we may have in mind a very different sort of concept, one that belongs more to biography than to biology. Human beings not only are alive; they *have lives* as well. A person who speaks of, say, 'the life of Bobby Fischer' is using the word in this sense.

It is easy to overlook this distinction in English, since one word does double duty. The distinction would be easier to spot if the language provided two words. None the less, the difference between being alive and having a life is clear enough. If we were to describe Bobby Fischer as a living being, we could say that he is an animal of the species *homo sapiens*, that he has a heart and liver and brain and blood and kidneys that function together in a certain way, and so forth. If we were to describe his *life*, however, we would mention an entirely different set of things. The facts of a person's life are facts about history and character:

Bobby Fischer was born in 1943 and grew up in New York City; he learned to play chess at age six and devoted himself to the game single-mindedly thereafter. He became the United States Champion at 14 and dropped out of high school; he won the world championship in 1972 and has been a recluse ever since. He has always suspected Russian players of trying to cheat him, and more generally, trusts almost no one. He was involved with an off-beat religious cult in California, but that ended in a public dispute. At last report, he was devoting his days to researching the theory that the world is run by an international conspiracy of Jews.

These are some of the facts of his life. They are not biological facts.

If the concept of life is ambiguous in this way, then so is the concept of the sanctity of life. The doctrine of the sanctity of life can be understood as placing value on things that are alive. But it can also be understood as placing value on *lives* and on the interests that some creatures, including ourselves, have in virtue of the fact that they are the subjects of lives. Very different moral views will result, depending on which interpretation one chooses.

The distinction between being alive and having a life has not been carefully observed in either the Eastern tradition or the

Western tradition. But the emphasis in both has been on the protection of living creatures. In the Eastern tradition this is abundantly clear. The Jain monk sweeps the ground before him, so that insects are not crushed beneath his feet. But insects, while they are doubtlessly alive, do not have lives. They are too simple. They do not have the mental wherewithal to have plans, hopes, or aspirations. They cannot regret their pasts, or look forward to their futures. Plants, toward which Schweitzer recommends reverence, are not even conscious. An ethic of reverence for *lives* would find little here with which to concern itself.

The Western tradition is a bit more complicated on this point. The doctrine of the sanctity of life is taken to protect only humans, and humans do have lives; so it might appear that the Western doctrine is concerned with lives. However, the Western doctrine is more concerned with the fact of being human than with the fact that humans have lives. The sanctity of life is interpreted as applying to *all* humans, even those that do not have lives, such as hopelessly deformed babies who cannot mature into children, and persons in irreversible comas. In the Western tradition, little attention has been paid to the difference between humans who have lives and those who don't.

This is the fundamental mistake that I think underlies both the Eastern and the Western doctrines. The sanctity of life ought to be interpreted as protecting lives in the biographical sense, and not merely life in the biological sense. There is a simple, but I think conclusive, argument for this.

From the point of view of the living individual, there is nothing important about being alive except that it enables one to have a life. In the absence of a conscious life, it is of no consequence to the subject himself whether he lives or dies. Imagine that you are given the choice between dying today and lapsing into a dreamless coma, from which you will never awaken, and then dying ten years from now. You might prefer the former because you find the prospect of a vegetable existence undignified. But in the most important sense, the choice is indifferent. In either case, your *life* will end today, and without that, the mere persistence of your body has no importance. Therefore, in so far as we are concerned to protect the interests of the individuals whose welfare is most directly at stake, we should be primarily concerned with lives and only secondarily with life.

This does not mean, of course, that being alive is unimportant. In the great majority of cases involving humans it is very important, for one cannot have a life if one is not alive. But the importance of being alive is only derivative from the more fundamental importance of having a life.

The moral rule against killing

In the course of growing up, each of us learns a large number of rules of conduct. Which rules we learn will depend, of course, on the kind of society we live in, the kind of parents and friends we have, and so on. We may learn to speak truthfully, to keep clean, to work hard at our tasks, to leave off strong drink, and to avoid harming others. Sometimes, however, we may learn to follow a rule without ever understanding its *point*—we learn to 'go by the book' without understanding why the book says what it does. In most cases this may work out well enough, for the rule may be designed to cover all ordinary circumstances. But when faced with unusual circumstances, we may be in trouble.

Consider someone learning to drive a car. He learns to stop for red lights, to signal before turning, and the rest. Following these rules, things go smoothly. Then, while driving along a highway, he suddenly and unexpectedly finds himself in an emergency situation in which he will crash into another car if he does not violate one of the rules. If he understands the point of the rules he has learned, he will know that they were not meant to be followed in such circumstances. In fact, because the rules were designed to ensure that accidents will not occur, he will paradoxically be more faithful to their intent if he breaks them than if he obeys them.

It is the same with moral rules. It is important to understand their point because otherwise we will not be able to judge intelligently when to make exceptions to them. Without this understanding, following the rules tends to be taken as an end-in-itself. Indeed, we may even come to think it a mark of virtue that we will not *consider* making exceptions. When this happens, morality degenerates into a rigid rule-worship that makes little sense.

We need a way of understanding the point of the rule against killing. The traditional Western view says a lot about who may be killed, and when, but it provides very little understanding of the point of the rule. On the other hand, our discussion of the ambiguity of 'life' does provide a way of understanding the rule's point. The point is not to preserve as many living things as possible, but to protect the interests of individuals who are the subjects of lives. It is a *derived* rule, inferred from a more fundamental rule having to do with the protection of lives. It is as though we had formulated the rule by reasoning thus: 'It is morally important to protect lives, and the individuals who are the subjects of lives. If those individuals are killed, their biographical lives, and not just their biological lives, will be destroyed. Therefore, such killing is wrong.'

When will exceptions to the rule be justified? The traditional understanding of the rule suggests three types of justification: first, non-human animals may be killed, since they are not covered by the rule at all; second, persons who are not 'innocent' may be killed because they have forfeited their right to life—this is said of criminals and enemy soldiers; and third, even innocent persons may be killed provided that the killing is not intentional and a greater good is being served.

Our new understanding suggests a type of justification that has not previously been noticed. If the point of the rule against killing is the protections of lives, then we may notice that *in some cases killing does not involve the destruction of a life*. A person in irreversible coma, or an infant with such defects that it will never mature, is not the subject of a life; so they fall outside the scope of the rule thus understood. In killing such persons, or allowing them to die by neglect, the justification isn't that their lives are being traded off against some 'higher value', or that an exception is being made from some dire necessity. It is simply that the point of the rule, in such cases, is lost.

Some practical implications

We have, then, if I may speak somewhat grandly, a new understanding of the sanctity of life. The practical implications are different from the implications of both the traditional Eastern and Western doctrines, and in each case, I believe the new understanding provides a better ethic. A few examples will illustrate why this is so, and will make the nature of my suggestion clearer.

Human vegetables

In 1939 an immigrant named Repouille, living in California, killed his thirteen-year-old son with chloroform. The boy, one of five children in the family, had suffered a brain injury at birth that left him virtually mindless, blind, mute, deformed in all four limbs, and with no control over his bladder or bowels. His whole life was spent in a small crib.

Repouille was tried for manslaughter in the first degree— apparently the prosecutor was unwilling to try him for first-degree murder, even though that charge could have been brought—but the jury, obviously sympathetic with him, brought in a verdict of *second*-degree manslaughter. From a legal point of view their verdict made no sense, because second-degree manslaughter presupposes that the killing was not intentional. Obviously the jury was intent on convicting him of only the mildest possible offence, so they ignored this legal nicety. They further indicated their desire to forgive the defendant by accompanying the verdict with a recommendation for 'utmost clemency' in sentencing. The judge agreed with them and complied by staying execution of the five-to-ten-year sentence and placing Repouille on probation. He never went to jail.

All this happened more than forty years ago, but it could have happened yesterday. Neither the legal situation, nor the moral climate which nurtured it, have changed. Such killings still occur, the law still officially condemns them, and the courts are still reluctant to impose heavy penalties.

The law condemns such killings because it reflects the Western tradition concerning the sanctity of life. The Western tradition does not distinguish between the life of a normal, healthy person and the 'life' of Repouille's son lying in the crib: both are sacred. So the law does not officially recognize any difference between killing a normal, healthy person and killing Repouille's son: both are murder. Yet the human beings who must deal with such cases—the judges and juries—are obviously uncomfortable with this attitude.

An ethic which emphasized the protection of lives and not mere biological life would say that the judges and juries are right. Repouille's son was alive, but the tragic brain injury prevented him from ever having a life. Thus, on the view I am proposing, it is a mistake to speak of 'the sanctity of life' in this instance.

This is easy enough to say, but difficult to apply in such a heartbreaking case. We feel a natural sense of identification with other humans, probably for deep biological reasons, no matter how unfortunate they are. But such feelings, however natural, may not have a rational basis. We may ask of Repouille's son whether his 'life' did *him* any good. Did it have any value from *his* point of view? And immediately we encounter the crucial problem that he did not *have* a point of view, in any but the most primitive sense.

He was, of course, conscious in a rudimentary way, and so was probably able to experience some physical pleasures and pains. This may lead some people to reject the view I am suggesting. But the capacity to experience simple pleasures and pains is not much, if it is the only capacity one has. The sensations experienced will not be endowed with any significance by the one experiencing them; they will not arise from any human activities or projects; they will not be connected with any coherent view of the world.

Nevertheless, one could maintain that the bare capacity to suffer and enjoy is enough to make the protection of life morally important. One could say that, *if* one were willing to extend equal moral protection to mice, fish, and toads, who, after all, can also experience pleasure and pain. However, I see no reason to go on in this way. The better course is to realize that the ethics of killing and the ethics of causing pain involve fundamentally different issues, and the two ought to be kept separate. The rule against causing pain applies to all creatures capable of suffering, and that includes Repouille's son; but something more is required to come under the protection of the rule against killing. On the view I am suggesting, the rule against killing protects creatures that have lives.

Defective infants

As I remarked in Chapter 1, the ancient Greeks and Romans did not object to the killing of deformed infants. Christianity took a very different attitude, and allowed no moral distinction between normal and abnormal babies. The Christian view has prevailed, and throughout most of Western history infanticide has been regarded as a great evil.

Recently, however, this situation has begun to change. The change has been prompted by advances in medical technology that have made it possible to keep many babies alive that previously would have died. In such cases, some parents and doctors have quietly decided against treating these infants. Not much publicity was given to this until 1973, when three doctors 'went public' in a pair of articles in *The New England Journal of Medicine*.

These articles caused great public controversy. Physicians were aware of such practices, but the general public was not. In one of the articles, Drs Raymond Duff and A. G. M. Campbell described how they had let forty-three defective babies die in the Yale–New Haven Special Care Nursery. In the other, Dr Anthony Shaw of the University of Virginia Medical Center discussed his own handling of such cases. Like Duff and Campbell, Shaw said that he had sometimes allowed defective babies to die when the parents refused permission for needed treatment. When these articles appeared, there was some fear that the doctors would be arrested. But that did not happen, and despite continuing controversy, such practices have now become commonplace.

Shaw argued that the new medical techniques pose a new dilemma: does it follow from the fact that we *have* a new life-preserving technique that we should *use* it? In some instances, wouldn't we be better off without it? He wrote:

Each year it becomes possible to remove yet another type of malformation from the 'unsalvageable' category. All pediatric surgeons, including myself, have 'triumphs'—infants who, if they had been born 25 or even five years ago, would not have been salvageable . . . But how about the infant whose gastrointestinal tract has been removed after volvulus and infarction? Although none of us regard the insertion of a central venous catheter as a 'heroic' procedure, is it right to insert a 'lifeline' to feed this baby in the light of our present technology, which can support him, tethered to an infusion pump, for a maximum of one year and some months?

Among the 43 infants allowed to die at the Yale–New Haven Hospital were 15 with multiple anomalies, 8 with trisomy, 8 with cardio-pulmonary disease, 7 with meningomyelocele, 3 with other central nervous system disorders, and 2 with short-bowel syndrome. Duff and Campbell argued that non-treatment was justified because, in each case, 'prognosis for meaningful life was extremely poor or hopeless'.

Does the non-treatment of these infants violate the sanctity of life? Duff and Campbell comment, 'If this is one of the consequences of the sanctity-of-life ethic, perhaps our formulation of the principle should be revised.' Such a revision is, of course, exactly what I am proposing. On my revision, the question to be asked is whether these babies have any prospect of a life in the biographical sense.

The infant described by Dr Shaw obviously has no such prospect. The baby could be kept alive by a central venous catheter for less than two years; then it would die. It would be conscious during that time—it might be aware of having its diaper changed (although it would not know *what* was happening), and of being hungry, and of the pain associated with its medical condition—but that is about all. It is no better off than Repouille's son; it will never have a life, and so the doctrine of the sanctity of life will have no application.

The terminally ill

The story of Matthew Donnelly is sadly typical of a whole range of cases:

Skin cancer had riddled the tortured body of Matthew Donnelly. A physicist, he had done research for the past thirty years on the use of X-rays. He had lost part of his jaw, his upper lip, his nose, and his left hand. Growths had been removed from his right arm and two fingers from his right hand. He was left blind, slowly deteriorating, and in agony of body and soul. The pain was constant; at its worst, he could be seen lying in bed with teeth clenched and beads of perspiration standing out on his forehead. Nothing could be done except continued surgery and analgesia. The physicians estimated that he had about a year to live.

Mr Donnelly begged his brother to shoot him, and he did.

Euthanasia is, of course, illegal, at least in the United States. But is it immoral? There is one clear argument in favour of it, namely, that it puts an end to such suffering. But in the Western tradition this is not considered sufficient reason to set aside the prohibition on killing. The dying person is 'innocent', and therefore comes under the rule against killing the innocent.

An ethic that is concerned with lives would lead to a different conclusion. It would have us ask what effect killing Mr Donnelly would have on his biographical life. In the case of someone in an irreversible coma, such as Karen Quinlan, the answer is that killing her would have had no effect whatever on her life: her life was already over; it ended when she entered the coma. Matthew Donnelly's life, however, was still in progress when his brother shot him. So a superficial answer would be that killing him destroyed his life.

Less superficially, we may compare the life Donnelly would have had if he were not killed with the life he would have had if he were killed. Then we can see the difference euthanasia makes. The two lives are exactly the same, except that one is a year longer. The extra year, however, is not spent on any activity or project which Donnelly thinks worth while; it is spent lying in bed, blind, deformed, teeth clenched. Is his life better with or without this year? Surely, if Donnelly believed that this extra year would add nothing of value to his life, that is a reasonable judgement. The sanctity of life, if it were interpreted as protecting lives and the interests people have in virtue of being the subjects of lives, would offer no objection to euthanasia in this case.

Non-human animals

The most striking difference between the Eastern and Western traditions is in their attitudes toward non-human animals. One tradition grants all animals the full protection of the sanctity of life; the other gives them virtually no protection at all. As I have already suggested, we need to find some reasonable middle ground.

Do animals have lives? Some of them clearly do not. Having a life requires some fairly sophisticated mental capacities, which simple animals do not have. Consider, however, a psychologically complex animal such as the rhesus monkey. Rhesus monkeys live together in social groups; they have families and care for one another; they communicate with one another; they engage in complicated activities; they have highly individualized personalities. And they are clever: one team of researchers noted that they 'can indeed solve many problems similar in type to the items used in standard tests of human intelligence'. Although their lives are not as complicated as ours, emotionally or intellectually, there seems no doubt that they do have lives. They are not merely alive.

It should come as no great surprise that other animals have lives; after all, *we* are animals—we are products of the same evolutionary forces that have shaped the rest of the animal kingdom—and our kinship with other creatures shows in all sorts of ways. In explaining how humans work, it is often necessary to remember this evolutionary kinship. A recent example, from *Newsweek*: A small boy falls through the ice and is under freezing water for twenty minutes. By the time he is brought up, he is 'clinically dead'—skin ashen, no heartbeat, no breathing, pupils fixed and dilated. At the hospital, his body temperature is measured at 85 degrees. But he survived. How? We can explain this because we know that we are the evolutionary descendants of aquatic mammals:

Such a state of hypothermia drastically reduced his brain's metabolic rate and its need for oxygen, greatly prolonging the time he could survive without adequate circulation. At the same time, Jimmy was helped by the 'mammalian diving response', a reflex triggered by immersion in cold water that diverts blood from the extremities and most of the internal organs and sends it to the heart and brain. The same mechanism permits whales, seals and other aquatic mammals to hunt for long periods underwater. Vestiges of the reflex remain in humans, and, according to Dr Michael Davidson of Philadelphia's Germantown Hospital, it is especially powerful in children. 'Hypothermia and the mammalian diving response worked together to help the child,' notes Dr Harold Rekate of Cleveland's University Hospitals.

Psychologists also are aware of our links with other animals and take advantage of it. Rhesus monkeys are so much like humans that they are favourite research animals for psychologists seeking to learn what makes us tick—if, for example, a researcher wants to know something about maternal behaviour, and his 'ethics' forbids doing a controlled experiment with a human mother and child, he may use a rhesus monkey mother and child, assuming that whatever is true of them is also true of us.

Of course we do not know a great deal about the lives of the members of most other species. To make intelligent judgements about them we need the sort of information that can be gained by observing animals in their natural homes, rather than in the laboratory or in other artificial environments such as zoos. Learning about animals by watching them in zoos is something like learning about people by observing them in prison. A widely used psychology textbook tells the story of a baboon colony in the London Zoo, where investigators

observed many instances of bloody fighting, brutality, and apparently senseless violence. Some of the females were torn to pieces, and no infant survived to maturity. From these observations, it was concluded that such violence was typical of the 'wild' baboons . . . But later, when baboons were studied under natural conditions in Africa, in the 'wild', it was discovered that they lived in well-organized, peaceful groups, in which the only aggressive behavior was directed at predators and intruders.

Such discoveries are all the more impressive because, unlike the rhesus monkey, the baboon is not a creature we *expect* to exhibit 'human' qualities.

This is true of many other species. When dogs and wolves are studied in their natural habitats, it is found that the lives of individual animals, carried out within pack societies, are surprisingly complex and diverse. But we are only beginning to appreciate the richness of the animal kingdom. Take the octopus, for example—a creature we surely would not suspect of being very psychologically complicated. It is a mollusc—like a clam—but it has the most complex central nervous system of all invertebrates, apparently developed originally to control the many gripping-pads along its tentacles. It has a home, stakes out a territory, and fights other octopuses that invade its territory, but not to the death. Observers believe that it shows emotions like fear and anger by changing its skin-colour (an ability which also allows it to blend with its surroundings when natural enemies are nearby). When fighting its prey, it shows no emotion, but when fighting other octopuses it does show emotion. Its intelligence has been tested in such ways as giving it food in a jar, and seeing if it can figure out how to screw the top off. The animal does figure this out, in a couple of minutes.

Now we do not know very much about octopuses, and I am not mentioning all this in order to argue to the definite conclusion that they do have lives. I only want to point out the way in which new information can make a difference to our view of animals' lives. Even this meagre information makes the octopuses seem very different from what we imagined before.

In our present state of semi-ignorance about other species, the situation seems to be this. When we consider the mammals with which we are most familiar, it is reasonable to believe that they do have lives in the biographical sense. They have emotions and cares and social systems and the rest, although perhaps not in just the way that humans do. Then the further down the phylogenetic scale we go, the less confidence we have that there is anything resembling a life. When we come to bugs, or shrimps, the animals pretty clearly lack the mental capacities necessary for a life, although they certainly are alive.

The moral view suggested by this is that animals are protected by the sanctity of life *to the extent that* they have lives. Most of us already recognize the truth of this—we think that killing a human is worse than killing a monkey, but we also think that killing a monkey is a more morally serious matter than swatting a fly. And when we come to plants, which are alive, but where the notion of a biographical life has no application whatever, the moral qualms about killing have vanished altogether. If the understanding of the sanctity of life I have suggested is correct, these feelings have a rational basis: in so far as we have reason to view other creatures as having lives, as we do, we have reason to think they come under the protection of the sanctity of life, if we do.

On my version of the sanctity of life, then, the higher animals ought to have serious moral protection—to kill a rhesus monkey or a chimpanzee might not require as strong a justification as killing a person, but it is nevertheless a serious matter. The protection becomes weaker, however, as we consider progressively simpler animals, until we reach the clams and snails and bugs whose 'lives' count for little. Thus, we have found the reasonable middle ground between the two extremes represented by the Eastern and Western traditions.

Morality and religion

The word 'sanctity' has religious associations, and so the phrase 'sanctity of life' suggests a religious doctrine as well as an ethical idea. However, the doctrine I have proposed is not a religious doctrine at all; it is an ethical idea which may be accepted or rejected on its own merits, by religious people or by non-religious people.

The separation of morality and religion does not necessarily mean the rejection of religion, any more than the separation of science from religion must mean the rejection of religion. The great religions connected theological ideas with ideas about the origin and nature of the physical world. Most of these quasi-scientific ideas have turned out to be false. This has been difficult to accept: the Church has only recently begun to concede its mistreatment of Galileo, and it has yet to come to terms fully with Darwin. But, however painful the recognition, the proper relation between science and religion now seems clear, at least in its main outlines. Physics and chemistry and biology and the other sciences have their own standards of truth and their own methods of discovering it. Theological ideas might be superimposed on what science discovers—for example, it might be said that God created the non-geocentric universe by willing the Big Bang, or that God produced humans by willing evolution. The theological claims might be true, or they might be false; that is not the point. The point is that the truth of the scientific claims does not depend in any way on the truth of the theological claims; nor does the discovery of scientific truth depend on one's having a theological perspective.

Many religious people are willing to accept this kind of independence for science, but are unwilling to accept a similar independence for ethics. To them, ethics without religion is unthinkable. Yet such a separation is implicit within the Christian tradition, which holds that moral truths are truths of reason binding on all people regardless of their religious convictions or lack of them. St Thomas Aquinas, the greatest of all the theologians, taught that the source of moral knowledge is the individual conscience, and that 'conscience is the dictate of reason'. One never sins, he says, when following one's conscience. Daniel Maguire, a contemporary Catholic thinker, echoes this when he emphasizes that Christians are not absolutely bound by the moral 'authority' of the Church. 'Historical Catholic ethical theory', he says, allows individuals to act on any moral view that is supported by 'good and serious reasons.' Maguire says this in the context of a discussion of euthanasia, and he insists that Christians are free to follow their consciences on this matter despite the Church's traditional opposition.

One discovers what is right and wrong by exercising one's reason. As with science, theological claims may then be superimposed—one may say, as Aquinas did, that reason is the voice of God. But the truth of the moral judgements, and our ability to make them, does not depend on the truth of the theological claims. That is why it is possible for believers and non-believers to share the same moral universe.

I shall not discuss theology. The view I am defending is non-theological, although not anti-theological, in that it sees the point of morality as the good of creatures on earth. In particular, the value of life is not the value it has for God, nor the value it may be assigned within any religious perspective. The value of life is the value it has *for the beings who are the subjects of lives*. But this must be carefully stated; it is easily misunderstood. In speaking of the value a life has for the subject of that life, I am not advocating any sort of moral subjectivism. To say that something has value *for someone* does not mean that it has value because he or she *believes* it is valuable. Nor does it mean that it has value only because someone consciously *cares* about it. Instead, it means this: something has value for a person if its loss would *harm* him (regardless of what he happens to believe or care about). The loss of my eyes would harm me: in a perfectly plain sense, it would be a bad thing, not for the universe, but for *me*. Similarly, the value of my life is primarily a value that it has for me, in the sense that I am the person who would be harmed by its loss. The rule against killing should be understood as a rule intended to protect individuals against that loss. That, in my opinion, is the proper non-theological starting-point for an ethic of life and death.

3 DEATH AND EVIL

Death and suffering

Why is it wrong to kill people? No doubt the question is too simple, because killing people is not *always* wrong; the rule has exceptions. However, there is always a strong presumption that it is wrong, and this presumption may be set aside only in special cases and for powerful reasons. Thus, when we ask why killing is wrong, we mean: why is there such a strong presumption against it?

It is a strange question, for two reasons. First, it brings into question something that we usually take for granted; the wrongness of killing may seem too obvious to need explanation. Second, it is an *unclear* question, in the way that philosophical questions are often unclear, at least when they are first posed. It is hard to tell, in advance, just what a satisfactory answer will be like. It is unlike questions such as 'What is the specific gravity of aluminium?' Here we know that the answer will be a number, and, moreover, we know how to go about discovering which number is the right one. There is a well-established procedure which, if followed faithfully, will yield the correct answer. But how will we recognize the correct answer to the question 'Why is it wrong to kill people?' if we find it? Here, as often happens in philosophy, we are to some extent groping in the dark, or better, in a kind of half-light, in which we can see that there is a problem, but not the exact shape of the problem.

Nevertheless, it is obvious enough where to start. The wrongness of killing is undoubtedly connected with the fact that the victim ends up dead. But why is *that* such a bad thing? Why is it bad to die? It is easy to see why it may be bad for people other than the victim himself. Those who love him may grieve over his death, and those who were depending on him for one thing or another may suffer because, being dead, he will be unable to perform as expected. But considerations of this kind will not provide a full account of why killing is wrong. Killing is wrong because of what is done to the victim himself, and not merely because of what happens to the survivors. A satisfactory account of the wrongness of killing must be based on an explanation of why death is a bad thing *for the person who dies*.

Epicurus' argument

Not everyone has agreed that death is bad. Some philosophers have argued that there is nothing evil about death, and that fearing it is therefore irrational. The most famous argument to this effect was devised by Epicurus, and repeated with approval by such figures as Lucretius and Montaigne. Epicurus' equanimity did not come from any optimistic view of death as merely a passage to a different and better life. If 'death' *were* followed by some sort of afterlife, then what we think of it should depend on what sort of life follows—if we go to heaven, death might be a splendid thing; and if we go to hell, it is clearly terrible for that very obvious reason. But Epicurus held no such view. He thought of death as annihilation, the absolute end of one's existence. Yet he still believed there was nothing bad about it. In a letter to one of his followers, he wrote:

Become accustomed to the belief that death is nothing to us. For all good and evil consists in sensation, but death is deprivation of sensation . . . So long as we exist death is not with us; but when death comes, then we do not exist. It does not then concern either the living or the dead, since for the former it is not, and the latter are no more.

The argument presented in this passage has three main steps.

1. First there is the hedonistic principle which says that the only things intrinsically good or bad for a person are pleasant or unpleasant experiences—'all good and evil consists in sensation'. It is unpleasant, for example, to suffer pain, or to feel depressed, worried, embarrassed, frustrated, frightened, or bored. So these are all intrinsically bad. But, according to this principle, things *other than* experiences are bad only in so far as they cause one to have unpleasant experiences. Disease, for example, is bad because it causes pain, and, when it is incapacitating, because it causes one to feel frustrated at being unable to do what one wants. Goods are explained in a similar manner: pleasant experiences are intrinsically good, and other things are good only in so far as they cause pleasant experiences.

2. Does death cause one to have unpleasant experiences? (Or for that matter, pleasant ones?) Epicurus points out that 'So long as we exist death is not with us; but when death comes, then we do not exist.' A person's death cannot cause him to have unpleasant experiences while he is alive because his death has not yet occurred; and after he dies it cannot cause him unpleasant experiences because he no longer exists, and has no experiences at all.

3. Therefore, although a person's death may be a bad thing for others—it may cause them to feel grief or frustration—it cannot be a bad thing for the person himself.

This argument is an example of one of the most fascinating philosophical phenomena: like Zeno's arguments for the unreality of motion, it attempts to prove false something that we all know— or think we know—to be true. Therefore, it is tempting to dismiss it as mere sophistry, for surely, one might think, there must be *something* wrong with it. That is an understandable reaction. However, like Zeno's arguments, there may be something to be learned by asking *what* is wrong with it.

Death, dying, and being dead (with a digression on the time of death)

An obvious but misguided reaction to the argument is to object that, contrary to what Epicurus says, death can be quite painful— think for example of the agony experienced by someone dying of a horrible disease. This objection is misguided because it confuses *death* with *dying*, which are different notions. The difference is that dying is a process, which goes on through a period of time, while death is an event which occurs *at* a certain time. While he is dying, a person is still alive: the process of dying, and not the event of death, is the source of the pain.

In the literature on medical ethics, the idea that death is an event is sometimes resisted on the grounds that there is no one point in the process of dying which is *the* point at which death takes place. The transition from living person to corpse is often a very gradual one, involving various changes. When is the exact moment death occurs? When spontaneous respiration ceases? When the heart stops? When the patient has an isoelectric electroencephalogram? As an empirical matter, the choice seems arbitrary. Therefore, it is concluded, there is no one event which is death.

There is obviously something to this, but it is important to keep the conceptual as well as the medical facts straight. The logical relation between dying and death is analogous to the relation between travelling towards a destination and arriving. By asking the same questions, we might come to doubt whether *arriving* is an event. Exactly when does an air traveller arrive in Philadelphia? When the aeroplane first broaches the space over the city? When the plane touches the airport runway? When the passenger sets foot off the plane? It seems arbitrary which moment we designate the moment of arrival; nevertheless, the *concept* of arrival is the concept of a momentary event. It is a fact about language that we cannot say, with good sense, 'She arrived in Philadelphia from 12.18 to 12.33,' but must rather say, 'She arrived *at* 12.33.' The example of arrival shows that the exact time at which an event takes place may be underdetermined by the facts.

Death is like this. The concept of death is the concept of a momentary event; but precisely when it takes place is underdetermined by the physiological facts, so that we are free, within limits, to set the time of death where we choose. In making this choice, practical considerations may come into play. One such practical consideration has to do with organ-transplant surgery. When a transplant is in the offing, we want to remove the donor's organs as soon as possible, before they begin to deteriorate; but of course we do not want to remove them before he is dead.

When is the organ-donor *really* dead? That, as we have seen, is the wrong question to ask, because it assumes there is some one moment which is *the* moment of death. Instead, we may ask, 'At what point is it morally all right to declare him dead?'—or even, 'At what point is it morally all right to remove his organs?' That may help us to decide among the several possible 'moments of death'. At what point does the donor no longer have any use for the organs? The most reasonable answer is when he has lost all consciousness and there is no possibility of his ever regaining it. At that point, his life is over, and we cannot possibly be harming him by removing his heart or kidney or whatever. Therefore, there is no moral reason (at least, none having to do with *his* welfare) why we should not fix the time of death as soon as possible after the permanent cessation of consciousness.

Medical expertise comes in to tell us which of the possible 'times of death' is associated with the irrevocable loss of consciousness.

Studies show that consciousness is possible when and only when certain sorts of brain activity are possible. This means that 'brain death' precludes any restoration of consciousness: at that point, we can be sure the donor's organs are no longer of any use to him. So, it is morally all right to fix the time of death at that point.

'Brain death' is currently the most popular option among physicians and legislators who must choose when to declare people dead. I believe this is the best approach; but it is not commonly understood *why* it is best. It is not because 'the facts' dictate that a person is dead when and only when he suffers brain death. It is not that a person *really* dies then. Empirical considerations only establish limits within which a decision must be made. The final decision is determined by moral considerations, which argue for fixing the time of death at the point at which consciousness is no longer possible.

At any rate, the importance of the distinction between death and dying for Epicurus' argument is clear enough. A person who is dying is still alive, and so is able to suffer; his death, whenever it occurs, is simply the termination of this process, after which suffering is no longer possible. Epicurus' argument maintains that death cannot be the source of unhappiness, but it does not imply that dying cannot be unpleasant.

There is one other related notion to be distinguished, that of *being dead*. Epicurus interprets the fear of death as based on the misconception of death as some sort of mysterious, possibly unpleasant condition. We may ask, 'What is it like to be dead?' and, being unable to answer, find it a strange and unsettling prospect. Against this, Epicurus assumes that the question itself is radically misconceived: being dead isn't like anything at all; it is simply the *absence* of experience. The 'state' you will be in after you die is exactly comparable to the 'state' you were in before you were born, and it is 'unimaginable' to you for exactly the same reason, namely, that there is nothing to imagine.

The fear of death

So dying—which is a process that takes place while one is still alive—but not death or being dead, can be the source of unhappiness. So far, Epicurus' argument seems unassailable. But we have not yet taken notice of the fact that the *anticipation* of death can cause one unhappiness. People, after all, can know in advance that they are going to die, and they dread it; so mustn't we admit that, contrary to what Epicurus says, death can be the source of unhappiness?

This objection is not hard to answer. People do fear their own deaths, but they fear a great many other things as well, and we do not always conclude that a thing is bad merely because it is feared. Some people fear enclosed places, but we do not assume on that account that there is anything bad about being in an enclosed space. Rather, because there *isn't* anything bad about it, we conclude that there is something wrong with those people. They may not be able to help themselves, of course; one does not choose to be claustrophobic. Nevertheless their fears are unfounded, since there is no good reason to fear enclosures.

The point of Epicurus' argument is to show that, in the same way, there is no good reason to fear death. If death is not an evil when it comes, we ought not to fear it in advance. The fact that some people do fear it is irrelevant; for the explanation of their fear might be their own ignorance or irrationality, and not the 'evil' of death itself. To show that death is bad we will have to show not only that some fear it, but that there is reason to fear it. As Epicurus put it,

The man speaks but idly who says that he fears death not because it will be painful when it comes, but because it is painful in anticipation. For that which gives no trouble when it comes, is but an empty pain in anticipation.

I believe Epicurus was right in what he said about death and suffering. Except possibly for the pain of anticipation, death cannot cause suffering for the person who dies, and the pain of anticipation cannot be invoked as evidence that death is bad. If we assume, then, that 'all good and evil consists in sensation', Epicurus was right: death is not an evil.

The unanswered question about killing

Epicurus intended his argument as a contribution to human happiness: by removing death from the list of things we worry about, he meant to make us more contented with our lot. That is a laudable enough intention. But the argument, if successful, would do more than that: it has another, less benign consequence. It would not only remove a certain rationale for fearing death; it would deprive us of any adequate rationale for the prohibition of murder. If death is not an evil, why should we object to killing? If, in killing someone, we are doing something that 'is nothing to him', then why is it wrong? We would be left with three possible reasons why murder might be prohibited, but each of them is inadequate:

First, we could still object to killings in which the victim is made to suffer a lot of pain before he dies. But then we would be objecting to the infliction of pain and not to the killing. This would not provide an adequate justification for the prohibition on murder because quick, painless killing would still be unobjectionable. Second, we could object to killing people whose survivors would suffer on account of their deaths—but again, on this way of looking at things, the killing of people without dependants would be all right.

There remains only one way, within the hedonistic framework, of trying to explain what is wrong with killing. We might appeal to the idea that, in causing someone's death, we prevent him from enjoying pleasures in the future: we might say that killing someone is wrong because it deprives him of pleasures he *would have* experienced had he continued to live. This is also unsatisfactory, though, since it would permit the killing of people simply on the grounds that their future lives could be expected to contain less happiness than unhappiness. But the wrongness of killing does not depend on the victim's future expectations in this way. If someone *wants* to go on living, even though his life is unhappy, killing him is simple murder.

Our conclusion about Epicurus' argument is, therefore, this: once the hedonistic conception of good and evil, expressed in the first step, is granted, his conclusion follows; and with that conclusion we are unable to account for either the evil of death or the wrongness of killing. It is the hedonistic conception of good and evil that leads to these problems.

Hedonism

Hedonism is, without doubt, the most elegant theory of good and evil ever conceived. It is, first of all, beautifully *simple*. Only one thing is taken as fundamentally good, and only one as fundamentally evil. The assumption of other basic goods and evils is unnecessary, since all other goods and evils are to be explained in terms of suffering and enjoyment. Moreover, because only one thing is viewed as fundamentally good, and one as fundamentally evil, there is a theoretically pleasing *unity* among all goods and evils: no matter how disparate the group of things we regard as good or bad, in the end they must all be seen as good or bad *for the same reason*, namely, because of their connection with enjoyment or suffering. And there is even a connection between enjoyment and suffering, since they are both states of consciousness, or, as Epicurus put it, 'sensations'. So there is an even deeper kind of unity in the fundamental conception.

In addition, there is no mystery about *why* the basic good is good, or why the basic evil is evil. Suffering is so obviously an evil, just on account of what it is like, that argument would be superfluous; and the same goes for enjoyment as a good. Moreover, no matter how much people disagree about 'values', we can expect every rational person to agree about this. It is no wonder, then, that hedonism has been such an appealing view, even to the present day.

But is hedonism *true*? One might doubt that it is true simply because of the problems it creates in connection with killing. But we need to see, in a more systematic way, what its deficiencies are. There are, in my opinion, two principal mistakes involved in this view. They might be called the *logical* mistake and the *metaphysical* mistake.

The logical mistake

Wonmug was a somewhat stupid but very vain college student interested in physics. The other students would amuse themselves by making fun of him; but to his face they pretended to have great respect for his intellect. As a result, Wonmug came to believe himself to be their intellectual leader. The others thought this very funny.

Soon Wonmug's teachers joined in the joke, giving him much higher grades than he deserved and writing effusive comments on his papers. When he applied for admission to graduate school, the physicists enlisted their friends at other universities. Gradually, the entire scientific establishment came to participate in the charade. Wonmug was given a Ph.D. 'with distinction', and offered a faculty position at a distinguished university. His research was in fact inconsequential, but it was acclaimed by all his colleagues, and he didn't know the difference.

Eventually the whole world was playing along, and the joke continued for forty-five years. Wonmug was cheered at scientific meetings; his picture was twice on the cover of *Time*; and he was fêted at the White House. Finally, he was awarded the Nobel Prize. As Wonmug delivered his pompous acceptance speech, the woman he loved, but who ridiculed him behind his back, sat beside him beaming with false pride, and the members of the Swedish Academy could barely keep from laughing. When Wonmug died he sincerely believed himself to have been the greatest and most beloved figure in science since Einstein.

This ludicrous story is, of course, fictitious, but it is worth thinking about in connection with hedonism. Was Wonmug a fortunate individual, or an unfortunate one? Did he have a good life, or not? In an obvious way he was very fortunate. He received honours that most of us can only dream about. But of course there was something radically wrong. Although he *thought* he achieved great things in science, he really achieved nothing. Although he *thought* he had many friends, he really had no friends. But what is wrong with that? Hedonism says that all the things we value— knowledge, achievement, the love and respect of other people—are good *only in that they cause pleasant states of consciousness*. It is only the states of consciousness that are good 'in themselves'. Wonmug, in fact, had all the states of consciousness associated with achieve- ment, respect, and the rest. So according to hedonism he had everything good associated with those things. His life was just as good as Einstein's, and maybe even better.

Hedonism seems mistaken on this point, but how can the mistake be explained? From the outside, knowing about the deception, we see him as a pathetic figure, the butt of an elaborate joke. He is happy only because he is ignorant of what is going on. And if he were to dis- cover what is really happening, he would also come to see himself in this way, and his happiness would be shattered. But why would his happiness be diminished? The answer is that what *he* values (and what we value too) is such things as achievement and friendship. It is because he values these things, and because he thinks he has them, that he is happy. His happiness would be diminished because he would learn that he really does not have the things he values.

This is what I termed the 'logical mistake'. In saying that achievement and friendship are good because they make us happy, hedonism gets things the wrong way round. They are not good because they make us happy. Rather, having them (and other things like them) makes us happy because we recognize them *as goods*. To explain their value, then, we have to look elsewhere than to the conscious states that accompany them.

Death is like this. It is a bad thing for the person who dies, but not because of the conscious states that accompany it. (As Epicurus observed, there are no conscious states that accompany it.) Its evil is to be explained in other ways. *What* other ways is suggested by considering the second kind of hedonistic mistake.

The metaphysical mistake

To assess a theory such as hedonism, we may consider some of the particular kinds of misfortune that a person may sustain, and ask whether in fact those misfortunes can adequately be explained in the recommended terms.

One kind of misfortune, which should be 'home ground' for hedonism, is physical injury—a broken arm, for example. Suppose we ask why it is a misfortune to be physically injured. Part of the answer will indeed be found in the pain and misery which go with it: a broken arm hurts, and that is bad. But this is only part of the answer. There are also the activities from which one is barred by the injury; these must be considered as well. A broken arm is a greater misfortune for an athlete than for a scholar because it will disrupt his normal activities to a greater degree. The scholar's life may go on as usual, with only a minimum of inconvenience; the athlete, however, will not be able to go about his normal business. This is bad for him not merely because he will fret and worry over it—on the contrary, even if he were quite cheerful about the mishap, the fact that a portion of his life has been upset in a way that he would not have wished would still constitute a misfortune for him.

The more severe the injury, the more important this sort of consideration becomes: think of a promising young pianist whose hands are permanently damaged in an automobile accident, so that she can no longer play. It is tempting to think this is a misfortune for her simply because it will make her so unhappy. But this is surely an anaemic view of the matter, and not merely because stronger language would be required to do justice to her despair. If we dwell exclusively on her distress over what happened, we miss the essential nature of the tragedy. To see why this is a tragedy, we must pay attention to what she is unhappy *about*, and to the life she could have led were it not for the accident. She could have had a life as a concert pianist, but now she cannot. *That* is the tragedy. Once again, even if she is unhappy over this, we must not think her unfortunate *merely* on that account. This confuses the order of things: it is not that she is unfortunate because she is so unhappy, but that she is unhappy because she recognizes a misfortune—the loss of the ability to play—for the bad thing it is. We could not eliminate her misfortune by getting her to cheer up.

Thus hedonism makes a kind of *metaphysical* error. It implies that, in order to understand the goods and evils to which people are subject, the only elements of human nature we need to consider are the capacities to suffer and enjoy: it is only the capacity for suffering that makes people vulnerable to misfortune, and it is only the capacity for enjoyment that enables anything to be good for them. The example of the pianist suggests that this is too impoverished a picture. To understand some evils, we need to consider people as more than receptacles of happiness and unhappiness. We need to consider them as beings who have hopes, aspirations, and desires that may or may not be fulfilled; we need to consider them as the subjects of lives with possibilities that may or may not be realized. Something may be bad for a person, not only because it causes unhappiness, but because it disappoints a hope, or precludes a possibility for his life.

The evil of death is like this. When a person dies, not merely some but *all* his hopes, aspirations, and desires are frustrated, and all the possibilities for his life are cancelled. Actually, the 'all' here is a little too sweeping; some qualification is needed, and I will come to that shortly. Nevertheless, this points us in the right direction. To see why death is an evil, we need to examine the concept of a life, and see how death may affect a life badly, by putting an end to it.

The concept of a life

Generally speaking, death is a misfortune for the person who dies because it puts an end to his life. Like many philosophical theses, this is more complicated than it first appears. Death is a misfortune, not because it puts an end to one's *being alive* (in the biological sense), but because it ends one's *life* (in the biographical sense). To explain the thesis—to show how the termination of one's life can be a bad thing—we need to examine some aspects of what it means to have a life.

Complete and incomplete lives

The contingencies of human existence determine the general shape of our lives. Because we are born physically weak and without knowledge or skills, the first part of our lives is a process of growth, learning, and general maturation. Because we will not live much longer than seventy-five years, and because in the last years we will decline mentally and physically, the projects and activities that will fill our lives cannot be planned for much longer than that. The forms of life within human society are adjusted to these dimensions: families care for children while they are small and are acquiring a basic understanding of the world; schools continue the educational process; careers last about forty years; and people normally retire some time between sixty and seventy.

A life can, therefore, be complete or incomplete; it can run its course, or be cut short. Bertrand Russell lived an extraordinarily full life. Born in 1872, he lived ninety-seven years, during which time he was twice married and raised a family; he travelled the world and enjoyed the friendship of such as George Bernard Shaw, H. G. Wells, and Ludwig Wittgenstein; he published seventy-one books and pamphlets, including many that made fundamental contributions to human thought, and was awarded the Nobel Prize; and he was internationally famous as a political and moral propagandist. Compare this with the life of another philosopher, Frank P. Ramsey, who died in 1930 at the age of twenty-six. Ramsey's life had hardly begun; he had achieved only a little of what he could have achieved. The two deaths were, therefore, very different. Ramsey's death was a tragedy, while Russell's death was only the occasion for solemn reflection on a life well lived.

The tragedy of Ramsey's death was threefold. First, there was the sense of *incompleteness*. It was as though a story was only half-told; we had the beginning, and intimations of the middle, but no idea of what the ending might be. Second, there was the sense of futility connected with the fact that Ramsey's life to that point had been *training* him for something that now could not take place. He had been educated and studied philosophy and the foundations of mathematics; prepared now for fundamental work in these fields, he died before he could do it. And third, there was the sense of unfulfilled promise: Ramsey *could have* done great things; but death prevented it. None of this could be said of Russell, whose life was complete, and so Russell's death was not comparably tragic.

This does not mean that Russell's death was not a bad thing in its own way, but we must be careful in describing how it was bad. Even Russell's personal friends, saddened by his passing, must have realized that his life was rich, successful, and in some important sense complete. If there was anything bad about the death, it is because we are able to view a life as in principle open-ended, as always having further possibilities that still might be realized, if only it could go on. There were still desires that Russell could have satisfied; there were still ambitions he might have accomplished. These thoughts make sense of seeing evil even in this death.

Our equanimity about his death, however, is due to our conception of life as bounded by the natural human contingencies. If those contingencies were different, our conception of a life's possibilities would be different. In reality, the possibilities for Russell's life had been exhausted by age and the feebleness it brings; thus thoughts about what he still might have done are largely fanciful. But suppose people lived to be a hundred and fifty, and at ninety-seven Russell was still vigorous and only half-done with the tasks he could naturally expect to accomplish. Then his death would be as tragic as Ramsey's; but then, too, our conception of what a life can contain would be changed, and so the reasons for judging the death tragic would be changed.

The stages of a life

The stages of a life are not isolated or self-contained parts. They bear relations to one another that must be understood if any part of the life is to be understood.

We cannot understand what a medical student is doing, for example, if we do not appreciate the way in which her present activity is preparation for the stages of her life which will come later. She wants to be a doctor, and live the kind of life that doctors have: apart from that, her present activity makes no sense. (Thus death at an early age renders this part of the life *pointless*.)

Moreover, the *evaluation* of one stage of a life may require reference to what came before. To be a door-keeper, with a small but steady income sufficient to pay the rent on a modest apartment, might be a laudable achievement for one who previously was a homeless drunk; but for one who was a vice-president of the United States, caught taking bribes, the same existence might be a sign of failure and disgrace. (This is of course a fictitious example, since we know this is not what happens to American vice-presidents caught taking bribes.)

Thus the fact that people have memories, and are able to contemplate their futures, is important in explaining why they are able to have lives. Without these capacities, one could not see one's present condition as part of a larger, temporally extended existence; and one could have neither regrets nor aspirations.

Consider the plight of someone in whom the connections of memory have been severed. A striking example of this is described by Oliver Sacks, a professor of neurology at the Albert Einstein School of Medicine. Sacks has a patient, whom he calls Jimmie R., suffering from Korsakov's syndrome, which is associated with braindamage produced by alcohol. Jimmie remembers his life vividly up to 1945, when he was nineteen years old. After that, he remembers nothing. He is a bright, alert man who will talk to you intelligently when you are introduced; but two minutes later he will not remember having met you before and the conversation will start again. (Dr Sacks has been 're-meeting' him regularly for nine years.) He believes he is still nineteen and that it is still 1945; but this is not because he is deluded in the way of someone who thinks he is Napoleon. He is rational enough; he simply has no memory of anything that has happened between then and now. When shown himself in the mirror he panics and thinks something terrible has happened to his face. Soon, though, he forgets having seen the mirror and the worry disappears.

Of course, Jimmie cannot have a normal life because he cannot do any of the things that constitute a life—he cannot relate normally to other people, hold a job, or even take care of his basic needs by shopping for food. (He is cared for in an institution.) But his lack of memory deprives him of a life in a deeper sense: without memory, he cannot conceive of his present state as connected with any other part of himself; plans, even intentional actions become impossible in any but a truncated sense. Without these connections, even the simplest feelings and attitudes lose their objects and meaning. Sacks recorded this conversation with Jimmie:

'How do you feel?'

'How do I feel,' he repeated, and scratched his head.

'I cannot say I feel ill. But I cannot say I feel well. I cannot say I feel anything at all.'

'Are you miserable?' I continued.

'Can't say I am.'

'Do you enjoy life?'

'I can't say I do . . .'

'You don't enjoy life,' I repeated, hesitating somewhat. 'How then *do* you feel about life?'

'I can't say I feel anything at all.'

'You feel alive though?'

' "Feel alive" . . . Not really. I haven't felt alive for a very long time.'

After nine years of trying to deal with this case, Dr Sacks's own conclusion is continuing bafflement about '. . .whether, indeed, one [can] speak of an "existence", given so absolute a privation of memory or continuity'. We can, of course, speak of an 'existence' —Jimmie R. exists. But Dr Sacks's point is clear enough. Without the continuity that memory makes possible, a life, in any but the most rudimentary sense, is unattainable.

Multiple lives

We sometimes speak of a person's having more than one life: a bigamist may be said to 'lead two lives'. This is not merely an idle way of speaking; it has a point. Lives are characterized by sets of interconnected projects, concerns, and relationships. A person may be said to 'lead two lives' when there are two such sets, held rigidly separate, with little or no interaction between elements of the sets. The bigamist has two sets of relationships which must be kept absolutely apart—it is important that the members of one household not even know of the other's existence. Thus it is natural to speak of him as going back and forth between two lives.

Similarly, someone who moves to a distant city to start a new profession may be said to take up 'a new life'. Suppose a woman who was a prostitute in Miami moves to Los Angeles to become the proprietor of a clothing shop. She will spend her time on an entirely new set of activities, she will have a new set of friends—everything will be different. Like the bigamist, she may not even want her friends in Los Angeles to know about her life in Miami. Hence, a new life.

On some occasions, the effect of physical injury is to leave a patient alive and able to lead a life, but not the same life he had before. The famous 'Texas burn case', often discussed in the literature of medical ethics, is a case of this type. In 1973 a young man known as 'Donald C.' was horribly burned over 68 per cent of his body by an exploding gas line, and left blind, crippled, without fingers, and deformed in other ways as well. He was kept alive in the hospital for two years by a series of extraordinary and painful treatments; but all these treatments were against his will. Wanting to die, he continually demanded to be removed from the protective environment of the hospital. The doctors refused. He attempted to commit suicide, but was physically unable to bring it off. Finally, to justify keeping him in the hospital against his wishes, a psychiatrist was brought in to examine him, in the expectation that he would testify that Donald was incompetent. But, after interviewing him, the psychiatrist refused to do that, pronouncing—to the surprise of the physicians—that the patient was perfectly rational. So the young man was given the right to leave the hospital. But then, in a dramatic reversal, he changed his mind, and he is still alive today.

Now what could be said in defence of the judgement that this man's desire to die was rational? I believe focusing on the notion of his *life* (in the biographical sense) points us in the right direction. He was, among other things, a rodeo performer, a pilot, and what used to be called a 'ladies' man'. His life was not the life of a scholar or a solitary dreamer. What his injury had done, from his point of view, was to destroy his ability to lead the life that made him the distinctive individual he was. There could be no more rodeos, no more aeroplanes, no more dancing with the ladies, and a lot more. Donald's position was that if he could not lead *that* life, he didn't want to live.

Donald's physicians, in resisting his demand to die, argued in effect that he could take up a different sort of life, and that this different life might come to have some value for him. That is what he eventually did. The physicians may naturally think that these later developments vindicate their refusal to let Donald die, but Donald himself disagrees. Nine years after his ordeal, he appeared before a group of medical students to insist, with some bitterness, that the doctors had been wrong to refuse his demand. Although one may feel some sympathy with the doctors' view, it isn't hard to see Donald's point. We may applaud the courage he eventually showed in making a new life for himself, but we shouldn't miss noticing that his old life was gone. That is why his despair was not merely a temporary hysterical reaction to his situation.

The temporal boundaries of a life

L. C. Morris was a 63-year-old Miami man who was shot in the head one night in 1970 when police mistook him for a roof-top sniper. The damage to his brain was extensive, but he did not die. He lived on, after a fashion, in a nursing home, where for more than three years he was fed through a tube running to his stomach and periodically turned to prevent bedsores. His body had private attendants round the clock; the cost of maintaining it alive was $2,600 per month. The emotional cost to Mrs Morris cannot be calculated. Under the strain of daily visits to see him, her health deteriorated and she too had to be hospitalized. When told in 1972 that her husband might live for two more years, she replied, 'He died back in 1970. We know that.'

At the same time that Mr Morris was in his coma, Miguel Martinez was also lying unconscious in a hospital. Martinez, a well-known Spanish athlete, had been injured in a soccer game in 1964 and remained in a coma until he died eight years later. When he died, his family announced, 'Miguel died at the age of 34 after having lived 26 years.'

Mrs Morris's statement that her husband died in 1970 was simply false. The Martinez's melodramatic statement was paradoxical. Yet it is easy to see the point in both cases. The *lives* of these two men were over when they entered the comas, even though both remained alive for some time longer. Both families realized that being alive, in the absence of having a life, was not very important.

These cases illustrate that the temporal boundaries of one's life need not be the same as the temporal boundaries of one's being alive—one may remain alive long after one's life is over. Now some people, as we have noted, do not want to be kept alive in such circumstances; they may even leave specific instructions to this effect in 'living wills'. It is an interesting question why these instructions should be respected. If hedonism were true, there would be no reason for respecting these wishes *having to do with the person's own interests.* Because the person will never know whether he lived on in the coma, he cannot be angry or otherwise unhappy about it; so no harm is done to him even if he is kept alive indefinitely. But I have argued that hedonism is mistaken on this point. People are vulnerable to misfortune, not only because they are capable of suffering unhappiness, but because they may have desires that may be frustrated; and, moreover, the misfortune of frustrated desire does not *consist in* the unhappiness this might cause, even if unhappiness is caused. Thus the way is open for us to regard ignoring the patient's wishes in this matter as an offence to *him.* He will not know that we have ignored his wishes, but that does not matter; for even if he did know, the wrongness of it would not depend on his being unhappy about it.

This has the following strange consequence: a person may suffer misfortune even after he is dead. Suppose, for example, a person's life has been spent in trying to accomplish projects to which he attaches great value. Whether the life is a success or a failure may depend, partly, on the success of these projects; and he may or may not live to see the outcome. There is no good reason (unless one is under the spell of a view such as hedonism) to think it is any *less* a misfortune for him if the crucial events occur after he dies. Of course, he will not *know* what has happened to his projects; but what of that?

One man who suffered such misfortune is Nietzsche. In writing about him Philippa Foot was not concerned with any of the matters we have been considering, but she found it natural to say that

Few philosophers can ever have suffered more than Nietzsche those special misfortunes that may come to a man after his death. That his unpublished manuscripts should have been in the hands of an unscrupulous sister ready to twist his doctrines to serve the cause of an anti-semitism that he loathed; that he should have been taken as a prophet by an intellectually and morally despicable regime; that he should have been execrated not only for those parts of his writings that are, precisely, execrable, but also on account of numberless misunderstandings; that even his non-Nazi disciples should have often defended him in a childish, hysterical way.

These perversions of Nietzsche's work are now widely recognized for what they are, and so his reputation has risen. If my account is correct, this is a good thing, not just for posterity, but for him.

More and less complex lives

In discussing non-human animals, I observed that some of them do apparently have lives, and that those lives range from very simple to quite complex, although none approach the social, emotional, or intellectual complexity of (normal) human lives. And I suggested that the natural moral conclusion should be that their lives are to be protected by the rule against killing in proportion to the complexity of the life—the more complex the life, the more objectionable the killing.

But why does complexity matter? Why is it morally important? This question has not often been discussed by moral philosophers. One philosopher who has discussed it is Edward Johnson; he thinks that, in fact, mental complexity does *not* count for anything. Why, he asks, should we think that the life of a creature is less valuable simply because its mental capacities are not as complex as our own? He can think of three possible answers—that more complex beings experience greater pleasures and pains; that they are capable of different sorts of personal relationships; and that mental complexity is intrinsically valuable—and rejects each of them in turn.

But there is another, more natural explanation that Johnson does not consider. Complexity matters because, when a mentally complex being dies, much more can be said about why its death was a bad thing. A young woman dies: it is bad because she will not get to raise her children, finish her novel, learn French, improve her backhand, or do what she wanted for Oxfam; her talents will remain undeveloped, her aspirations unfulfilled. Not nearly so much of this kind could be said about a less sophisticated being. Her death is worse because there are *more reasons* for regretting it. Thus, if we had to choose between the death of a human and the death of a dog, there is reason to choose in favour of the human.

When comparisons are made between humans and other animals, this idea may be easy enough to accept. As I remarked before, it conforms fairly well to what we already instinctively feel about the animals. It explains not only why we feel that killing a human is worse than killing a dog, but why killing a dog is a more morally serious matter than squashing a bug. However, there are other implications of this idea that are more unsettling. Let me mention two such implications, one less radical and one more radical.

The less radical, but still somewhat unsettling, implication is that in most cases the life of a 'normal' human is to be preferred to the life of a mentally retarded human. This is contrary to the thought that every human life is equally sacred. Thus, it may be a hard idea to accept, for on the face of it it *sounds like* an unacceptable denigration of the mentally handicapped.

But it does not imply that the lives of the mentally handicapped are to be held cheap, or that they may be killed at will. It implies only a comparison that might come into play in a theoretical situation of 'forced choice'. The life of a mentally defective human will typically be simpler than the life of a normal human, in the same way that the life of a non-human animal is simpler; and so this idea would dictate that, in a situation of forced choice—if you *must choose* between the death of the retarded person and the death of the normal person—there is reason to choose in favour of the normal person. The reasoning is exactly the same as in the earlier comparison: where the life of the mentally more complex creature is at issue, there are more reasons why the death would be a bad thing.

I call this the 'less radical' implication because it is not quite so contrary to our normal views as it may at first appear to be. Although we may be inclined to endorse 'the equal worth of all human lives' almost by reflex—it sounds so noble, who could deny it?—not many of us really believe this high-sounding principle. Suppose you were to hear of the death of a severely retarded person at the same time as you heard of the death of the young woman in the previous example. Would you think the two deaths equally tragic? You would not have to be an especially radical thinker to see that there are important differences.

The more radical implication becomes apparent when we remember that severely retarded humans might have *less* complex mental abilities than those of some non-human animals. Then, according to the principle we are considering, there would be reason to prefer the life of the animal to that of the human. This may seem at first wildly implausible, for on the traditional view the lives of humans have special value simply because they are human, independent of any other considerations. I will discuss the idea that there is something morally special about being human—an idea that I believe should be rejected—in the next chapter, and so I ask that you suspend judgement on this matter for a few more pages.

Conclusion

Death is an evil for the person who dies because it forecloses possibilities for his or her life; because it eliminates the chance for developing abilities and talents; because it frustrates desires, hopes, and aspirations; and because it leaves parts of lives pointless and whole lives incomplete.

These results reinforce the conclusion of Chapter 2. In Chapter 2, I argued that the moral rule against killing should be construed as protecting lives and the interests of beings who are the subjects of lives. In this chapter, we have asked why it is bad to die, and we have seen that the explanation is connected with various aspects of the concept of a life. From a theoretical point of view, this leaves matters rather tidy. The explanation of the point of the rule against killing, and the explanation of why it is bad to die, should fit together. And, on the account presented here, they do.

4 'INNOCENT HUMANS'

The case of Baby Jane Doe

On 11 October 1983, an infant known to the public only as 'Baby Jane Doe' was born in New York and subsequently transferred to the State University of New York (SUNY) Hospital in Stony Brook. Baby Jane Doe suffered from multiple defects including spina bifida (a broken and protruding spine), hydrocephaly (excess fluid on the brain), and, perhaps worst of all, microencephaly (an abnormally small brain). A computerized tomography scan (CAT-scan) indicated that part of her cerebral cortex was missing altogether. The parents were told that without surgery, the infant would die within two years; with surgery, she would have a fifty-fifty chance of surviving into her twenties—but even then she would be severely mentally retarded and physically impaired, paralysed, epileptic, unable to leave her bed, and there would be a continuous high risk of such diseases as meningitis. In the face of all this, the parents chose not to authorize the surgery.

This decision was similar to many others made by parents in recent years. Since the landmark paper by Duff and Campbell in the *New England Journal of Medicine* over a decade ago, the facts about such choices have been well known. Considering this, the case of Baby Jane Doe would not have been newsworthy had it not been for the intervention of third parties. But there was intervention, and the push-and-pull that followed illustrates the depth of the division that exists, not only among the public, but between the branches of the American government as well. The executive and legislative branches actively sought, and are still seeking, to limit the range of parental choice in such cases; while the courts have more or less consistently championed the right of the parents to decide.

First, a lawyer named Lawrence Washburn, who represents

some conservative right-to-life groups, successfully petitioned the New York State Supreme Court to order that the surgery be performed on Baby Jane. However, higher courts in New York quickly overturned the order, calling Washburn's suit 'offensive'. He then asked the US Supreme Court to order the surgery, but the Supreme Court declined to hear the case.

Then the executive branch of the federal government got into the act. The federal government provides medicare and medicaid (State-funded medical insurance) payments to hospitals, but hospitals that practise unjust discrimination are not eligible for these funds (although the point of the regulations, at least before this case, seems to have been that agencies cannot practise discrimination *in employment* and still be eligible for federal funds). So the Department of Justice filed suit demanding access to the SUNY Hospital's records in order to determine whether a 'handicapped person'—Baby Jane Doe—was being discriminated against. This suit was subsequently dismissed in the federal court, with the judge declaring that:

The papers submitted to the court demonstrate conclusively that the decision of the parents to refuse consent to the surgical procedures was a reasonable one based on due consideration of the medical options available and on a genuine concern for the best interests of the child.

Washburn, however, did not give up. After all this had taken place, he asked the Federal District Court once again to appoint a guardian who would have access to the baby's records. This time the judge fined Washburn $500 under a rule that allows judges to discipline lawyers who are trying 'to harrass or to cause unnecessary delay or needlessly increase the cost of litigation'.

Coincidentally the US Department of Health and Human Services was formulating a new set of guidelines to govern hospitals in dealing with such cases. (These guidelines were prompted by public controversy over earlier, similar cases.) The final regulations were released during the week of Washburn's $500 fine. The guidelines required hospitals to post notices stating that 'nourishment and medically beneficial treatment . . . should not be withheld from handicapped infants solely on the basis of their present or anticipated mental or physical handicap'. The notices went on to encourage anyone suspecting such a thing to report it on the twenty-four-hour telephone 'hotline' maintained for this purpose by the DHHS.

Once again, the executive branch's 'final regulations' were promptly struck down by the courts. On 23 May 1984, Judge Charles L. Brieant of the US District Court for the Southern District of New York declared them to be 'invalid, unlawful, and without statutory authority'. The American Medical Association, which had opposed the guidelines, declared itself to be 'elated' by this turn of events. But within five months Congress had responded by passing *new* 'Baby Doe' legislation, requiring States receiving federal child-abuse prevention grants to adopt rules covering 'medical neglect'. And once again, the AMA promised to fight the legislation in court.

The fundamental issue

The debate over this case, both in the courts and in the Press, centred partly on the question of the confidentiality of hospital records, but more prominently on the question of parental autonomy—the question of whether the parents have the right to decide when their children will have such surgery. But these are not really the central issues. The more fundamental question concerns the value of the infant's life. If, in fact, Baby Jane Doe's life merits the very same moral protection as that of a normal human being, then I think we should all agree that the conservatives are right, and the parents should not be allowed to refuse the treatment. Suppose it *were* a normal child, and the parents were rejecting a procedure which would allow it to proceed to a normal life. Then how many of us would defend their 'right to choose'? Would you say that I have the right to deny appropriate medical care for my (normal) fourteen-year-old son? Of course not. The view that parents *do* have the right to decide in cases like that of Baby Jane Doe presupposes that such children's lives are not being assigned the same value. The conservatives, on the other hand, are assuming that their lives *should* be given the same value, and so they say parents should not be permitted discretion. That is what really separates the two groups.

Often, people are reluctant to face up to this fundamental issue. We hear them say things like 'Only God can decide when a life has value', or 'We do not have the *right* to decide that a human life has no value.' It is worth pausing to consider why people say such things. First, there is the clear suggestion that the value of human life is just too big an issue for us to tackle; it seems somehow *presumptuous* to take a position, especially if, by taking the wrong position, we run the risk of condemning some humans unjustly. Moreover, as conservatives are wont to emphasize, there is a fear that somehow we will poison our moral sensibilities if we entertain the thought that some lives are worth less than others. Patrick J. Buchanan, once an aide to President Nixon, then a syndicated newspaper columnist and television pundit, and now a speechwriter for President Reagan, had this to say about Baby Jane Doe:

Once however, we embrace this utilitarian [sic] ethic—that Man has the sovereign right to decide who is entitled to life and who is not—we have boarded a passenger train on which there are no scheduled stops between here and Birkenau.

Once we accept that there are certain classes—i.e. unwanted unborn children, unwanted infants who are retarded or handicapped, etc.—whose lives are unworthy of legal protection, upon what moral high ground do we stand to decry when Dr Himmler slaps us on the back, and asks us if he can include Gypsies and Jews?

Taken as a piece of reasoning aimed at supporting the conservative approach, this argument is not difficult to refute. (It is a version of the 'slippery-slope' argument that I discuss in some detail in Chapter 10, pp. 170–80 below.) However, in addition to whatever rational force they have, such remarks have the rhetorical effect of intimidating the opposition—Buchanan is saying, in effect, '*My* side occupies the moral high ground.' And nervous liberals often reveal that they are ready to concede this when they refuse to join the issue. Instead of replying directly, they try to avoid the question of the value of life and redirect attention to some smaller matter such as the parents' right to decide. But this cannot be done, for any conclusion about the smaller issue will simply presuppose an answer to the larger one. It is a mistake to think that the question of the value of the child's life can be side-stepped by pretending that the issue is only one of parental autonomy.

There is no good reason why we should be reluctant to face the question of the value of life head-on. It is a big question, but it is not intractable. Of all moral questions, this is one on which we *should* have a rational view. Nor will our sensibilities be corrupted by considering the possibility that the conservatives are wrong. For one thing, each of us already believes that different human lives have different values, whether we realize it or not. Nobody really thinks that all lives are equal. Suppose one had to choose between Karen Quinlan dying, and say, the American opera singer Beverly Sills dying—does anyone really think it would be an indifferent choice? Or, if you do not like the image of choosing, simply imagine that you were to hear, after the fact, that both these women had died. Would anyone, including Patrick Buchanan, really think that the two deaths were equally tragic? (The comparable tragedy, in the case of Karen Quinlan, was not her dying, but her going into the irreversible coma in the first place.) These simple questions show that, contrary to what conservatives might suggest, the division of 'lives' into more valuable and less valuable is already an established part of our moral common sense.

This point has been recognized, implicitly at least, even by the most conservative figures. Dr C. Everett Koop, Surgeon General of the United States, was a leader in the effort to compel aggressive treatment for Baby Jane Doe. At a Press conference discussing the case, he said 'This is a fight for a principle of this country that every life is individually and uniquely sacred.' But, after proclaiming it, he could not maintain this as an absolute principle. When confronted with the example of anencephaly—babies born without brains—he conceded that *their* lives need not be given the same importance.

Subnormal lives

In his essay on suicide, first published in 1783, David Hume declared that 'The life of a man is of no greater importance to the universe than that of an oyster.' But even if Hume was right, there is no particular cause to despair. Our lives may have importance to us—it may be a bad thing to die *for the person who dies*—even if the universe is indifferent. Thus, it is possible to formulate a general, rationally defensible answer to the question of when a life has value, even while admitting that 'from the point of view of the universe' we are indescribably small and insignificant.

In Chapters 2 and 3 I argued that it is *having a life* and not merely *being alive* that is of value to the individual. Human beings are complex creatures who have a rich mix of desires and aspirations.

They enjoy pleasures and suffer pains; they are curious, and want to understand themselves and the world around them. They are gregarious; they form friendships and seek the company of others like themselves. They accomplish things, although sometimes they are frustrated in the attempt. And of course much more of this kind could be said. Our lives are the sum of all this. A person's life is, quite literally, all he has, and so the value of his life, to him, is beyond calculation.

All this is true of what we might call a 'normal' human life. But when we begin to consider subnormal lives, the assessment of value changes. By a 'subnormal' life I mean one from which the various valuable elements have been removed. Consider a life in which there is no possibility of satisfying one's desires or aspirations; or a life in which friendships are impossible; or one filled only with pain, from which the possibility of enjoyment has been eliminated. Such a life will not have the value which it otherwise might have had. This judgement is not an attempt to impose some 'outside' perspective on the person's situation. The point is that such a 'life' will not have as much value *for the subject of that life*.

Let me put this argument in a different way. When we think about the value of life, we may easily be mesmerized by the idea that there is something special about *life*. And so there is—a person's life, as I said, is all he has, and so its value is very great. But in another respect, there is nothing special about this question. We may approach it by using the same general principles that come into play when we think about any question of value. One such principle is this:

If something is (positively) valuable because it contains certain elements, and those elements are removed and are not replaced by anything equally valuable, nor is that loss compensated in any other way, then that thing is made less valuable as a result.

The argument about subnormal lives is simply an application of this general principle to the specific issue of life. A person's life has value because it contains the elements I mentioned, and others like them. When they are removed, and are not replaced by anything of equal value, it follows that the value of the life must be diminished.

Baby Jane Doe is, without doubt, alive; moreover, if her existence were prolonged by surgery, she would remain alive for perhaps twenty years. But this is not, by itself, important. As we have seen, merely being alive does one no good unless it enables one to have a life.

The crucial question is, therefore, *Would she have a recognizably human life?* We are told that she would lack the mental and physical abilities to engage in even simple human activities; she would not be capable of normal associations with other people, of being curious about the world and having that curiosity satisfied, of enjoying the things that people enjoy, and much more. It would not, in short, be a human life, in any sense other than that she would be a member of the biological species who is alive.

What conclusion, then, should we reach about this case? It is tempting to cling to the old saws: 'Every human life, no matter how pitiful, has the same inherent value.' Or, as Dr Koop put it, 'every life is individually and uniquely sacred'. But, once we have distinguished between the two senses of 'life', the old saws look muddled rather than noble. (Is it being alive, or having a life, that has 'the same inherent value'?) The inescapable conclusion is that Baby Jane Doe, tragically, does not have even the prospect of a life; and thus we cannot appeal to 'the value of human life' as an objection to non-treatment in her case.

It is misleading to think of her as a 'handicapped person', as conservative commentators, and apparently the United States Department of Justice, would have us do. It is a clever rhetorical ploy—we all agree that handicapped people should receive every possible benefit; therefore, if we could be persuaded to place Baby Jane Doe in this category, we would have to agree that it is wrong to deny her aggressive medical care. But, to think of Baby Jane Doe as a handicapped person is somewhat like thinking of Karen Quinlan as a handicapped person. Typical handicaps—blindness, deafness, loss of limbs, partial paralysis, and even mild mental retardation—leave one fully capable of having a human life, even though the handicap makes things more difficult. Baby Jane Doe, on the other hand, like Karen Quinlan in her coma, lacks this capability. That is why categorizing her with 'the handicapped' is perverse. Lacking a life, or even the possibility of one, is not a 'handicap'.

If we accept the conclusion that Baby Jane Doe's life really is less valuable than that of a normal baby, will we, as Patrick Buchanan claims, 'have boarded a passenger train on which there are no scheduled stops between here and Birkenau'? In the first place, as I have already pointed out, the idea that some lives are more valuable than others is already a part of our moral common sense; it is not some insidious new thought which, once admitted, will corrupt our hearts and lead us into unimaginable wickedness. Moreover, our distinction between Baby Jane Doe's 'life' (or lack of it) and other, fuller human lives expresses a rational moral principle, whereas Dr Himmler's prejudices do not—it is nothing but rhetorical bullying to claim they are in the same category.

Normal humans have an equal right to life because they benefit equally from having a life. The capacity to live one's life is precious to one *no matter what type of person one is*, whether one is an athlete or politician, intellectual or labourer, man or woman, Oriental or occidental, Gypsy or Jew. That is also true, in a sense, of Baby Jane Doe: the capacity to live a life would be no less precious to her, if she had such a capacity. But, sadly, that is exactly the crucial capacity she lacks; and that is why her parents, in opting against surgery, were not doing her any harm.

'An innocent human'

Those who accept the dominant Western tradition concerning the value of life will not be happy with the preceding argument, for it does not address what they consider to be the most important facts about Baby Jane Doe. Baby Jane Doe is, after all, a human being— not a dog or a monkey—and traditionalists like to say *that* is what makes omitting treatment such a morally serious matter. What is important, it is urged, is not whether she is 'normal', but whether she is human. Moreover, she is an *innocent* human and, as such, her life cannot be said to have any less value than anyone else's.

In Chapter 1, we looked briefly at the history of these notions. (You may want to glance at pp. 11–14 again.) But we have not yet examined them critically. Now let us ask: Apart from the fact that these notions are honoured by the tradition, is there anything about being innocent, or being human, that puts one in a special moral category? Is there any *reason* we should accept the traditional view of their significance?

The limited importance of innocence

In announcing that he would seek a second term as President,

Ronald Reagan emphasized his support for a constitutional amendment allowing the States to prohibit abortion. He said, 'We must stop this slaughter of innocents.' He did not say 'babies' or 'children' or anything of that sort—he said 'innocents'. Nothing could better illustrate how the traditional perspective dominates our thinking than the fact that a politician would find this terminology so natural.

'Innocence', as the term is used in the tradition, obviously denotes something of moral significance. A non-innocent person is one who is unjustly threatening the life of another, or has unjustly killed another; and that does make a difference in how he may be treated. But the importance of the notion is much more limited than defenders of the tradition have realized.

Consider this. Suppose someone believes that all killing of humans is wrong; but for some reason, he changes his mind about euthanasia. He decides that voluntary euthanasia for persons suffering painful terminal illness is permissible. But all the other familiar types of killing he continues to think wrong: he condemns not only abortion and infanticide, but capital punishment, killing in war, and killing in self-defence. This would be a peculiar combination of views, but it is a possible one; and we are supposing it is his.

He now faces a problem of moral theory. He would like to have a principle that would summarize and support this combination of judgements. Previously, he followed the simple principle that killing human beings is always wrong. But what principle does he follow now? What principle, he asks, will permit euthanasia, while at the same time forbidding the other types of killing? The key to solving this problem, he sees, is that the candidate for euthanasia is in bad health, while the potential victims of the other types of killing are healthy. Thus he affirms the new, more sophisticated principle: the intentional killing of *healthy* humans is always wrong.

Other people, of course, may not share this man's peculiar opinions, and when he insists that killing in self-defence, for example, is wrong, they may demand to know why. Suppose he then offers this syllogism, which he considers decisive: The intentional killing of the healthy is always wrong; killing in self-defence is the intentional killing of the healthy; therefore, killing in self-defence is always wrong. Should the sceptics be impressed?

Obviously, they need not be at all impressed by this argument. Although it is formally valid, that's about all that can be said for it. The obvious question is, why should we accept the principle that the intentional killing of the healthy is always wrong? Doesn't this simply beg the question about self-defence? Of course, if one had *already* decided, on *other* grounds, that killing in self-defence and the other kinds of killing are wrong, and that the only permissible killing is euthanasia, *then* one might find the principle plausible. But if one had not already decided all that, there would be no reason at all to accept the principle.

The principle that it is always wrong to kill the healthy is, of course, silly. No one has ever defended it, and there is no reason anyone should. Yet the traditional prohibition upon killing the innocent is exactly analogous—and, it would seem, despite its venerability, it is equally silly.

Defenders of the traditional doctrine have used the prohibition upon killing the innocent as an argument against euthanasia, abortion, and the like, in an exactly similar manner. For example, after conceding a right to kill aggressors, the contemporary Jesuit scholar Gerald Kelly adds that

innocent human life is absolutely inviolable. By reason of this principle, we exclude all direct killing of the innocent, e.g. by . . . 'mercy killing,' by all direct abortion . . .

And Kelly's colleague, Bishop Joseph Sullivan, sounds the same theme:

it is never lawful for man on his own authority to kill the innocent directly. If this thesis is morally sound, if follows that mercy killing is never permissible.

Thus both writers think this argument is decisive: The intentional killing of the innocent is always wrong; euthanasia is the intentional killing of the innocent; therefore, euthanasia is always wrong. It would be easy to cite other writers who rely on the same argument. The traditional principle is no mere historical relic.

But the appeal to innocence is no better as an argument against euthanasia than the appeal to health is as an argument against killing in self-defence. The same sort of reaction is in order: why should we accept the principle? If we had *already* decided, on *other* grounds, that euthanasia, abortion, and the like are wrong, and that the only acceptable kinds of killing are in war, individual self-defence, and as punishment, *then* we might find the principle plausible. The early Christians had decided for reasons of political expediency that the line between acceptable and unacceptable killing should be drawn at just that point; and so they affirmed the principle. But what if we have not already made that choice? Then we would have no reason to affirm that principle, and so the argument from it should not persuade us. It merely begs the question.

Is it possible to defend the traditional principle by giving a general argument in its favour? There is one such argument implicit in the tradition. God, it is said, endows every human being with a right to life, so that—initially—no one may legitimately take the life of another. However, a person retains this right only so long as he respects the rights of others. If he attacks the lives of others, he forfeits his right to his own life. Now comes the key step of the argument: the right to life can be forfeited, *but it cannot be waived*. I can forfeit my right, and make it permissible for you to kill me, by attacking you, but I cannot make it permissible for you to kill me simply by asking you to do so. (Why may I not simply waive my right? Apparently because God forbids it.) From this it is concluded that the only situation in which killing is permissible is that in which the right to life has been forfeited. Hence the crucial importance of innocence.

To see what a peculiar argument this is, we may reflect for a moment on a different right—the right to property. If a person has a right to a certain piece of property—if he owns it—then no one may rightly take it away from him. He may, however, forfeit his right to that property by his own misconduct. For example, if he maliciously destroys something that belongs to another, his property may be taken away to replace what he has destroyed. But he may also waive his right by giving his property away—he may make someone a gift of it, or he may simply renounce his claim to the property, and invite others to take it away. If he does this, then whoever takes the property away is not violating his rights.

Why, then, may a person not simply renounce his right to life? Someone dying of a painful illness might very well want to do this. If such a person *asks* to be killed, it would not seem that the one who kills him violates his rights. At this point it becomes clear why the religious framework is indispensable for the traditional argument. A person's life is conceived as belonging, not to himself, but to God. That is why life is not like property; that is why a person may not dispose of his life on his own authority.

Is it possible to construct a non-theological argument to support the principle that the intentional killing of the innocent is always wrong? This principle, after all, has no specifically religious content, and it is presented as a principle of morality, binding on everyone, theist and non-theist alike. So a non-theological argument should be possible. But I doubt that a convincing argument can be found. Let me explain why, again referring to the silly rule about health.

It is simply irrelevant to urge, as a reason against killing in self-defence, that the one to be killed is healthy. The state of his health has nothing to do with the issue; what is relevant is that he is attacking you with deadly force, and that the only way to defend yourself is by killing him. If it is said of the aggressor, 'But he is healthy!' the reply will be, 'But what does *that* have to do with it?'

Similarly, it is irrelevant to urge, as a reason against euthanasia, that the one to be killed is innocent. The fact that he is not an aggressor has nothing to do with the issue; what is relevant is that he is dying wretchedly, and so forth. If it is said of the dying person, 'But he is innocent!' the reply may be, 'But what does *that* have to do with it?'

Innocence is essentially a negative notion: a person's innocence consists in his *not* having done certain things—he has not killed anyone, he is not attacking anyone or threatening anyone, and so on. (Foetuses and infants are often cited as paradigmatically innocent humans, and it is easy to see why, for they cannot have done any of these things to become not innocent.) The moral importance of innocence is, similarly, negative. If a person is innocent, then certain sorts of justifications for killing him *cannot* be used. Killing him cannot be justified because he has committed a heinous crime, deserving of death; for he has committed no such crime. Killing him cannot be justified on the grounds that he is our enemy in a just war, or on the grounds that he maliciously threatens the life of another, for if he is innocent he is not doing such things. The fact of innocence rules out these justifications of killing—but that is all it does. *It does not rule out other possible justifications.* That is why it is irrelevant to urge, against euthanasia, that the dying person is innocent. The argument about euthanasia is not an argument about innocence.

Of course I have only been using euthanasia as an example; the same point could be made in connection with abortion, suicide, infanticide, and all the rest. In the case of Baby Jane Doe, the fact that she is 'innocent' is as irrelevant as the fact that enemy soldiers are healthy. Any attempt to argue her case on such grounds will only commit the fallacy of importing considerations that are relevant in entirely different sorts of cases, and assuming that those considerations must play the same role in this case. But they do not.

Thus it seems highly unlikely that there could be a general argument centring on innocence that would establish, at one go, a principle which would govern the morality of killing in *all* areas. Because it relies on such a principle, the traditional doctrine appears to be be misguided in its most fundamental approach.

The unimportance of being human

I have already remarked on the importance our tradition attaches to being human. In this tradition, the moral law forbids killing *humans* while placing virtually no value on the lives of other animals. This has obvious implications for the other animals; they may be slaughtered at our whim. But it also has important implications in cases such as that of Baby Jane Doe. Baby Jane Doe is human—doesn't that count for something, even though she suffers grave 'handicaps'? 'All human beings have equal rights, simply because they are human' has been the rallying-cry of virtually every good cause in modern times: the struggle against slavery, the struggle against anti-semitism, the civil-rights movement, the defence of the impoverished and the handicapped, and more. Against this background, to deny that being human is enough to give one's life value may seem morally perverse.

But to deny the importance of being human is not to argue against these good causes; it is only to point out the fallacy of basing one's support for them on this particular principle. Membership of a biological species is not what makes one's interests morally important. This can be seen easily enough by imagining a species different from our own, but having the same capacities we have. Suppose we were visited by beings from another planet who, although unlike ourselves biologically, speak a language translatable into English. These extraterrestrials, we will suppose, have science and morality; they care for their families; they have a complex society; and so on. They are, in short, psychologically indistinguishable from us, except that they are technologically more advanced. Wouldn't it be just as wrong to murder one of these creatures, or otherwise harm one of them, as it would be to murder or harm a human? If someone thought they did not merit the same moral consideration, wouldn't that just be a new form of racism (which has been called 'speciesism')?

Again, to deny that species membership is important is not to deny that the interests of humans are important. Humans are psychologically complex creatures, with varied desires, aspirations, and relationships to one another—*that* makes it important to respect them, even though the fact that they are human, rather than, say, canine or Martian, is of little significance. It is individual characteristics, and not species membership, that makes beings morally special.

In recent years this point has been made with great force by partisans of the animal-rights movement, who have argued, correctly in my opinion, that it is wrong to discount the interests of non-human animals merely because they are not members of our species. To the extent that non-humans have the same individual characteristics as humans—for example, the capacity to suffer pain—we should treat them as we would treat humans. (Tormenting animals is wrong for exactly the same basic reason that tormenting humans is wrong, namely, that it *hurts*.) At the same time, to the extent that humans have different capacities—for example, the capacities to read, appreciate literature, and practise science—they may be treated differently. (Thus no one would suggest admitting non-humans to universities—or at least, not the non-humans with which we are presently familiar. Some day, extraterrestrials may qualify.) Morality, it would seem, requires that we adjust our treatment of creatures to their individual capacities.

This, however, has some radical consequences. Consider a severely retarded human, whose capacities are no greater, and perhaps are even less, than those of a chimpanzee. On what grounds could we justify treating the human better? If species membership is not itself a sufficient ground, it would seem that the chimp merits the same moral consideration. Although I believe this conclusion is unavoidable, it has been vigorously resisted—not surprisingly, since it goes against deeply ingrained feelings. But the only plausible way to resist this conclusion is by asserting that species membership is, after all, morally important.

Robert Nozick has taken exactly this line, and it is worth quoting him at some length. Here we see what a philosopher of undoubted intellect can produce in the effort to defend the traditional view:

> Normal human beings have various capacities that we think form the basis of the respectful treatment these people are owed. How can someone's merely being a member of the same species be a reason to treat him in certain ways when he [i.e., a severely retarded human] so patently lacks those very capacities? This does present a puzzle, hence an occasion to formulate a deeper view. We would then understand the inadequacy of a 'moral individualism' that looks only at a particular organism's character-istics and deems irrelevant something as fundamental and essential as species membership.

When faced with an apparently sound chain of reasoning that leads to a surprising result, we have two options. We could conclude that we have made a new discovery: the reasoning teaches us something (for example, that species membership is not in itself a morally significant matter) that we did not realize before. Or, if we find the surprising result hard to take, we might refuse to accept the reasoning. Here Nozick chooses the second path; and so he regards it as a 'puzzle' to explain why species membership is in fact impor-tant. To say this is a 'puzzle' is to *assume* that species membership *is* important, as though that were something we know to be true, and to take it merely as outstanding business to figure out why. Following up on this thought, he adds that 'Nothing much should be inferred from our not presently having a theory of the moral importance of species membership that no one has spent much time trying to formulate because the issue hasn't seemed pressing.'

Here we have run up against a fundamental issue of philo-sophical method. Do we trust arguments, and follow them wher-ever they lead, or do we trust our intuitions and reject argument when it does not lead in the 'right' direction? (I discuss this issue in more detail in Chapter 8, pp. 129–34 and 148–50 below.) There is no simple answer. If a chain of reasoning is implausible and unconvincing, and leads to a ridiculous conclusion, it may be wise to distrust the reasoning and examine it for possible mistakes. On the other hand, the present case is not like that. The reasoning which leads to the conclusion that species membership is not morally important is, to me at least, plausible and convincing, and the conclusion itself, upon reflection, seems right. So I see no reason to distrust it. Still, it is possible that Nozick (or someone else) might produce a persuasive argument to the contrary, in which case the whole matter would have to be reconsidered. But, in the face of the arguments to the contrary, it does not seem right simply to assume that species membership *must* be important.

Nozick makes two suggestions about the formulation of a 'deeper view'. The first is this:

The traits of normal human beings (rationality, autonomy, a rich internal psychological life, etc.) have to be respected by all, including any denizens of Alpha Centauri. But perhaps it will turn out that the bare species characteristic of simply being human, as the most severely retarded people are, will command special respect only from other humans—this is an instance of the general principle that the members of any species may legitimately give their fellows more weight than they give members of other species (or at least more weight than a neutral view would grant them). Lions, too, if they were moral agents, could not then be criticized for putting the interests of other lions first.

The 'general principle' to which Nozick refers seems to be an expanded version of something that most people find plausible, namely, that one is justified in giving special weight to the interests of one's family or one's neighbours. If it is proper to have special regard for one's family and neighbours, why not for one's fellow species members?

The problem with this approach is that we can define lots of groups to which we naturally belong, and it is not obvious (to say the least) that these group memberships are morally significant. Suppose it were suggested that we are justified in having special regard for members of our own *race*? That suggestion would rightly be rejected; but why? To resist the suggestion, it might be said that members of other races are rational, autonomous, and have rich internal psychological lives, as we do; therefore they should be treated with equal regard. But the Nozickian reply is that this only places us with respect to them as a 'denizen of Alpha Centauri' would be placed with respect to us. Since we have a *special* relation to members of our own race, which those denizens do not have, it may be reasonable for us to give them special treatment, even if the Alpha Centaurians have no reason to do so. If this way of thinking is to be rejected with respect to race, I see no good reason to accept it with respect to species. (The point is not that Nozick is a racist. He is not. The point is that, in attempting to justify discrimination based on species, he has inadvertently produced an argument which, if accepted, would justify racist discrimination as well.)

Nozick's second suggestion is, I believe, logically independent of the first:

We see humans, even defective ones, as part of the multifarious texture of human history and civilizations, human achievements and human family relations. Animals, even year-old mammals, we see against a different background and texture. The differences are enormous and endless. It will be asked, 'But what precise aspects of these endless differences legitimately make the moral difference?' This question assumes that something much simpler than the total differences between two rich tapestries (one richer than the other) will, by itself, constitute the morally relevant difference. Yet this need not be so. For the two organisms, human and other mammal, we can state a difference. One is part of one tapestry, one of another. But if we are asked to state the morally relevant difference between all of human civilization and the animal kingdom, we may find ourselves, understandably, without any succinct answer.

Such a grand proposal is difficult to assess, but three comments seem relevant. First, it is easy to distinguish various 'tapestries' *within* human history. Oriental history and civilizations have developed and endured, throughout most of history, with very little interaction with the West. We could then rewrite this entire passage (substituting 'Westerner' for 'human' and 'Oriental' for 'mammal') as a justification for treating Westerners better. (The same trick might be tried for 'Europeans' and 'Africans'.)

Second, this proposal ignores the fact that the defective human in question *has had nothing at all to do with* the history and civilizations being cited. Certainly, when we think of the Greeks and Romans, the medieval cathedrals, the rise of modern science, the great civilizations of China and India, and all the rest, we are filled with awe—and if we associate the defective human with all that, it may seem plausible that she has some special status. But what exactly is her connection with all that? Only that she is a member of the same species as the beings who have done all of it. Thus, the talk of history and civilization seems to add little to the original unadorned talk about species membership.

Third, both proposals seem to provide more of an explanation than a justification of our feelings. Suppose we ask *what explains* (not what justifies?) our feeling that humans are morally special? Part of the answer might be that *we* are human, and this prejudices us in a way that the Alpha Centaurians are not prejudiced. Another part of the answer might be that humankind has a magnificent history. Reflecting on that history we are awe-struck, and, associating this magnificence with the human race, we tend to have a special regard for all humans, simply because they are human. (As Nozick says, we see them against this background and texture.) These considerations go some way towards explaining our feelings, and that is why Nozick's suggestions are plausible. But *justifying* those feelings is a different matter. The other arguments I have given suggest that, considered as justifications, they are much weaker.

Thus, an examination of Nozick's proposals does nothing to decrease confidence in the original proposition that species membership is not itself a morally important matter. On the contrary, the inability of a thinker of Nozick's ingenuity to come up with anything better than this only increases that confidence.

The belief that species membership *is* important is one of those moral convictions that we feel, intuitively, *must* be true; and it is surprising that, on analysis, it turns out to be false. But appreciating its falsity leads to the improvement of our moral thinking in a variety of ways. In the case of Baby Jane Doe, appreciating the irrelevance of the fact that she is human frees us to focus without distraction on just those matters that *are* relevant—principally, that keeping her alive would do neither her nor her parents any good, for the only 'life' of which she is capable is merely biological.

My conclusion about Baby Jane Doe, then, is this. The facts are (1) that she is human, (2) that she is innocent, (3) that she is alive, and with constant care can remain alive for perhaps twenty years, and (4) that she does not and never will have a life. The first three are not enough to confer any value on her 'life', either singly or jointly. And the fourth means that her 'life' in the morally important sense will never exist; so, sadly, there is nothing to be concerned with, from a moral point of view.

5 SUICIDE AND EUTHANASIA

Barney Clark's key

There are signs that our society is moving away from a rigid insistence that one may never choose the time of one's death. The case of Barney Clark is a conspicuous recent example.

On 2 December 1982 Barney Clark became the first human to receive a permanent artificial heart. The retired Seattle dentist seemed ideally suited for the new procedure. He was dying of a heart disease that did not respond to other treatments and, at sixty-one, he was considered too old for a conventional transplant. Otherwise he was in good physical condition. Psychologically, he also seemed right: Margaret Miller, a social worker on the implantation evaluation committee at the University of Utah, where the operation was performed, commented, 'He had a very strong will to live, had an intelligent, thorough understanding of his disease and what his option was, was a flexible person, and had a loving, supportive family.'

Barney Clark's 'option', while no doubt preferable to death, was not without its drawbacks. Unlike a transplant, the artificial heart would not leave him fully mobile. For the rest of his life he would be tethered to a bulky compressor by two six-foot hoses. So everyone involved was uncertain about what the quality of his life would be, either in terms of physical discomfort or in terms of restrictions upon his activities. One of the attending physicians, interviewed on television, was asked about this. 'Will he have a good life? That's not for us to say,' he responded. 'Barney Clark will be the judge of that.'

The implantation received an enormous amount of publicity, almost all of it ecstatic over the new technology. However, buried among the enthusiastic newspaper and magazine articles hailing the great breakthrough was one small item that struck a different note. It was reported that Barney Clark had been given a key that he could use to turn off the compressor if he should wish at any time to cease living tied to the machine.

'If the man suffers and feels it isn't worth it any more, he has a key that he can apply,' said Dr Willem Kolff, head of the University of Utah's Artificial Organs Division, inventor of the artificial kidney, and founder of the artificial heart program.

'I think it is entirely legitimate that this man whose life has been extended should have the right to cut it off if he doesn't want it, if life ceases to be enjoyable,' he added.

'The operation won't be a success unless he is happy. That has always been our criteria—to restore happiness.'

Considering the dominant ethical tradition of our culture, this is a remarkable thing for Dr Kolff to have said. As we have seen, most Western moralists have denied that a person has the right to end his life even in the most extreme circumstances when it is filled with terrible suffering. Yet Dr Kolff offered the even more radical idea that Barney Clark could end his life if he was merely unhappy. He was ascribing to Clark a very wide-ranging discretionary power. It was reminiscent of what Epictetus said about choosing death: 'If the room is smoky, if only moderately, I will stay; if there is too much smoke I will go. Remember this, keep a firm hold on it, the door is always open.' As part of the official arrangements concerning the new artificial heart, Barney Clark was given the key to the door.

He never used the key. Fifteen weeks after the history-making operation, Barney Clark died. But although he never used it, the fact that he was given the key is significant for our social stance regarding voluntary death.

What the key signified

What were the ethical implications of giving him the key? First, it was an acknowledgement that in this case suicide would have been permissible. The element of acknowledgement is important. In the past we had often refrained from condemning suicides when they were performed in desperate circumstances; but we had never, as a society, openly acknowledged the permissibility of the act. Our society's position—if I may use so broad a notion—was expressed in the condemnation of suicide by both Christian and Jewish authorities, and by a legal system that still, in many jurisdictions, forbids it. Giving Barney Clark his key involved a new social stance.

Indeed, the public adoption of this stance seemed to be the only point of giving him the key. He certainly did not need a key to disconnect himself from the compressor. He could have done that by unplugging it, or by cutting the cords with a knife, or in any number of other ways. Why, then, give him a key? Obviously, it was a way of saying that cutting the connection would be all right. The key symbolized the social acceptability of the act.

Second, this stance has implications for other related issues of life and death. It is only a very small step from accepting Barney Clark's potential suicide to accepting voluntary euthanasia—after all, the only difference between suicide and euthanasia is that, in the former, one does the deed oneself, while in the latter one solicits the help of others. And if it is permissible to do the deed oneself, how can it be wrong to enlist aid? If it is permissible for Barney Clark to turn the key, how can it be wrong for a friend to turn it for him?

Many people will doubt that Barney Clark's key has these implications. (Some may even think it insulting to him and his doctors to suggest as much.) Those who approve of him being provided with the key, but who do not approve of euthanasia, will wish to deny the connection. But the connection, in my opinion, is quite firm. If we accept one, we have started on a path that leads logically to the other.

Suicide

Those who disagree might begin by balking at the very first step— they might refuse to agree that the use of the key would be suicide. After all, it might be pointed out quite correctly that not every act of self-destruction is suicide. The mother who runs into a burning building to save her child, and perishes, is not a suicide. Neither is the soldier who sacrifices his life to protect his comrades. Other cases are uncertain. Was Socrates, who drank the hemlock at the order of the Athenian court, a suicide? Or Captain Oates, who courageously walked away from Scott's last expedition, into a blizzard, to relieve his companions of an unmanageable encumbrance? Just as there is doubt about such cases, there may also be doubt about the case of Barney Clark's key.

To resolve the doubt, we need some way of distinguishing those self-destructive acts that are suicides from those that are not. We need an account of what suicide is. Two approaches might be taken in trying to provide such an account. One approach is to try to formulate a precise definition of suicide, stating exactly what conditions must be satisfied for an act to fall into this category. Here, for example, is one such definition, from a recent study by Tom L. Beauchamp:

A person commits suicide if:
  (1) that person intentionally brings about his or her own death;
  (2) others do not coerce him or her to do the action; and
  (3) death is caused by conditions arranged by the person for the purpose of bringing about his or her own death.

If we apply this analysis to the examples mentioned above, we see that the heroic mother is no suicide because it was no part of her purpose to bring about her own death—her purpose was only to save her child, and so condition (3) is not satisfied. A similar explanation reveals why the soldier is not a suicide. It also turns out, on this analysis, that Socrates did not commit suicide, for he was coerced to drink the hemlock, and that violates condition (2). And what of Captain Oates? Scott wrote:

He slept through the night before last, hoping not to wake; but he woke in the morning—yesterday. It was blowing a blizzard. He said, 'I am just going outside and may be some time.' He went out into the blizzard and we have not seen him since . . . We knew that poor Oates was walking to his death, but although we tried to dissuade him, we knew it was the act of a brave man and an English gentleman.

Beauchamp believes that the captain did commit suicide, although heroically. But some doubt remains, even in terms of Beauchamp's own analysis. Remembering condition (3), we need not say that his death was part of his purpose; perhaps, like the mother and the soldier, his only purpose was to aid his companions.

The application to Barney Clark's circumstances is, however, clear. If he had used the key, he would have intentionally brought about his own death, without having been coerced; and moreover, his demise would be caused by a condition—the cessation of the artificial heart—that he would have arranged for the purpose of bringing it about. The analysis fits the case snugly. He would have been committing suicide.

However, this approach to understanding what suicide is—defining it through a set of necessary and sufficient conditions—has a built-in limitation. Suppose someone feels, intuitively, that the use of the key by Barney Clark would *not* be suicide. He would not be compelled to change his mind simply because Beauchamp's account—or any other similar account, for that matter—yields a contrary result. He could reply that, since the analysis gives the 'wrong' result in this case, the analysis must be mistaken. He could say that we need a different analysis, with a different set of defining conditions, that would give a result which matches his intuition. The problem here is perfectly general: we test the correctness of any such analysis by reference to the results it yields in individual cases, and if we feel strongly enough about the individual case we can always reject the offending analysis.

This has led some thinkers to try a second approach, which is very different. It begins by observing that, for many people, 'suicide' is an emotionally charged word: it designates something towards which they have a negative attitude. For those people, and there are a lot of them, to label an act 'suicide' is not merely to describe it but to stigmatize it.

Such attitudes influence what people are willing to classify as suicide. If people strongly disapprove suicide, and there are cases of self-destruction they admire—the woman saving her child, or Captain Oates sacrificing himself for the good of the expedition—they will insist on describing the act in some other way. The word 'suicide' will not be used. This is obviously true of those within the great Catholic tradition: because they think suicide is a mortal sin, Roman Catholics are led to deny that admirable acts of self-destruction are 'really' suicides, and traditional casuistry has devised ingenious ways of classifying them as something else. On the other hand, for those who take a more neutral position on the morality of self-destruction, suicide may be accepted as a broader, more inclusive category, and admirable acts of self-destruction can simply be regarded as admirable suicides.

Following this line of thought, it is tempting to conclude that there is no *one* concept of suicide, but different concepts—a wider and a narrower concept—that one will adopt depending on what attitude one takes. If so, this explains why any definition like Beauchamp's will meet resistance. Such definitions, it will be said, mistakenly treat 'suicide' as a factual, descriptive notion, when it is essential to recognize that, for many people, it has an emotional content as well.

This also explains why people might disagree about whether the use of Barney Clark's key would be suicide. Those who have no special negative feelings about the matter may think nothing of saying it would be suicide. But those who strongly disapprove suicide—or even think it is a mortal sin—may find the use of the word in this context insulting not only to Clark but to the physicians attending him as well. They will look for other words to describe what is going on.

Other descriptions are not hard to find. Here are three of them, two suggested by Barney Clark's doctors and one suggested by the religious–philosophical tradition.

1. In the statement by Dr Kolff that I have already quoted, he said, in justification of giving the key, '*The operation won't be a success* unless he is happy' (emphasis added). The suggestion seems to be that if the key were used it would be comparable to Clark having died on the operating table, as the result of some medical failure. Reinforcing this thought, Dr Kolff adds 'That has always been our criteria [of success]—to restore happiness.'

The problem with this can be brought out by considering the difference between the operation being a success and it serving its ultimate purpose. It will have been a success if Clark is restored to good physical condition—if he is made once again healthy, except for the artificial heart. The criterion of success is medical, not psychological. The ultimate purpose of the operation, enabling Clark to be happy, is another thing. It cannot be right to say that the operation won't be successful unless Clark is happy, any more than it can be right to say that an appendectomy won't be performed successfully if the patient doesn't subsequently have a happy life. This simply confuses different things. Thus it cannot be right to view his potential suicide simply as the conclusion of an unsuccessful surgical procedure.

2. Still another suggestion is made in the Press report from which I quoted:

When Clark signed the consent form for the operation approved by the Food and Drug Administration, he was specifically given the right to withdraw from the experiment at any stage, including after the surgery.

'Of course the only way to make the decision afterwards is to have the option of turning the juice off,' said Dr Robert Jarvik, developer of the Jarvik-7 heart placed in Clark.

The consent form included the words 'I understand I am free at any time to withdraw my consent to participate in this experimental project, recognizing that the exercise of such an option after the artificial heart is in place may result in my death.' So, on this way of thinking, if Barney Clark used his key he would only be withdrawing from an experiment, which, of course, any experimental subject has the right to do.

This way of thinking seems more than a little disingenuous. Of course, this was the *first* implantation of the artificial heart, and so the operation was experimental in that sense. But the use of the key could hardly be regarded as 'only' withdrawing from the 'experiment', when the withdrawal means the immediate, intended death of the subject. (The disingenuousness of the consent form's wording is clear enough: it says 'the exercise of such an option after the artificial heart is in place *may* result in my death'. *May?!*) In these circumstances withdrawing from the experiment would be a way of killing oneself, just as surely as if one used a gun. Perhaps Clark would be withdrawing *and* committing suicide, simultaneously. The use of one description does not preclude the other.

3. There is a familiar idea in the literature of medical ethics that might be thought useful in dealing with Barney Clark's key. The idea is that *the use of extraordinary means to prolong life is not morally mandatory*. This is an old thought, developed within the tradition of Catholic moral theology, but widely accepted by non-Catholics. The application to the case of Barney Clark might go like this:

(1) Our duty to prolong life is not absolute; there are circumstances in which we may permissibly choose not to do so. The distinction between ordinary and extraordinary treatments is relevant to this choice. If life can be prolonged using ordinary means, we must do so. But if extraordinary means are required, it is permissible to omit those means.

(2) The use of the artificial heart to keep Clark alive is an example of 'extraordinary' treatment, if anything is. It was extraordinary both

in terms of rarity—he was the only patient in the world receiving such treatment—and expense—the heart cost more than $150,000 to install and maintain.

(3) So, in using his key, Barney Clark would have been doing something perfectly permissible. He would merely be choosing to omit extraordinary means of prolonging his life.

(4) Therefore, because his act would have been permissible, it should not be confused with 'suicide', which is morally much more problematic.

There are a number of problems with this idea. In the first place, omitting a treatment, even an extraordinary one, may be a way of choosing death—it may be the means one uses to terminate one's life—and so be a way of committing suicide. There is nothing in the one description that rules out the other. This is especially clear when the use of the 'extraordinary treatment' may prolong one's life *indefinitely*.

But there is a second and more fundamental reason for objecting to this way of thinking, namely that the distinction between ordinary and extraordinary treatments, on which it is based, is fraught with difficulty. The distinction is supposed to be useful because it is supposed to divide morally mandatory treatments from morally optional ones. But it does not do that. I go into this in some detail in Chapter 6, pp. 96–100 below, so I will not duplicate that discussion here.

These three ways of thinking about Barney Clark's key all try to defend its use by focusing on aspects of the case that are, at best, peripheral. But in trying to understand why the use of the key may be permissible, we will surely do better to focus directly on the central facts of the case. The central facts are that Clark could have found himself in a miserable position, from which there was no escape in life; a position in which the activities that make life worthwhile were impossible for him; and that, moreover, it was *his* life that was at issue. Certainly it must be these facts, and not any business about what makes an operation successful, or the status of experimental subjects, or extraordinary treatments, that justified the key.

The link to euthanasia

The point of insisting that Barney Clark would be committing suicide is to underscore the fact that he would be terminating his life intentionally, by his positive action and not 'merely' by omission, and that this would be (at least part of) the purpose of the act and not merely an incidental by-product. Once we face up to these facts, the implication regarding euthanasia is inescapable.

The connection with euthanasia is made by way of a general principle of moral reasoning: a principle which says, roughly, that if it is all right for a person to bring about a certain situation, then it is all right for that person to enlist the freely given help of others in bringing it about. This principle expresses a simple idea. Suppose there is no moral objection to my drinking a beer, or planting a garden. It follows that there is no moral objection to someone helping me (at my request) to drink a beer or plant a garden.

We must be careful, however, not to state this principle *too* roughly. It will not do to say, simply, that if a person has the right to do an act then he has the right to delegate someone else to do it for him. Stated in this careless way, the principle is false—there are obvious counter-examples. If you invite me to your party, I may have the right to attend, but not necessarily the right to have someone else go in my place; or, a man may have the right to sleep with his wife, without having the right to delegate that privilege. What complicates matters is that, in each of these cases, the rights of third parties are involved. (It violates your rights for me to send someone else to the party, and the wife's rights for the man to send someone else to her bed.) Therefore, the principle must be stated in this more careful way:

If it is permissible for a person (or if a person has the right) to do a certain action, or bring about a certain situation, then it is permissible for that person (he or she has the right) to enlist the freely given aid of someone else in doing the act or bringing about the situation, provided that this does not violate the rights of any third parties.

We may now state more precisely the implication for euthanasia of Barney Clark's key. Giving Clark the key was, as I have already remarked, a way of sanctioning the self-termination of his life—it was a way of saying that it would be all right for him to commit suicide. But, if it is all right for a person to commit suicide, it follows from the above principle that it would be all right for that person to solicit assistance, provided that no third party's rights are violated in the process. In this way the permissibility of euthanasia follows from the permissibility of suicide—a result that probably will not surprise any thoughtful person.

Two very different conclusions could be drawn from all this. Some might conclude that, if Barney Clark's key has these implications, then it was wrong to give it to him. They might urge that I have been describing a 'slippery slope' down which we must not slide. But I would draw a different conclusion. Giving Barney Clark the key symbolized an attitude towards his circumstances, and towards his rights within those circumstances, that is more decent, more humane, than the contrary attitude which has often prevailed in our society. There may indeed be a slippery slope here. But if we went to the bottom of this particular slope, our attitudes towards suicide and euthanasia would have become not worse but better.

6 DEBUNKING IRRELEVANT DISTINCTIONS

Distinctions made in traditional medical ethics

A moral system makes distinctions in order to recognize important differences between various kinds of cases. Where distinctions are made, cases will be set apart for separate consideration and possibly different treatment. Where distinctions are not made, the same cases may be lumped together for similar treatment. We can assess a moral system, then, by examining the distinctions it holds important.

Traditional medical ethics, as it applies to questions of life and death, embraces a number of time-honoured distinctions. The most important of these are incorporated into statements of medical ethics such as the American Medical Association's 1973 policy statement on 'The Physician and the Dying Patient'. This was a remarkably short document, considering the complexity of the issues involved. But, in the space of only three sentences, it alluded to almost every key idea on the subject in our tradition. Although it was produced by Americans, it expresses views common in every Western nation. It said, in its entirety:

The intentional termination of the life of one human being by another—mercy killing—is contrary to that for which the medical profession stands and is contrary to the policy of the American Medical Association.

The cessation of the employment of extraordinary means to prolong the life of the body when there is irrefutable evidence that biological death is imminent is the decision of the patient and/or his immediate family. The advice and judgement of the physician should be freely available to the patient and/or his immediate family.

Several moral judgements are expressed here. Mercy-killing is clearly condemned; it is 'contrary to that for which the medical profession stands'. But at the same time, allowing patients to die (by ceasing treatment) is condoned, at least in some circumstances. Even if he may not kill a patient, a physician may nevertheless sometimes allow death by standing by and 'doing nothing'. Now, if it is sometimes all right to allow a patient to die, the question naturally arises: *When* is it all right? The AMA policy statement provides an answer. It mentions four conditions, all of which must be satisfied before cessation of treatment is permissible.

First, the patient's death must not be part of the doctor's or the medical staff's *intention*. (The 'intentional' termination of life is forbidden.)

Second, the cessation of treatment is permissible only if 'biological death is imminent'. I take this to mean that the patient must be suffering some fatal condition which we cannot cure, and that death is expected in the reasonably near future even if we do everything possible to prevent it.

Third, 'extraordinary' means must be needed to keep the patient alive. Extraordinary means of prolonging life may (sometimes) be omitted; the implication is that, by contrast, 'ordinary' means may not be omitted.

Finally, the right to make this decision is reserved to the patient and/or the immediate family—I take this to mean that, before it is permissible for the doctor to cease treatment, the patient or the family must request it or at least approve it.

These were the guidelines set out by the medical establishment in 1973; however, it is remarkable how little these policies corresponded to the actual behaviour of physicians. In fact, in many cases patients were being allowed to die when these conditions were *not* all satisfied. Here are some examples:

(1) In most cases, babies born with Down's syndrome (popularly called 'mongolism') are in no immediate danger of dying; with only the normal pediatric care, they will proceed to a 'normal' infancy. However, in some cases there may be an additional difficulty, an intestinal blockage (duodenal atresia) that prevents food from passing through. Surgery may be required to remove the blockage; otherwise, the baby will die. At the time of the 1973 AMA statement, it had become fairly common in cases of this type for the parents and doctor to decide not to perform the operation. In these cases, the babies were allowed to die even though 'biological death' was not 'imminent'.

This particular type of non-treatment has since become quite controversial, and is now rare in American hospitals. However, it is easy enough to point out other cases in which life-sustaining treatment is omitted, even though with treatment there would be little danger of imminent death. The case of Baby Jane Doe, discussed in Chapter 4 above, is such a case.

(2) An 89-year-old man, hopelessly senile and hospitalized for a variety of maladies, contracts pneumonia. Seeing that further treatment is pointless, nothing is done for the pneumonia, and he dies. But pneumonia is treatable with penicillin—a perfectly 'ordinary' drug. Therefore, it is not an extraordinary treatment that has been omitted. He could have been kept alive at least a little longer by ordinary means, but he was allowed to die anyway.

(3) Another old man, senile and with heart disease, is judged beyond hope. The doctor orders that if his heart should fail again nothing be done to interfere. (This practice is called 'no-coding'—shorthand for entering a code on the patient's chart directing that no action is to be taken to prolong his life.) But the permission of the family is not sought; this is considered to be a 'medical decision' within the sphere of the physician's authority.

These sorts of cases occur frequently in modern hospitals. I do not mention them in order to suggest that these doctors are acting wrongly; I am only pointing out that the AMA statement did not describe a code of ethics that doctors actually follow. The statement was more faithful to the orthodox moral ideas that have developed within the Western philosophical–religious tradition than to the hard experience of medical practitioners. I am going to be fairly critical of the main ideas embodied in this statement—I believe that they are mistaken—but, if their practice is any indication, many doctors would agree.

In 1982 the AMA issued a more general set of guidelines with the title 'Principles of Medical Ethics'. Unlike the 1973 statement, this one included comment on a variety of matters, and went into some detail in discussing them. Four paragraphs were devoted to the treatment of hopeless or terminal cases:

Quality of life. In the making of decisions for the treatment of seriously deformed newborns or persons who are severely deteriorated victims of injury, illness or advanced age, the primary consideration should be what is best for the individual patient and not the avoidance of a burden to the family or to society. Quality of life is a factor to be considered in determining what is best for the individual. Life should be cherished despite disabilities and handicaps, except when prolongation would be inhumane and unconscionable. Under these circumstances, withholding or removing life supporting means is ethical provided that the normal care given an individual who is ill is not discontinued.

*   *   *

Terminal illness. The social commitment of the physician is to prolong life and relieve suffering. Where the observance of one conflicts with the other, the physician, patient, and/or family of the patient have discretion to resolve the conflict.

For humane reasons, with informed consent a physician may do what is medically indicated to alleviate severe pain, or cease or omit treatment to let a terminally ill patient die, but he should not intentionally cause death. In determining whether the administration of potentially life-prolonging medical treatment is in the best interest of the patient, the physician should consider what the possibility is for extending life under humane and comfortable conditions and what are the wishes and attitudes of the family or those who have responsibility for the custody of the patient.

Where a terminally ill patient's coma is beyond doubt irreversible, and there are adequate safeguards to confirm the accuracy of the diagnosis, all means of life support may be discontinued. If death does not occur when life support systems are discontinued, the comfort and dignity of the patient should be maintained.

We can see, in these paragraphs, a kind of struggle between conflicting ethical ideas. On the one hand, the quality of a person's life is explicitly made relevant to the decision of whether the life should be prolonged, and it is implied that the relief of suffering is equally as important as the prolongation of life. Moreover, the pointlessness of life-support for persons in irreversible comas is explicitly acknowledged. All this must please those who see traditional medical ethics as in need of reform. At the same time, the sterner ideas of the 1973 statement are unchanged: it is still forbidden to cause death intentionally, and it is still forbidden to omit ordinary means of treatment. (The terminology 'extra-ordinary means' has been eliminated, but the distinction between ordinary and extraordinary means is still being assumed—it is now said to be the difference between 'life supporting means' and 'the normal care given an individual who is ill'.)

In this chapter, I will focus on two of the distinctions that are assumed here: the distinction between intentional and non-intentional termination of life, and the distinction between ordinary and extraordinary means of treatment. In the next chapter I will take up the even more important distinction between killing and letting die. All of these distinctions are, I believe, of doubtful importance.

Intentional and non-intentional termination of life

Both the AMA statements condemn 'the *intentional* termination of the life of one human being by another'. The word 'intentional' is no mere stylistic ornament; it introduces a complicated moral doctrine with a long history. The basic idea is that, in evaluating an act, we must take into account the intention with which it is performed. Is it wrong to terminate someone's life? It depends, among other things, on whether the termination is intentional—if it is, the termination is wrong; if not, it may be all right.

In Chapter 1 (pp. 15–17) I outlined some of the history of this doctrine. As an illustration, I used the example of a military bombing raid that would destroy both an armaments factory and some surrounding civilian homes. The commander may order such a raid with different intentions: he might order it for the purpose of inflicting civilian casualties and thereby demoralizing the enemy; or he might order it strictly for the purpose of destroying the armaments factory. In the first instance, the raid would be forbidden, but in the second instance it might be all right. In Chapter 1 I did not say anything critical about this doctrine. Now I want to argue that the basic idea is unacceptable.

In his *Provincial Letters* Pascal criticized the doctrine by having an imaginary Jesuit say 'Our method of direction of intention consists in proposing to oneself, as the end of one's actions, a permitted object. As far as we can we turn men away from forbidden things, but when we cannot prevent the action at least we purify the intention.' Anthony Kenny remarks that Pascal was satirizing the doctrine. Be that as it may, Pascal had put his finger precisely on its main weakness. In the bombing example, the same civilians are killed, and the same factory is destroyed, *regardless of the intention*. If the act is wrong with one intention, how can it be right with another? It is hard to see how the transformation from wrong to right can be made simply by 'purifying the intention'.

Despite Pascal's argument, which has been repeated many times, the doctrine has not disappeared from moral debate. On the contrary, it is as influential now as it ever has been—it pops up in the most unexpected places, such as in the AMA policies. And it is vigorously defended in the academic journals. A contemporary statement of the doctrine is provided by Thomas D. Sullivan, who says that:

the intentional termination of human life is impermissible irrespective of whether this goal is brought about by action or inaction. Is the action or refraining *aimed at* producing death? Is the termination of life *sought, chosen, or planned*? Is the intention deadly? If so, the act or omission is wrong.

Although I believe it is a sound objection, I will set Pascal's argument aside, and concentrate instead on a different sort of argument against the traditional view. I want to focus on what the traditional view implies about the moral relation between act and intention. On this view, an act that is otherwise permissible may become impermissible if it is accompanied by a bad intention. The intention makes the act wrong. I shall argue that this view of the relation between act and intention is mistaken.

Consider the following example. Jack visits his sick and lonely grandmother, and entertains her for the afternoon. He loves her and his only intention is to cheer her up. Jill also visits the grandmother, and provides an afternoon's cheer. But Jill's only concern is that the old lady will soon be making her will; Jill wants to be included among the heirs. Jack also knows that his visit might influence the making of the will, in his favour, but that is no part of his plan. Thus Jack and Jill do the very same thing—they both spend an afternoon cheering up their sick grandmother—and what they do may have the same consequences, namely influencing the will. But their intentions are quite different.

Jack's intention was honourable and Jill's was not. Could we say on that account that what Jack did was right, but what Jill did was not right? No; for Jack and Jill did the very same thing, and if they did the same thing, in the same circumstances, we cannot say that one acted rightly and one acted wrongly. Consistency requires that we assess similar actions similarly. Thus if we are trying to evaluate their *actions*, we must say about one what we say about the other.

However, if we are trying to assess Jack's *character*, or Jill's, things are different. Even though their actions were similar, Jack seems admirable for what he did, while Jill does not. What Jill did— comforting an elderly sick relative—was a morally good thing, but we would not think well of her for it because she was only scheming after the money. Jack, on the other hand, did a good thing *and* he did it with an admirable intention. Thus we think well, not only of what Jack did, but of Jack.

The traditional view says that the intention with which an act is done is relevant to determining whether the act is right. The example of Jack and Jill suggests that, on the contrary, the intention is not relevant to deciding whether the act is right or wrong, but instead is relevant to assessing the character of the person who does it, which is another thing entirely.

Is it any different if the example concerns more important issues of life and death? A massively necrotic bowel condition in an infant is out of control. Dr White realizes that further treatment offers little hope of reversing the dying process and will only increase suffering; so he does not submit the infant to further treatment, even though he knows this decision will hasten death. However, Dr White does not seek, choose, or plan that death, so it is not part of his intention that the baby dies. His intention is only to refrain from increasing suffering.

Dr Black is faced with a similar case. A massively necrotic bowel condition in an infant is out of control. He realizes that further treatment offers little hope of saving the baby and will only increase its suffering. He decides that it is better for the baby to die a bit sooner than to go on suffering pointlessly; so, with the intention of letting the baby die, he ceases treatment.

According to the traditional analysis, Dr White's action was acceptable, but Dr Black acted wrongly. However, this assessment faces the same problem we encountered before. Dr White and Dr Black did *the very same thing*: their handling of the cases was identical. Both doctors ceased treatment, knowing that the baby would die sooner, and both did so because they regarded continued treatment as pointless, given the infants' prospects, and because they opposed further suffering. So how could one's action be acceptable and the other's not? There was, of course, a subtle difference in their attitudes towards what they did. Dr Black may have said to himself, 'I want this baby to die now, rather than later, so that it won't suffer more; so I won't continue the treatment.' A defender of the traditional view might condemn Dr Black for this, and say that his character is defective (although I would not say that); but the traditionalist should not say that Dr Black's *action* was wrong on that account, at least not if he wants to go on saying that Dr White's action was right. A pure heart cannot make a wrong act right; neither can an impure heart make a right act wrong. As in the case of Jack and Jill, the intention is relevant, not to determining the rightness of actions, but to assessing the character of the people who act.

There is a deeper lesson to be learned if we ask what underlying feature of morality accounts for this point and makes it true. We need, first, to shift our stance. We have been considering situations in which we have to assess an action that has already been performed. But let us imagine a situation in which the crucial act has not yet been performed, and one is trying to decide what to do. Suppose you are trying to decide, like Dr White or Dr Black, whether to continue the infant's treatment. Remember that *the rightness or wrongness of an act is determined by the reasons for and against it.* You will, therefore, want to consider the reasons for and against this particular act. What are those reasons?

On the one hand, if treatment is ceased the baby will die very soon. On the other hand, the baby will die eventually anyway, even if treatment is continued. It has no chance of growing up. Moreover, if its life is prolonged, its suffering will be prolonged as well, and the medical resources used will be unavailable to others who would have a better chance of a satisfactory cure.

In the light of all this, you may well decide against continued treatment. But notice that there is no mention here of anyone's intentions. *The intention you would have, if you decided to cease treatment, is not one of the things you need to consider. It is not among the reasons for or against the action.* That is why it is irrelevant to determining whether the action is right.

Incidentally, this may also explain the justice of Pascal's 'satire'. The words put into the imaginary Jesuit's mouth seem silly; that is why his speech seems satirical. But if the intention were among the reasons for or against the act then what the imaginary Jesuit says would be perfectly logical. After one had taken account of the other reasons, and decided that an act is permissible on those grounds, the question of intention would arise. If the person's likely intention is found unacceptable, this could be changed by altering his attitude—by 'purifying the intention'. Thus, the only thing needed to see the justice of Pascal's satire is that we consider, not the situation in which we are assessing an already-performed action, but the situation in which a person is deciding what to do. In the situation of choice, it is clear that talk about intentions simply is not helpful.

Ordinary and extraordinary means of treatment

Another part of the traditional view is that, in deciding whether a treatment may be omitted, a lot depends on whether the treatment is 'ordinary' or 'extraordinary'. Extraordinary treatments are morally optional; they may or may not be used, depending on the other circumstances. Ordinary treatments, however, are mandatory; doctors are simply failing in their duty if they omit ordinary treatments.

The obvious question is what these terms mean. What distinguishes an extraordinary treatment from an ordinary one? How do we tell the difference? Two approaches are possible. One I call the common-sense approach; the other the approach by stipulative definition.

The common-sense approach takes the terms 'ordinary' and 'extraordinary' at face value. An extraordinary treatment is one that is rare, difficult, or expensive. An ordinary treatment is, by contrast, common and inexpensive. Of course, this is not terribly precise—it does not say *how* uncommon or *how* expensive a treatment must be before it becomes extraordinary. The common-sense approach would leave this open to some extent, as a matter of judgement in each case. Moreover, a treatment that was extraordinary may become ordinary, as medical technology advances and the treatment becomes cheaper and more common. A sense of history is helpful in understanding this approach. In earlier times, when medical science was less well developed, there were fewer treatments available and the technology involved was less costly. In those times, a distinction between ordinary and extraordinary treatments had less point. But, as medicine developed into the enormously expensive, technological business it is today, the number of exotic and costly treatments increased dramatically. At the same time, the new technology enabled doctors to treat conditions that might best be untreated (for example, terribly deformed infants that previously were regarded as 'mistakes of nature', which nature mercifully disposed of shortly after birth). The use of the notion of 'extraordinary' treatment must be understood against this background.

The common-sense approach provides an easy, natural way of understanding what is meant by these terms. However, if we interpret the terms in this way, the traditional moral doctrine is clearly false, for it is obvious that it is sometimes permissible to omit ordinary treatments.

Suppose that a diabetic long accustomed to self-administration of insulin falls victim to terminal cancer, or suppose that a terminal cancer patient suddenly develops diabetes. Is he in the first case obliged to continue, and in the second case obliged to begin, insulin treatment and die painfully of cancer, or in either or both cases may the patient choose rather to pass into diabetic coma and an earlier death? . . . What of the conscious patient suffering from painful incurable disease who suddenly gets pneumonia? Or an old man slowly deteriorating who from simply being inactive and recumbent gets pneumonia? Are we to use antibiotics in a likely successful attack upon this disease which from time immemorial has been called 'the old man's friend'?

These examples are provided by Paul Ramsey, a leading theological ethicist. Even so conservative a thinker as Ramsey is sympathetic with the idea that, in such cases, life-prolonging treatment is not mandatory: the insulin and the antibiotics need not be used. Yet insulin and antibiotics are 'ordinary' treatments—they are common, easily administered, and cheap. There is nothing exotic about them.

So, on the common-sense approach, the distinction between ordinary and extraordinary treatments does not have the significance traditionally attached to it. It does not mark a difference between optional and non-optional modes of treatment. Extraordinary treatments may sometimes be omitted, and sometimes not, depending on the circumstances. But ordinary treatments *also* may sometimes be omitted and sometimes not. Knowing that a treatment is one or the other, then, is of no particular help in deciding whether the treatment is omittable.

For this reason, more sophisticated defenders of the traditional doctrine do not take the common-sense approach. Instead, they stipulate definitions of 'ordinary' and 'extraordinary', and then claim that in these special senses the terms mark a difference between permitted and forbidden omissions. Fr. Gerald Kelly, S J, has formulated one of the most influential set of stipulative definitions. He says:

Ordinary means of preserving life are all medicines, treatments, and operations, which offer a reasonable hope of benefit for the patient and which can be obtained and used without excessive expense, pain, and other inconvenience.

Extra-ordinary means of preserving life are all those medicines, treatments, and operations which cannot be obtained without excessive expense, pain, or other inconvenience, or which, if used, would not offer a reasonable hope of benefit.

Using these definitions, it turns out that the insulin and antibiotics *would* be extraordinary treatments in the examples I quoted, because their use 'would not offer a reasonable hope of benefit'. Thus the two approaches lead to very different results in particular cases.

If we take the stipulative definition approach to understanding the meaning of 'ordinary' and 'extraordinary', then the traditional moral doctrine seems to be true—that is, it seems true that ordinary treatments should never be omitted, while extraordinary treatments can be omitted. After all, what possible reason could be given for omitting a treatment that offers the patient a reasonable hope of benefit, without involving excessive expense, pain, or other inconvenience? And isn't it equally obvious that a treatment that does *not* offer such a hope of benefit, while being excessively expensive and painful, need not be used? Using these definitions, the traditional doctrine is quite plausible.

Nevertheless, there is something wrong here: the definitions cheat. The cheat-words are 'excessive' and 'benefit'. Because of the way these words function in the definitions, the definitions turn out not to provide a useful distinction after all.

First, notice the work being done by the word 'excessive'. It is said that a treatment is extraordinary if it cannot be obtained without *excessive* expense or pain. But when is an expense 'excessive'? Is a cost of $10,000 excessive? If it would save the life of a young woman and restore her to perfect health, $10,000 is cheap. But if it would only prolong the life of Ramsey's cancer-stricken diabetic a short while, perhaps $10,000 is excessive. The same goes for pain. It might be worth enduring quite a bit of pain to recover one's health; but the same amount of pain may be excessive if it only prolongs dying a little bit.

The point is not merely that what is excessive changes from case to case. The point is more fundamental. It is that what is excessive *depends on* whether it is a good thing for the life to be prolonged. If continued life would be desirable for the patient (perhaps because the quality of life would be good), then a considerable expenditure of resources would not be excessive; but if continued life is not so desirable (perhaps because its quality is bad), then that same expenditure would be excessive. The point is that the judgement about the desirability of treatment must be made *before* we can make any judgement about what is 'excessive'.

Second, we should notice the use of the word 'benefit' in the definitions. It is said that ordinary treatments offer a reasonable hope of *benefit*, while extraordinary treatments do not. How do we determine whether a treatment will benefit the patient? Remember that we are talking about life-prolonging treatments; the 'benefit', if any, is the continuation of life. Whether continued life is a benefit depends on the details of the particular case. For a person with a painful terminal illness, a temporarily continued life may not be a benefit. For a person in irreversible coma, such as Karen Quinlan, continued biological existence is almost certainly not a benefit. On the other hand, for a person who can be cured and resume a normal life, life-sustaining treatment definitely is a benefit. Again, the point is not just that whether a treatment is a benefit varies from case to case. The point is that in order to decide whether life-sustaining treatment is a benefit we must *first* decide whether it would be a good thing for the life in question to be prolonged.

The upshot is that these definitions do not mark a distinction that can be used to help us decide when treatment may be omitted. We cannot, by using the definitions, identify which treatments are extraordinary, and then use that information to determine whether the treatment may be omitted. For the definitions require that we must *already* have decided the moral questions of life and death—we must already have decided whether the use of the treatment is a good thing—*before* we can answer the question of whether the treatment is extraordinary. Thus, the judgement of ordinariness or extraordinariness cannot figure in the reasoning which leads to the conclusion that the treatment should or should not be used.

The definitions do *appear* to mark an important distinction, and this appearance is easy to explain. The matters to which the definitions refer—expense, pain, and benefit—are quite important. In fact, if we are trying to decide whether to omit a treatment, the reasons for and against the omission might very well have to do with expense, pain, and benefit. So far, so good. The mistake creeps in when we start to think that these matters characterize different *types of treatment*. They do not. The different types of treatment (insulin, antibiotics, and so on) are related to pain, expense, and benefit in different ways at different times. The moral is that these matters should be brought into our discussions through the front door, as important matters in their own right, rather than through the back door, as though they were important only as characterizing different types of treatment.

We are brought, then, to this conclusion about the distinction between ordinary and extraordinary means. If we take the common-sense approach, the traditional doctrine is false. On the other hand, if we take the stipulative definition approach, the distinction is useless in practical decision-making. In either case, the distinction provides no help in formulating an acceptable ethic of letting die.

The effect of debunking irrelevant distinctions

The two distinctions I have discussed are widely accepted by physicians, and, as one might expect, there are practical consequences. Consider, for example, the well-known case of Karen Quinlan, to which I have already referred several times. In April 1975 this young woman ceased breathing for at least two fifteen-minute periods, for reasons that were never made clear. As a result, she suffered severe brain damage, and, in the words of the attending physicians, was reduced to 'a chronic persistent vegetative state' in which she 'no longer had any cognitive function'. Accepting the doctors' judgement that there was no hope of recovery, her parents sought permission from the courts to disconnect the respirator that was keeping her alive in the intensive-care unit of a New Jersey hospital.

The trial court, and then the Supreme Court of New Jersey, agreed that Karen's respirator could be removed. So it was disconnected. However, the nuns in charge of her care in the

Catholic hospital opposed this decision and, anticipating it, had begun to wean her from the respirator so that by the time it was disconnected she could remain alive without it. So Karen did not die. Those who thought it right that Karen be allowed to die were indignant at the nuns' behaviour. One prominent Catholic scholar commented angrily, 'Some nuns always were holier than the church.' (Official Church doctrine sees nothing wrong with 'pulling the plug' in such circumstances.) Karen remained alive for ten additional years. In June 1985 she finally died, of acute pneumonia. Antibiotics, which would have fought the pneumonia, were not given.

Little attention was paid to the fact that during that additional decade Karen was *still* being kept alive by artificial means. She was alive because one life-support device was *not* disconnected: the intravenous (IV) tube (or the nasogastric tube) that supplied nourishment to her body. Without this device she would, of course, have starved to death. Thus, there was still one additional plug that could have been pulled, without which she could not possibly have survived.

When the original judgement was made that Karen's case was hopeless, and that there was no longer any point in maintaining her body alive, why weren't *all* the plugs pulled? It is because distinctions are made among the various life-support systems; in the terms we have been discussing, the respirator is counted as an 'extraordinary means', which can be omitted, while the provision of nourishment is considered an 'ordinary means', which may not be omitted. Thus did the influence of this distinction keep this unfortunate woman alive.

The 1982 AMA policy statement quoted at the beginning of this chapter speaks to this kind of case, and implies that the distinction between supplying food and water and supplying other forms of life-sustaining treatment is indeed important. Notice the curious final sentence of the passage that was quoted: it is said that, '*If death does not occur when life support systems are discontinued*, the comfort and dignity of the patient should be maintained' (italics added). If *all* life-support systems, including the provision of food and water, were discontinued, then of course death could not but occur. Food and water seems to be a prime example of the 'normal care' that may not be omitted. Some philosophers and theologians agree that the provision of food and water is morally 'different' from other forms of life-support; to them, unplugging a respirator is merely refusing a treatment that has become grotesque, whereas starving a person seems somehow inhuman.

But the courts have now begun to reconsider this matter. The New Jersey court that authorized the disconnection of Karen Quinlan's respirator did not authorize disconnecting the feeding tubes. However, in two more recent cases, the courts found no difference between the two procedures.

The Case of Clarence Herbert. In August 1981, two California physicians, Dr Robert Nejdl and Dr Neil Barber, were charged with murder when they terminated intravenous feeding for a 55-year-old patient named Clarence Herbert. Herbert had suffered a heart attack while in the recovery room following an operation. He went into a coma and was placed on a ventilator and an IV set-up. After the judgement was made that he was unlikely to recover, his family requested that the life-sustaining equipment be removed. The ventilator was removed, and two days later the IV was taken away. Then Mr Herbert died.

A nurse, who did not approve of all this, copied the patient's charts and took them to the authorities, who filed charges against the doctors. The magistrate hearing the case dismissed the charges, and when the State took the case to the appeals court, the appeals court affirmed the magistrate's decision.

The prosecutors objected to the removal of all the life-sustaining equipment, but the argument in court focused especially on the cessation of the intravenous feeding. The appeals court seemed to take it for granted that it was permissible to discontinue the respirator. The question that occupied attention was whether there is an important difference between the respirator and the IV. The judge said there is not, and offered this principle:

Medical procedures to provide nutrition and hydration are more similar to other medical procedures than to typical human ways of providing nutrition and hydration. Their benefits and burdens ought to be evaluated in the same manner as any other medical procedure.

Thus, if it is permissible to allow a patient to die by unplugging a respirator, this judge said that it is equally permissible to disconnect an IV tube.

The Case of Claire Conroy. Claire Conroy was a mentally incompetent 84-year-old woman suffering from 'organic brain syndrome', which involves permanent brain damage. During the legal controversy that came to surround her case, a judge visited her and said 'She does not speak. She lies in bed in a fetal position. She sometimes follows people with her eyes, but often stares blankly ahead . . . she has no cognitive or volitional functioning.'

The controversy began in July 1982 when Mrs Conroy developed necrotic ulcers on her foot as a result of diabetes. She had been in a nursing home for three years, and now she was moved to a hospital where doctors recommended that her leg be amputated. Mrs Conroy's guardian would not permit the amputation, and also demanded that the nasogastric tube supplying nutrition be removed. The doctor would not remove the tube, and so the guardian obtained a court order to force its removal. But before it could be removed, the patient died.

Because of the general interest and importance of the case, the New Jersey appeals courts continued to deliberate the legal issues involved, even though Mrs Conroy's death had rendered the practical point moot. In mid-1983 an appeals court reversed the trial court's order that the tube be removed. The appeals court held that, in removing the nasogastric tube, the doctors would be purposefully killing the patient, and so would be committing murder. The judge declared:

If the trial judge's order had been enforced, Conroy would not have died as the result of an existing medical condition, but rather she would have died, and painfully so, as the result of a new and independent condition: dehydration and starvation. Thus she would have been actively killed by independent means.

But this decision was not allowed to stand. In January 1985 a higher authority, the New Jersey Supreme Court, ruled that providing food and water is just another way of artificially prolonging life. Speaking for the court's 6–1 majority, Justice Sidney M. Schreiber wrote that 'The pain and invasiveness of an artificial feeding device, and the pain of withdrawing that device, should be treated just like the results of administering or withholding any other medical treatment.' Thus the higher court ruled that, if it could be shown that Claire Conroy would not have wished the treatment continued, or that the treatment did not serve her best interests, the gastro-intestinal tube could have been removed.

Predictably, 'right-to-life' groups were not happy with this outcome. The New Jersey Right to Life Committee immediately issued a statement saying that 'food and water are basic human needs' that should never be taken away. Apparently Karen Quinlan's parents agreed, at least to some extent. On the day Justice Schreiber's opinion was released, their lawyer said they 'had no intention' of seeking permission to disconnect the tubes keeping Karen alive.

These examples illustrate the practical consequences of distinguishing among the 'means' that may be used to sustain life. It is also easy to identify practical consequences of the other distinction we have discussed, between intentional and non-intentional termination of life. Opponents of euthanasia have sometimes conceded that it is permissible for a doctor to give a terminal patient an injection of pain-killing drug sufficient to cause death, provided that no smaller dosage will alleviate the pain, and that the doctor's *intention* is not to kill but is only to relieve the pain. (Of course, these same people deny that it is permissible to give a lethal injection with the intention of causing death.) This is the official position of the Catholic Church, as summarized in the recent *Vatican Declaration on Euthanasia*:

But the intensive use of painkillers is not without difficulties, because the phenomenon of habituation generally makes it necessary to increase their dosage in order to maintain their efficacy. At this point it is fitting to recall a declaration by Pius XII, which retains its full force. In answer to a group of doctors who had put the question: 'Is the suppression of pain and consciousness by the use of narcotics . . . permitted by religion and morality to the doctor and the patient (even at the approach of death and if one foresees that the use of narcotics will shorten life)?'

The pope said: 'If no other means exist, and if, in the given circumstances, this does not prevent the carrying out of other religious and moral duties: Yes.' In this case, of course, death is in no way intended or sought even if the risk of it is reasonably taken; the intention is simply to relieve pain effectively, using for this purpose painkillers available to medicine.

But if one doubts the validity of the traditional distinction between intentional and non-intentional killing, one will think this makes little difference, except to make death available arbitrarily in some circumstances but not others. Joseph Fletcher compares the orthodox view with the opinion of St Alphonsus Liguori, a nineteenth-century theologian who thought it wrong to commit suicide, but all right to leap from a high window, knowing that it would cause certain death, provided that the building were on fire and one's thoughts were firmly fixed on escaping the blaze.

The effect of rejecting such distinctions is to focus attention on the patient's welfare and best interests. Once the irrelevant considerations have been set aside, we will simply ask what is best for the patient. Thus, the point of debunking is not only theoretical but practical. In the cases of Karen Quinlan, Clarence Herbert, and Claire Conroy, the issue will be only whether it serves *their* interests to keep them alive. If the answer is 'No', then it does not matter whether the means being used are 'extraordinary' (a respirator) or 'ordinary' (an IV tube). Either may be discontinued. And in the euthanasia case, the question will be whether, from the patient's own point of view and (if possible) in his own judgement, it is best that his life be ended. If the answer is 'Yes', it will not matter whether the instrument is an overdose of pain-killer or a straightforward injection of some deliberately lethal substance. The decision will be made based on what is best for the patient, and on what the patient reasonably wants, and that is all. The 1982 AMA statement is on the right track when it begins by saying that 'the primary consideration should be what is best for the individual patient'. But then, unfortunately, too many qualifications are added. The effect of debunking irrelevant distinctions is to focus even more emphatically on that primary consideration.

7   ACTIVE AND PASSIVE EUTHANASIA

Killing and letting die

The idea that it is all right to allow patients to die is an old one. Four centuries before Christ Socrates said of a physician, with approval, 'bodies which disease had penetrated through and through, he would not have attempted to cure . . . he did not want to lengthen out good-for-nothing lives'. In the centuries that followed neither the Christians nor the Jews significantly altered this basic idea: both viewed allowing to die, in circumstances of hopeless suffering, as permissible. It was killing that was zealously opposed.

The morality of allowing people to die by not treating them has become more important as methods of treatment have become more sophisticated. By using such devices as respirators, heart-lung machines, and intravenous feeding, we can now keep almost anybody alive indefinitely, even after he or she has become a 'human vegetable' without thought or feeling or hope of recovery. The maintenance of life by artificial means is, in such cases, sadly pointless. Virtually everyone who has thought about the matter agrees that it is morally all right, at some point, to cease treatment and allow such people to die. In our own time, no less a figure than the Pope has reaffirmed the permission: Pius XII emphasized in 1958 that we may 'allow the patient who is virtually already dead to pass away in peace'. The American Medical Association policy statements quoted in the preceding chapter are in this tradition: they condemn mercy-killing, but say it is permissible to 'cease or omit treatment to let a terminally ill patient die'.

Thus the medical community embraces, as part of its fundamental code, a distinction between active euthanasia and what we might call 'passive euthanasia'. By 'active euthanasia' we mean taking some positive action designed to kill the patient; for example, giving a lethal injection of potassium chloride. 'Passive euthanasia', on the other hand, means simply refraining from doing anything to keep the patient alive. In passive euthanasia we withhold medication or other life-sustaining therapy, or we refuse to perform surgery, and so on, and let the patient die 'naturally' of whatever ills already afflict him. It is the difference between *killing people*, on the one hand, and merely *letting people die* on the other.

Many writers prefer to use the term 'euthanasia' only in connection with active euthanasia. They use other words to refer to what I am calling 'passive euthanasia'—for example, instead of 'passive euthanasia' they may speak of 'death with dignity'. One reason for this choice of terms is the emotional impact of the words: it *sounds* so much better to defend 'death with dignity' than to advocate 'euthanasia' of any sort. And of course if one believes that there is a great moral difference between the two, one will prefer a terminology that puts as much psychological distance as possible between them. But nothing of substance depends on which label is used. I will stay with the terms 'active euthanasia' and 'passive euthanasia' because they are the most convenient; but other terms could be substituted without affecting my argument.

The belief that there is an important moral difference between active and passive euthanasia has obvious consequences for medical practice. It makes a difference to what doctors are willing to do. Consider this case: a patient dying from incurable cancer of the throat is in terrible pain that we can no longer satisfactorily alleviate. He is certain to die within a few days, but he decides that he does not want to go on living for those days since the pain is unbearable. So he asks the doctor to end his life now, and his family joins in the request.

One way the doctor might comply with this request is simply by killing the patient with a lethal injection. Most doctors would not do that, for all the reasons we have been considering. Yet, even so, the physician may sympathize with the dying patient's request and feel that it is reasonable for him to prefer death now rather than after a few more days of suffering. The active/passive doctrine tells the doctor what to do: it says that although he may not administer the lethal injection—that would be active euthanasia, which is forbidden—he *may* withhold treatment and let the patient die sooner than he otherwise would. It is no wonder that this simple idea is so widely accepted, for it seems to give the doctor a way out of his dilemma without having to kill the patient, and without having to prolong the patient's agony.

I will argue, against the prevailing view, that active and passive euthanasia are morally equivalent—there is no moral difference between them. By this I mean that there is no reason to prefer one over the other as a matter of principle; the fact that one case of euthanasia is active, while another is passive, is not *itself* a reason to think one morally better than the other. My argument will not depend on assuming that either practice is acceptable or unacceptable. Here I will only argue that the two forms of euthanasia are morally equivalent: either both are acceptable or both are not. They stand or fall together. Of course, if you already think that passive euthanasia is all right, then you may conclude from this that active euthanasia must be all right, too. On the other hand, if you believe that active euthanasia is immoral, you may want to conclude that passive euthanasia is also immoral. Obviously, I prefer the former alternative; however, nothing in the argument of this chapter will depend on that.

Practical consequences of the traditional view

I will discuss the theoretical shortcomings of the traditional view at some length. However, I also want to emphasize the practical side of the issue. Employing the traditional distinction has serious adverse consequences for patients. Consider again the man with terminal cancer. Basically, the doctors have three options. First, they can end his life now by a lethal injection. Second, they can withhold treatment and allow him to die sooner than he otherwise would—this will take some time, however, so let us say that he would die in one day. And third, they could continue treatment and prolong his life as long as possible—say, for five days. (The exact numbers do not matter; they are merely for the purpose of illustration.) The traditional view says that the second, but not the first, option may be chosen.

As a practical matter, what is wrong with this? Remember that the justification for allowing the patient to die, rather than prolonging his life for a few more hopeless days, is that he is in horrible pain. One problem is that, if we simply withhold treatment, it will take him *longer* to die, and so he will suffer *more*, than if we administered the lethal injection. Why, if we have already decided to shorten his life because of the pain, should we prefer the option than involves more suffering? This seems, on the face of it, contrary to the humanitarian impulse that prompts the decision not to prolong his life in the first place. I think I can understand why some people oppose euthanasia in any form—the view that prefers option three is mistaken, in my opinion, but it has a certain kind of integrity. A preference for the first option is also understandable. But the view which makes option two the top choice is a 'moderate' position that incorporates the worst, and not the best, of both extremes.

The cruelty lurking in the distinction between killing and letting die may also be illustrated by a very different kind of case. Down's syndrome (mongolism) is sometimes complicated by duodenal atresia (blocked intestine), and the unfortunate infant cannot obtain nourishment. In such cases, the parents and doctors have sometimes decided not to perform the surgery necessary to remove the blockage, and let the baby die. Here is one doctor's account of what happens then:

When surgery is denied [the doctor] must try to keep the infant from suffering while natural forces sap the baby's life away. As a surgeon whose natural inclination is to use the scalpel to fight off death, standing by and watching a salvageable baby die is the most emotionally exhausting experience I know. It is easy at a conference, in a theoretical discussion, to decide that such infants should be allowed to die. It is altogether different to stand by in the nursery and watch as dehydration and infection wither a tiny being over hours and days. This is a terrible ordeal for me and the hospital staff—much more so than for the parents who never set foot in the nursery.

This is not the account of a doctor who opposes the practice he is describing. On the contrary, Dr Anthony Shaw, the author of this account and one of the most frequently cited writers on the subject, supports the morality of letting these infants die. He is troubled only by the 'ordeal' he seems to think is necessary. But why is the ordeal necessary? Why must the hospital staff 'stand by in the nursery and watch as dehydration and infection wither a tiny being over hours and days'? What is gained from this, when an injection would end its life at once? No matter what you think of the lives of such infants, there seems to be no satisfactory answer. If you think that the babies' lives are precious and should be protected, then of course you will oppose killing them *or* letting them die. On the other hand, if you think death is a permissible choice here, why shouldn't you think the injection at least as good as letting the infant 'wither'?

Let me mention another, even more bizarre, practical consequence of the traditional doctrine. Duodenal atresia is not part of Down's syndrome; it is only a condition that sometimes *accompanies* it. When duodenal atresia is present, a decision might be made to let the baby die. But when there is no intestinal blockage (or other similar defect requiring surgery), other Down's babies live on. Let us focus on this fact: *some Down's infants, with duodenal atresia, die, while other Down's infants, without duodenal atresia, live.* This, I wish to suggest, is irrational.

To bring out the irrationality of this situation, we may first ask *why* the babies with blocked intestines are allowed to die. Clearly, it is not because they have blocked intestines. The parents do not despair, and opt for death, over this condition which often could easily be corrected. The reason surgery is not performed is, obviously, that the child is mongoloid and the parents and doctors judge that because of *that* it is better for the child not to survive. But notice that the other babies, without duodenal atresia, are *also* mongoloid—they have the very same condition which dooms the ones with the blocked intestines—and yet they live on.

This is absurd, no matter what view one takes of the lives and potentials of such infants. Again, if you think that the life of such an infant is worth preserving, then what does it matter if it needs a simple operation? Or, if you think Down's syndrome so terrible that such babies may be allowed to die, then what does it matter if some babies' intestinal tracts are *not* blocked? In either case, the matter of life and death is being decided on irrelevant grounds. It is the Down's syndrome, and not the intestines, that is the issue. The issue should be decided, if at all, on *that* basis, and not be allowed to depend on the essentially irrelevant question of whether the intestinal tract is blocked.

What makes this situation possible, of course, is the idea that there is a big moral difference between letting die and killing: when there is an intestinal obstruction we can 'let the baby die', but when there is no such defect there is no choice to be made, for we must not 'kill' it. The fact that this idea leads to such results as deciding life or death on irrelevant grounds is one reason, among others, why it should be rejected.

The Bare Difference Argument

The Equivalence Thesis, as I will call it, says that there is no morally important difference between killing and letting die; if one is permissible (or objectionable), then so is the other, and to the same degree. More precisely, it is a claim about what does, or does not, count as a morally good reason in support of a value judgement: the bare fact that one act is an act of killing, while another act is an act of 'merely' letting someone die, is not a morally good reason in support of the judgement that the former is worse than the latter.

It is compatible with the Equivalence Thesis that there may be *other* differences between such acts that are morally significant. For example, the family of an irreversibly comatose hospital patient may want their loved one to be allowed to die, but not killed. In that case, we have at least one reason to let the patient die rather than to kill him—the reason is that the family prefers it that way. This does not mean, however, that the distinction between killing and letting die *itself* is important. What is important is respecting the family's wishes. (It is often right to respect people's wishes even when we think those wishes are based on false beliefs.) In another sort of case, a patient with a painful terminal illness may want to be killed rather than allowed to die because a slow, lingering death would be agonizing. Here we have reason to kill and not let die, but once again the reason is not that one course is intrinsically preferable to the other. The reason is, rather, that the latter course would lead to more suffering.

I will argue that the Equivalence Thesis is true. It should be clear, however, that I will *not* be arguing that every act of letting die is equally as bad as every act of killing. There are lots of reasons, such as those I have just mentioned, why a particular act of killing may be morally inferior to a particular act of letting die, or vice versa. All I will argue is that, whatever reasons there may be for judging one act worse than another, the bare fact that one is killing, while the other is letting die, is not among them.

The Equivalence Thesis is one of those airy, abstract sorts of philosophical claims that may seem impossible to 'prove' one way or the other. But I think it is possible to give some fairly convincing reasons for accepting it. The practical considerations adduced in the previous section should go some way towards making the thesis plausible; yet those considerations do not add up to a rigorous argument. What follows is an attempt to provide something more compelling.

In the sciences we often want to know what influence is exerted by one element of a complex situation. The familiar procedure is to isolate the element of interest by studying cases in which everything else is held constant, while that one element is varied. Children are taught this idea in school by having them perform simple experiments. For example, does the colour of a combustible material affect whether it will burn? Children can see that it does not by trying—and succeeding —to burn bits of paper of different colours. Does the presence of air affect combustion? Most of us will remember placing a candle in a bell-jar and watching it go out after the oxygen is consumed, while a similar candle outside the jar continues to burn. By varying one element, we see what difference it makes.

We may try a similar 'experiment' with the distinction between killing and letting die. We may consider two cases which are exactly alike except that one involves killing where the other involves letting die. Then we can ask whether this difference makes any difference to our moral assessments. It is important that the cases be *exactly* alike except for this one difference, because otherwise we cannot be confident that it is *this* difference which accounts for any variation in the assessments. Consider, then, this pair of cases:

Smith stands to gain a large inheritance if anything should happen to his six-year-old cousin. One evening while the child is taking his bath, Smith sneaks into the bathroom and drowns the child, and then arranges things so that it will look like an accident. No one is the wiser, and Smith gets his inheritance.

Jones also stands to gain if anything should happen to his six-year-old cousin. Like Smith, Jones sneaks in planning to drown the child in his bath. However, just as he enters the bathroom Jones sees the child slip, hit his head, and fall face-down in the water. Jones is delighted; he stands by, ready to push the child's head back under if necessary, but it is not necessary. With only a little thrashing about, the child drowns all by himself, 'accidentally', as Jones watches and does nothing. No one is the wiser, and Jones gets his inheritance.

Now Smith killed the child, while Jones 'merely' let the child die. That is the only difference between them. Did either man behave better, from a moral point of view? Is there a moral difference between them? *If the difference between killing and letting die were itself a morally important matter, then we should say that Jones's behaviour was less reprehensible than Smith's.* But do we want to say that? I think not, for several reasons.

First, both men acted from the same motive—personal gain—and both had exactly the same end in view when they acted. We may infer from Smith's conduct that he is a bad man, although we may withdraw or modify that judgement if we learn certain other facts about him, for example, that he is mentally deranged. But would we not also infer the very same thing about Jones from his conduct? And would not the same further considerations also be relevant to any modification of that judgement?

Second, the *results* of their conduct were the same—in both cases, the cousin ended up dead and the villain ended up with the money.

Third, suppose Jones pleaded, in his defence, 'After all, I didn't kill the child. I only stood there and let him die.' Again, if letting die were in itself less bad than killing, this defence should have at least some weight. But—morally, at least—it does not. Such a 'defence' can only be regarded as a grotesque perversion of moral reasoning.

Thus, it seems that when we are careful not to smuggle in any further differences which prejudice the issue, the bare difference between killing and letting die does not itself make any difference to the morality of actions concerning life and death. I will call this the 'Bare Difference Argument'.

Now it may be pointed out, quite properly, that the cases of euthanasia with which doctors are concerned are not like this at all. They do not involve personal gain or the destruction of normal, healthy children. Doctors are concerned only with cases in which the patient's life is of no further use to him, or in which the patient's life has become a positive burden. However, the point will be the same even in those cases: the difference between killing and letting die does not, *in itself*, make a difference, from the point of view of morality. If a doctor lets a patient die, for humane reasons, he is in the same moral position as if he had given the patient a lethal injection for humane reasons. If the decision was wrong—if, for example, the patient's illness was in fact curable—then the decision would be equally regrettable no matter which method was used to carry it out. And if the doctor's decision was the right one, then the method he used is not itself important.

Counter-arguments

Our argument has brought us to this point: we cannot draw any moral distinction between active and passive euthanasia on the grounds that one involves killing while the other only involves letting someone die, because that is a difference that does not make a difference, from a moral point of view. Some people will find this hard to accept. One reason, I think, is that they fail to distinguish the question of whether killing is, in itself, worse than letting die, from the very different question of whether most actual cases of killing are more reprehensible than most actual cases of letting die. Most actual cases of killing are clearly terrible—think of the murders reported in the newspapers—and we hear of such cases almost every day. On the other hand, we hardly ever hear of a case of letting die, except for the actions of doctors who are motivated by humanitarian concerns. So we learn to think of killing in a much worse light than letting die; and we conclude, invalidly, that there must be something about killing which makes it *in itself* worse than letting die. But this does not follow, for it is not the bare difference between killing and letting die that makes the difference in these cases. Rather, it is the other factors—the murderer's motive of personal gain, for example, contrasted with the doctor's humanitarian motivation, or the fact that the murderer kills a healthy person while the doctor lets die a terminal patient racked with disease—that account for our different reactions to the different cases.

There are, however, some substantial arguments that may be advanced to oppose this conclusion. Here are three of them:

1. The first counter-argument focuses specifically on the concept of *being the cause of someone's death*. If we kill someone, then we are the cause of his death. But if we merely let someone die, we are not the cause; rather, he dies of whatever condition he already has. The doctor who gives the cancer patient a lethal injection will have caused his patient's death, whereas if he merely ceases treatment, the cancer and not the doctor is the cause of death. According to some thinkers, this is supposed to make a moral difference.

Ramsey, for example, urges us to remember that 'In omission no human agent causes the patient's death, directly or indirectly.' And, writing in the *Villanova Law Review*, Dr J. Russell Elkinton said that what makes the active/passive distinction important is that in passive euthanasia 'The patient does not die from the act [that is, the act of turning off a respirator] but from the underlying disease or injury.'

This argument will not do, for two reasons. First, just as there is a distinction to be drawn between being and not being the cause of someone's death, there is also a distinction to be drawn between letting someone die and not letting anyone die. It is certainly desirable, in general, not to be the cause of anyone's death; but it is also desirable, in general, not to let anyone die when we can save them. (Doctors act on this precept every day.) Therefore, we cannot draw any special conclusion about the relative desirability of passive euthanasia just on these grounds.

Second, the reason we think it is bad to be the cause of someone's death is that we think death is a great evil—and so it is. However, if we have decided that euthanasia, even passive euthanasia, is desirable in a given case, then we have decided that in *this* instance death is no greater an evil than the patient's continued existence. And if this is true, then the usual reason for not wanting to be the cause of someone's death simply does not apply. To put the point just a bit differently: There is nothing wrong with being the cause of someone's death if his death is, all things considered, a good thing. And if his death is *not* a good thing, then *no* form of euthanasia, active or passive, is justified. So once again we see that the two kinds of euthanasia stand or fall together.

2. The second counter-argument appeals to a favourite idea of philosophers, namely that our duty not to harm people is generally more stringent than our duty to help them. The law affirms this when it forbids us to kill people, or steal their goods, but does not require us in general to save people's lives or give them charity. And this is said to be not merely a point about the law, but about morality as well. We do not have a strict moral duty to help some poor man in Ethiopia—although it might be kind and generous of us if we did—but we *do* have a strict moral duty to refrain from doing anything to harm him. Killing someone is a violation of our duty not to do harm, whereas letting someone die is merely a failure

to give help. Therefore, the former is a more serious breach of morality than the latter; and so, contrary to what was said above, there is a morally significant difference between killing and letting die.

This argument has a certain superficial plausibility, but it cannot be used to show that there is a morally important difference between active and passive euthanasia. For one thing, it only seems that our duty to help people is less stringent than our duty not to harm them when we concentrate on certain sorts of cases: cases in which the people we could help are very far away, and are strangers to us; or cases in which it would be very difficult for us to help them, or in which helping would require a substantial sacrifice on our part. Many people feel that, in *these* types of cases, it may be kind and generous of us to give help, but we are not morally required to do so. Thus it is felt that when we give money for famine relief we are being especially big-hearted, and we deserve special praise— even if it would be immodest of us to seek such praise—because we are doing more than we are, strictly speaking, required to do.

However, if we think of cases in which it would be very easy for us to help someone who is close at hand and in which no great personal sacrifice is required, things look very different. Think again of the child drowning in the bathtub: *of course* anyone standing next to the tub would have a strict moral duty to help the child. Here the alleged asymmetry between the duty to help and the duty not to do harm vanishes. Since most of the cases of euthanasia with which we are concerned are of this latter type—the patient is close at hand, it is well within the professional skills of the physician to keep him alive, and so on—the alleged asymmetry has little relevance.

It should also be remembered, in considering this argument, that the duty of doctors towards their patients *is* precisely to help them; that is what doctors are supposed to do. Therefore, even if there were a general asymmetry between the duty to help and the duty not to harm—which I deny, and which I will discuss in more detail in the next chapter—it would not apply in the special case of the relation between doctors and their patients.

Finally, it is not clear that killing such a patient *is* harming him, even though in other cases it certainly is a great harm to someone to kill him. For we are going under the assumption that the patient would be no worse off dead than he is now (otherwise, even *passive* euthanasia would be unthinkable); and if this is so, then killing him is not harming him. For the same reason we should not classify letting such a patient die as a failure to help. Therefore, even if we grant that our duty to help people is less stringent than our duty not to harm them, nothing follows about our duties with respect to killing and letting die in the special case of euthanasia.

3. The third counter-argument appeals to a consideration that has often been mentioned by doctors. Allowing a patient to die is, normally, a rather impersonal thing, in the sense that the physician does not feel 'involved' in the death—the cancer, or whatever, causes the death, and the doctor has nothing to do with it. So, there is no reason for him to feel guilty or responsible for the death. But if the physician were to give a lethal injection, *he* would be responsible, and feelings of guilt would be inevitable.

I do not wish to minimize the importance of the psychological situation in which doctors and other health-care professionals may find themselves. No doubt, many people who are comfortable enough letting die would find it psychologically impossible to kill— they just couldn't bring themselves to do it, and if they did, they would be haunted by feelings of remorse. But, important as this is for the people involved, we should be careful not to infer too much from it. We are trying to figure out whether mercy-killing is *wrong*, and whether it is *morally different* from letting die. So, we should ask: If someone feels guilty about mercy-killing, is that evidence that it is wrong? Or, if someone feels guiltier about mercy-killing than about letting die, is that evidence that it is worse?

Guilt feelings may, of course, be irrational. Someone may *feel* guilty even when he has not done anything wrong. Thus, we should not conclude that something is bad simply because someone feels, or would feel, guilty about it. We must *first* decide whether the conduct is wrong, on the basis of objective reasons; and then, if it is wrong, we may view the feelings of guilt as justified. But if it is not wrong, the feelings of guilt are irrational and we may encourage the person suffering them not to feel so bad. At any rate, feelings of guilt and the judgement of real guilt are different matters, and we cannot validly argue that a form of conduct *is* wrong, or that one type of behaviour *is* worse than another, because of feelings of guilt or innocence. That gets things the wrong way round.

The physician's commitments

Some people find it especially difficult to accept the idea of *physicians* engaging in active euthanasia. Doctors, they remind us, are dedicated to protecting and preserving life; that is their special task. Thus we should not expect *them* to kill, regardless of whatever might be right for the rest of us. Passive euthanasia, however, is another matter; since it only involves withholding pointless treatment, there is nothing in the physician's special position to rule it out.

This idea has been used by some philosophers as the basis for a qualified defence of the active/passive distinction. It is said that the distinction is important for doctors, because of their special role, regardless of whether it is important for anyone else. We need to ask, then, whether there is anything in the doctor's position that makes it impossible for him to accept active euthanasia. According to this argument, the doctor has some sort of special commitment, which the rest of us do not have, which makes the ethics of his position different.

Is this true? Everything turns on the nature of the physician's commitment. Exactly what kind of commitment is it? It might be a moral commitment—a matter of what physicians believe to be morally right—or it might be some sort of professional commitment, having to do with their role in society. Professional commitments and moral commitments are very different, and so we should consider them separately. Therefore, let's look at them one at a time.

Moral commitments

Many doctors certainly do believe that active euthanasia is immoral. Indeed, that is one reason the medical community so firmly rejects the practice. However, we should remember that anyone, including doctors, might have moral beliefs that are mistaken. To discover the truth, we must look at the arguments that can be given for and against active euthanasia; if better reasons can be given for it than against it, then it is morally acceptable, regardless of what doctors (or anyone else) might think—and of course if better reasons can be given against it, it is wrong regardless of what anyone thinks. But the fact that someone believes something is wrong never entails, by itself, that it *is* wrong. And so the fact that doctors *believe* active euthanasia to be wrong cannot, by itself, justify the conclusion that it is wrong for them to practise it.

When thinking about this point, it is easy to fall into a certain confusion. Suppose someone mistakenly believes that something is wrong—he believes it is wrong, when in fact it is perfectly all right. If he goes ahead and does that thing, even though he believes it is wrong, he is certainly open to criticism—you may think him in some sense a morally defective person, for he should not have done what he thought was wrong. This is where the confusion can slip in. When we say 'He should not have done it' we do not mean that what he did was wrong. In *fact*, what he did was perfectly all right. Despite this, he behaved badly because he did what he *thought* was wrong. Thus, if doctors believe active euthanasia is wrong, we can say that, in this sense, they shouldn't practise it. But this will not mean that, if they did practise it, they would be doing the wrong thing.

What doctors believe is also relevant in another way. It is in general true that, other things being equal, people should be allowed to follow their own consciences. We should not, without very strong reasons, compel people to do what they think is wrong, *even if their beliefs are mistaken*. Otherwise, we do not respect their autonomy as rational beings. Thus, if a doctor believes that something is wrong, he should be permitted to refrain from it. For example, many doctors believe that abortion is immoral, and so they should not be (and in fact they are not) required to perform abortions, even though the procedure is legal and accepted by other doctors without qualm. The same might be true of active euthanasia: those physicians who disapprove of it should not have to engage in it. But it does not follow that other doctors, who take a different view, should be forbidden, and so it does not follow that it would be wrong for the medical profession in general.

Therefore, if we focus on the question of *moral* commitment, the argument we are considering fails. There is nothing in the idea of a doctor's moral commitments to support the notion that doctors are precluded from accepting active euthanasia—unless, that is, active euthanasia is objectively wrong, in which case *everyone's* moral commitments ought to forbid it.

Professional commitments

There are two ways in which doctors might be professionally committed against active euthanasia. First, it might be that doctors pledge themselves to shun it, by subscribing to an explicit professional code of conduct. For a long time the Hippocratic Oath was taken to be such a code, although now it seems to have become more a historical relic than an actual guide. (The oath forbids abortion, for example.) More recently, the American Medical Association's policy statements have condemned active euthanasia —but it is not the purpose of those statements to bind physicians, and as we have noted, various of their provisions are regularly ignored in hospitals. Therefore, if the 'professional commitment' against mercy-killing is supposed to be in virtue of a pledge to an explicit code, there doesn't seem to be such a code. (And even if there were, advocates of active euthanasia could argue that the code should be changed.)

There is, however, another possibility. Perhaps physicians are committed to certain things, not by having taken a specific pledge, but *simply in virtue of being physicians*. Roger Rigterink, a philosopher who defends the general argument we are considering, suggests this when he says, '*The point of medicine* is to preserve human life whenever it occurs,' and 'A profession can hardly authorize an activity *that is antithetical to its basic function*' (italics added). The idea is that there is something in the very conception of what it is to be a physician that rules out killing patients.

To evaluate this suggestion, let us consider a parallel argument drawn from another area of life. Suppose someone argued that, while it can sometimes be right to destroy an automobile, it can never be right *for a mechanic* to do such a thing. After all, the whole point of automobile mechanics is to repair cars and make them serviceable. In destroying a car, a mechanic would be going against the very nature of his profession. So, if an automobile is beyond salvaging, it may be acceptable for the owner to junk it, but he cannot expect the mechanic to have any part of such a thing.

Obviously, this is a silly argument. But why? It isn't because there is something less noble about automobile mechanics than there is about doctors; nor is it silly because cars lack special moral worth. (There is no 'sanctity of automotive life'.) It is a bad argument because the concept of a profession cannot be used to show that it is wrong for a professional to do something that falls outside that concept. Mechanics fix cars when they can be fixed; if, in consigning a jalopy to the junk-heap, he isn't acting 'as a mechanic', what of it? Similarly, if a doctor, in practising active euthanasia, wasn't acting 'as a doctor', what of it?

It might be objected that, in engaging in mercy-killing, the physician isn't merely doing something *outside* his professional role; he is doing something *incompatible* with it. However, the same can be said about the auto mechanic. If the point of that profession is 'to repair cars and make them serviceable'—and isn't that its point?—then it is equally incompatible with auto mechanics to junk cars. Nevertheless, we would think it very strange for a mechanic to insist that he can do nothing to help us junk cars without violating his calling.

Suppose, however, we admit for purposes of argument that the nature of medicine does somehow imply that those engaged in it cannot be involved in mercy-killing. Would that mean we must meekly accept the implied conclusion? No, for consider this: we can define a *different* profession, very much like medicine, but called (perhaps) 'smedicine'. Smedicine, as we will define it, is the profession which does everything it can to treat illness, cure disease, and repair the human body, so long as there is any point to it; but, when the possibility of a meaningful life is gone, smedicine helps to make the passage to death as easy as possible. We could argue that medicine, which (we are assuming) precludes this latter kind of help, is morally defective, and should be abandoned, to be replaced by the better practice of smedicine. If I thought that the concept of medicine precluded mercy-killing, that is exactly what I would argue, for 'medicine', thus conceived, would be forbidding its practitioners from doing what is in many instances the morally right thing.

There is, therefore, nothing in the physician's commitments that leads to the conclusion that the active/passive distinction is somehow valid 'for him'. If it is in general an unsound distinction, then it is as much unsound for him as for anyone.

Thomson's objection

The Bare Difference Argument relies on a certain method of reasoning, and some philosophers have suggested that this method is not sound. Judith Jarvis Thomson has urged that *something* must be wrong with this way of reasoning, because it leads to patently absurd conclusions. To demonstrate this, she offers an argument that is parallel to the one involving Smith and Jones, but which is obviously unsound:

Alfrieda knows that if she cuts off Alfred's head he will die, and wanting him to die, cuts if off; Bertha knows that if she punches Bert in the nose he will die—Bert is in peculiar physical condition—and, wanting him to die, punches him in the nose. But what Bertha does is surely every bit as bad as what Alfrieda does. So cutting off a man's head isn't worse than punching a man in the nose.

She concludes that, since this absurd argument doesn't prove anything, the Smith-and-Jones argument doesn't prove anything either.

If Thomson were right, we would have to scuttle the Bare Difference Argument and look elsewhere for support for the Equivalence Thesis. But I don't think she is right: the Alfrieda-and-Bertha argument is not absurd, as strange as it is. A little analysis shows that it is a sound argument and that its conclusion is true. The analysis is a bit tedious, but it is worth doing, for it clarifies the nature of the Bare Difference Argument and confirms its soundness.

We need first to notice that the reason it is wrong to chop someone's head off is, obviously, that this causes death. (I am setting aside secondary reactions having to do with messiness.) The act is objectionable because of its consequences. Thus, a different act with the same consequences may be equally objectionable. In Thomson's example, punching Bert in the nose has the same consequences as chopping off Alfred's head; and, indeed, the two actions are equally bad.

Now the Alfrieda-and-Bertha argument presupposes a distinction between the act of chopping off someone's head, and the results of that act, the victim's death. (It is stipulated that, except for the fact that Alfrieda chops off someone's head, while Bertha punches someone in the nose, the two acts are 'in all other respects alike'. The 'other respects' include the act's consequence, the victim's death.) This is not a distinction we would normally think to make, since we cannot in fact cut off someone's head without killing him. Yet in thought the distinction can be drawn. The question raised in the argument, then, is whether, *considered apart from their consequences*, head-chopping is worse than nose-punching. And the answer to *this* strange question is No, just as the argument says it should be.

The conclusion of the argument should be construed like this: the bare fact that one act is an act of head-chopping, while another act is an act of nose-punching, is not a reason for judging the former to be worse than the latter. At the same time—and this is perfectly compatible with the argument—the fact that one act causes death, while another does not, *is* a reason for judging the former to be worse. Thomson has specified, however, that in the cases of Alfrieda and Bertha there is no difference in this regard either; and so their acts turn out to be morally equivalent. So be it.

The parallel construal of the conclusion to the Smith-and-Jones argument is: the bare fact that one act is an act of killing, while another act is an act of letting die, is not a reason for judging the former to be worse than the latter. At the same time—and this is perfectly compatible with that argument—the fact that an act (of killing, for example) prevents suffering, while another act (of letting die, for example) does not, is a reason for preferring the former. So once we see exactly how the Alfrieda-and-Bertha argument *is* parallel to the Smith-and-Jones argument, we find that Thomson's argument is, surprisingly, quite all right. Therefore, it provides no reason for doubting the soundness of the style of reasoning employed in the Bare Difference Argument.

The Compromise View

Some philosophers concede that, in the case of Smith and Jones, there is no moral difference between killing and letting die; but they continue to maintain that in the euthanasia cases the distinction *is* morally important. Thus, it is suggested that the Bare Difference Argument commits an elementary fallacy—the fallacy of hasty generalization. It leaps from one example, in which the distinction appears to be unimportant, to the general conclusion that the distinction is *never* important. But why should this be so? Why should the only options be that the distinction is *always* important, or *never* important?

Perhaps the truth is simply that the difference between killing and letting die is sometimes morally important, and sometimes not, depending on the particular case you choose to think about.

I will call this the Compromise View. It is the most appealing alternative to the view I am defending, and of all possible views of the matter it most closely conforms to our pre-reflective intuitions. The Compromise View allows us to look at cases one at a time, and decide in each case whether the difference between killing and letting die is significant. What could be more reasonable?

In fact, I will argue, such a procedure is not reasonable at all. Logic requires that the distinction be always, or never, important. There is no middle ground. This may sound unattractively dogmatic. Nevertheless, it follows from some inescapable principles of reasoning.

The crucial question is this: Is it possible for a fact sometimes to count as a good reason in support of a moral judgement, and sometimes not? Imagine what it would be like if this were possible. I tell you that John is a bad man because he is stingy and a liar; you then observe that Frank is also a stingy liar, and so you conclude that he is a bad man as well. But I object, and say that although stinginess and dishonesty count against John, the same does not apply to Frank. Frank, I say, is a splendid fellow. I am *not* saying that, despite being a stingy liar, Frank has other qualities that compensate for this. I am saying something more radical—I take the fact that John is stingy and dishonest to be a good reason for judging him to be a bad man; but I do not take the fact that Frank has these qualities to be a reason for judging him badly. I am holding these qualities against John, but I am not holding these very same qualities against Frank at all, not even as something that needs to be compensated for.

Or, to take a different example: I say that you ought to vote for Brown, a candidate for public office, because she favours gun control. You point out that Black, her opponent, also favours gun control; therefore you say that I have not given any reason for preferring Brown over Black. But again, I object, and say that Brown's position is a reason in her favour, but Black's identical position is not a reason in Black's favour.

Surely, in both these cases, I am inconsistent. It would be perfectly all right to argue that Brown, but not Black, should be elected for other reasons. Perhaps we know more about them than that they both favour gun control: perhaps we also know that both candidates are strong supporters of affirmative action programmes, and that Brown has greater experience in dealing with governmental matters. Then we might tabulate what we know like this:

Reasons for voting for Brown
Brown favours gun control.
Brown supports affirmative action programmes.
Brown has greater experience.

Reasons for voting for Black
Black favours gun control.
Black supports affirmative action programmes.

We certainly may conclude that, all things considered, one ought to vote for Brown. In every respect save one, they are equally good candidates; and in the one respect in which they differ, Brown has the edge. So she is the candidate of choice, at least on this information. What we *cannot* do, without violating the requirement of consistency, is say that Brown's position on gun control (or her position on affirmative action) goes on the list in her favour, but that Black's position doesn't even go on the list.

There is a formal principle of reasoning involved here; 'formal' because it is a principle of logic that everyone must accept regardless of the content of his or her particular moral code. Let A and B stand for any actions, and let P stand for any property of actions. Then:

Principle I
If the fact that A has P is a morally good reason in support of the judgement that A ought (or ought not) to be done, and B also has P, then that is also a reason, of equal weight, for the judgement that B ought (or ought not) to be done.

The act 'voting for Brown' has the property 'being a vote for someone who favours gun control', and the act 'voting for Black' has the same property; so, if this provides a reason for voting for Brown, it also provides a reason for voting for Black.

The following corollary covers cases in which the merits of two acts are being compared:

Principle II
If the fact that A has P and B has Q is a morally good reason for preferring A over B, then if C has P and D has Q, that is a reason of equal weight for preferring C over D.

Thus, if we say that Brown's experience as compared with Black's is a reason for preferring Brown, then in any other similar election between an experienced and an inexperienced candidate, we must say this is a reason for preferring the former.

Superficially, there appear to be some counter-examples to this principle—that is, examples which show the principle to be unsound. Suppose we prefer Brown's experience over Black's in one election, but in another election we think it important to bring in a candidate from outside government—'fresh blood', as it is called. Doesn't this mean that, in one instance, we are taking experience as desirable, and in another instance taking it as undesirable—and can't this be all right? Of course this is all right—it certainly isn't irrational—but it does not violate the principle. It only appears that we have violated the principle because we have not specified the reasons accurately. The reason we sometimes prefer an 'inexperienced' candidate is not that he is inexperienced. It is because we think it likely that he will have a fresher approach, be more open to new ideas and be less bound by the mistakes of the past. And these are *always* good qualities in a candidate. Other apparent counter-examples to the principle may be explained away in a similar manner.

Now, with these principles in mind, let us return to the distinction between killing and letting die. You will recall that the Equivalence Thesis is a thesis about what does, or does not, count as a morally good reason in support of a value judgement. It says: the fact that one act is an act of killing, while another act is an act of letting someone die, is not a morally good reason in support of the judgement that either act is preferable to the other. The Compromise View, on the other hand, says that in some cases the distinction may be important, while in other cases it is not. In other words, the Compromise View implies this:

In some cases, the fact that *A* is letting die, while *B* is killing, is a morally good reason for preferring *A* over *B*. But in other cases, the fact that *C* is letting die, while *D* is killing, may *not* be a morally good reason for preferring *C* over *D*.

And this violates Principle II. This is what I meant when I said that the Compromise View is inconsistent with sound principles of moral reasoning. The reasonable-sounding compromise offered by this view is not tenable; and so we are stuck with the radical-sounding alternatives: either the distinction between killing and letting die is always important, or it never is.

What do advocates of the Compromise View actually say? Philippa Foot proposes a version of the Compromise View. She asks, 'When is this distinction morally relevant?' and answers 'in cases in which rights are in question'. It may violate a person's rights to kill him, she says, even when in the same circumstances it would not violate his rights to let him die. She adds that 'permission may make all the difference in such a case . . . if someone gives us the right to kill him, for his own good, by seriously consenting to the action, it then makes no moral difference whether we do kill him or rather allow him to die.'

Foot thinks it is 'obvious' that there is sometimes a moral difference between killing and letting die, especially 'when one thinks about the crucial question of rights'. She suggests that those who defend the Equivalence Thesis are confused about what they are denying; they 'seem simply to have misunderstood the position of their opponents'.

It would not be surprising if there were some misunderstanding here. Often, when people take sides on complex issues, and are determined to defend their views, misunderstanding occurs. People become more interested in scoring debating points, and proving themselves right, than in patiently analysing issues. Rather than being immune from this tendency, philosophers often seem to be among the worst offenders.

I can think of one way to bring the two sides on this issue a little closer together. I (and other defenders of the Equivalence Thesis) can easily concede that, in some cases, it may be permissible to let die but not to kill. Likewise, in other cases it may be permissible to kill but not to let die. This is perfectly compatible with the Equivalence Thesis. All the Equivalence Thesis requires is that, in such a case, it is some *other* feature of the case that makes the difference.

Permission may, indeed, be a crucial matter, as Foot says. Suppose I give you permission to let me die, but say that I do not want to be killed. Then it might be all right for you to let me die but not to kill me. (If it is the other way round—I give permission to be killed, but don't want to be allowed to die—the reverse may be true.) However, the *reason* one is permissible, but not the other, will not be that one is killing and the other is letting die. The reason will be, simply, that I permitted one but not the other.

Perhaps the Equivalence Thesis is misunderstood by those who reject it. Foot emphasizes that 'If one may, in particular circumstances, allow a man to die it does not *follow* that one may also kill him, even for his own good.' She apparently thinks this is a telling point against those of us on the other side of the issue. But it isn't; this is something we all agree on. Suppose, again, that someone wants to be allowed to die but does not want to be killed. In those 'particular circumstances', one may allow him to die; but, as she says, 'it does not *follow* that one may also kill him'. The Equivalence Thesis does not imply otherwise. The Equivalence Thesis only says that the reason one course, but not the other, is permissible, isn't simply the intrinsic 'moral importance' of the difference between killing and letting die. In this case that difference is *correlated* with another difference (between permission and objection) and this other difference is, indeed, morally important.

I do not know whether clearing away such misunderstandings, and exposing areas of common ground, will lead to agreement. It should at least reduce the extent of the disagreement, and clarify the differences that remain. Complete agreement is probably too much to hope for; that is rare in any branch of philosophy, and even rarer when philosophical theses lie so close to moral practice.

8 FURTHER REFLECTIONS ON KILLING AND LETTING DIE

The status of intuitions

In the previous chapter I argued that there is no moral difference between killing and letting die. In addition to its obvious importance for medical ethics, this thesis has other implications: it implies, for example, that our duty towards starving people is greater than we might have realized. In this chapter, I take up this issue, and present additional arguments for the Equivalence Thesis. This will also be a convenient place to comment on some questions of method in ethical theory.

Although we do not know exactly how many people die each year of malnutrition and related health problems, the number is very high, in the millions. The most common pattern among children in poor countries is death from dehydration caused by diarrhoea brought on by malnutrition. In 1983, not a particularly bad year, James Grant, Executive Director of the United Nations Children's Fund (UNICEF), estimated that 15,000 children were dying in this way every day. That comes to 5,475,000 children annually. Even if Grant's estimate was high by a factor of three, it is still a staggering number of deaths—and it includes only one way of death, among only one class of victims.

By giving money to support famine-relief efforts, each of us could save at least some of these people. By not giving, we let them die. The Equivalence Thesis suggests a harsh judgement about this behaviour, for it says there is no moral difference between letting die and killing. The question of famine relief provides another important test of this idea, for even if one is convinced that there is no difference in medical contexts—that active and passive euthanasia are morally the same—one might still balk at the idea in connection with famine relief. Moreover, there is likely to be more resistance to this application of the Equivalence Thesis because it affects more of us directly. Not many of us are ever in a position to choose active or passive euthanasia; but almost all of us are in a position to save lives by contributing money for famine relief. If the Equivalence Thesis is correct, we are all, morally speaking, murderers. On the face of it, this seems wrong. When reminded that people are dying of starvation while we spend money on trivial things, we may feel a bit guilty, but certainly we do not feel like murderers. In a famous essay, Philippa Foot writes:

Most of us allow people to die of starvation in India and Africa, and there is surely something wrong with us that we do; it would be nonsense, however, to pretend that it is only in law that we make a distinction between allowing people in the underdeveloped countries to die of starvation and sending them poisoned food. There is worked into our moral system a distinction between what we owe people in the form of aid and what we owe them in the way of non-interference.

No doubt this would be correct if it were intended only as a description of what most affluent people believe. Whether this feature of 'our moral system' is rationally defensible is, however, another matter.

Our 'intuitions' are our pre-reflective beliefs about what is right or wrong in individual cases—one might say, inelegantly, that they are our gut feelings. In the above quotation, Professor Foot expresses the common intuition that there *must* be an important moral difference between killing and letting die. What significance are we to attach to this feeling? Philosophers differ profoundly in what they think about intuitions. Some treat them with a great deal of respect. They trust intuitions and are suspicious of any moral view at odds with them. Those thinkers are often morally conservative, because their methodology inclines them to theories that systematize what (reasonable, sober) people already happen to believe. They have little use for radical claims like the Equivalence Thesis, for if the Equivalence Thesis is true it would mean that many of our intuitions must be rejected. When faced with arguments that purportedly 'prove' the thesis is 'true', these philosophers would rather dismiss the argument than reject the intuitions. Thomas Nagel sums up this approach when he says, 'I believe one should trust . . . intuitions over arguments . . . Given a knockdown argument for an intuitively unacceptable conclusion, one should assume there is probably something wrong with the argument that one cannot detect . . .' Other philosophers have a different attitude: they trust arguments more than intuitions. They are more comfortable with radical moral ideas because, when faced with persuasive arguments, they are willing to let the intuitions go.

The difference between these philosophers is not that they have different intuitions. They may have the same gut feelings. I take the second approach; but I have the same feelings as everyone else: when I think of the starving people I let die by not contributing more for famine relief, I do not feel like a murderer. I feel, intuitively, that there *must* be a difference. But on reflection I can find no reason to think that there really is a difference, and much reason to think otherwise; so I conclude that the intuition is mistaken. It may be observed, however, that the influence of arguments can eventually lead to a change in one's intuitions. In my own case, I find that my 'feeling' that I am not the moral equivalent of a murderer is much weaker than it used to be.

In other times the priority of argument would have been taken for granted; at least among philosophers, it would not have been questioned. But a change of mood began to come over philosophers early in this century, not in moral philosophy at first, but in metaphysics. The nineteenth-century idealists defended wildly implausible theses, such that time is unreal, or that physical objects do not exist, with elaborate but hard-to-refute arguments. In a series of influential essays, G. E. Moore asserted that we simply *know* these propositions to be false, as a matter of common sense. The implication was that arguments which go against common sense must contain some mistake, even if we cannot figure out what the mistake is. Moore himself spent little time trying to identify the specific errors in idealist arguments, and, as a result of his influence, it became acceptable to say: X is more certain than any argument that might be given against it. Arguments, when they lead to implausible conclusions, are not to be trusted.

It is in moral philosophy, however, that the appeal to common sense has been most widespread. In the twentieth century moral philosophers have been preoccupied with utilitarianism, which is by far the most impressive unified moral theory we have. Utilitarianism has provided the theoretical foundation of work not only in ethics but in economics and law and social science for decades.

Yet many thinkers have regarded utilitarianism as ultimately unacceptable, because it has consequences incompatible with our intuitions—our moral common sense. The basic idea of the theory is that right actions or social policies are those which produce the best results. It is a simple, powerful idea that, considered abstractly, is difficult to fault. When we turn to specific cases, however, it seems quite implausible. Suppose a Peeping Tom will get enormous pleasure from spying on young women, and suppose further that he will never be detected and will never embarrass them. The only consequences of his spying will be his own gain in pleasure, a good result. If utility is taken as the sole criterion of right action, his actions would be unobjectionable. Yet, intuitively, his behaviour seems outrageous. The women's rights are being trampled, regardless of whether they are aware of it. Other, similar cases come easily to mind, in which utilitarianism gives the 'wrong' outcome in specific cases. The theory, then, seems unacceptable.

This style of reasoning became very popular after the publication of W. D. Ross's *The Right and the Good* in 1930. During the 1950s and 60s Ross's intuitionist objections were reprinted alongside the classic utilitarian writings in virtually every standard textbook in moral philosophy, so that generations of students learned to think in this way. But notice what was happening. Conformity with 'intuition' was becoming the test of acceptability for moral theory. If a theory conflicts with one's pre-reflective beliefs, it was the theory, and not the beliefs, that was assumed to be defective.

In responding to the intuitionist objections, defenders of utilitarianism by and large did not challenge this approach. Most of them merely replied that, contrary to appearances, their theory did not have the counter-intuitive consequences. To demonstrate this they offered more sophisticated versions of the theory, often emphasizing that rules, and not individual actions, are the objects of utilitarian justification. Only a few, such as J. J. C. Smart in his *Outline of a System of Utilitarian Ethics*, chose the bolder course and admitted that the theory really does require the abandonment of some pre-reflective intuitions.

By the time John Rawls published his *A Theory of Justice* in 1971, the priority of intuition was commonly assumed. In Rawls's hands it was made into a matter of basic philosophical method. Moral philosophy, he said, is 'the attempt to describe our moral capacity', much as a linguistic theory is an attempt to describe our capacity for language. Native speakers are able to distinguish well-formed from ill-formed sentences, even without a theory for guidance. The task of linguistic theory is to formulate 'clearly expressed principles which make the same discriminations as the native speaker', so that we can understand the speaker's capacity *as if* it were guided by those principles. Similarly, we are able to judge intuitively that some actions are right, and others wrong; and the task of moral theory is to formulate principles that explain and justify those judgements:

what is required is a formulation of a set of principles which, when conjoined to our beliefs and knowledge of the circumstances, would lead us to make these judgements with their supporting reasons were we to apply these principles conscientiously and intelligently . . . These principles can serve as part of the premises of an argument which arrives at the matching judgements.

The trouble with this is that we have no guarantee that our intuitions are perceptions of the truth. The analogy with linguistics breaks down because grammaticalness is determined by the conventions of a group of speakers—in an important sense, common usage *cannot* be incorrect. If everyone said 'I is' rather than 'I am', and always had said it, it would be proper English. Right and wrong, however, are not determined in the same way—a common moral belief *can* be incorrect. If everyone believed, along with Aquinas and Kant, that the suffering of non-human animals has no moral importance, this could still be wrong. Our moral beliefs might be the result of prejudice, selfishness, or cultural conditioning. They might be left over from discredited religious or metaphysical systems. Countless irrational factors might be involved. The principles of a moral theory that remains faithful to all our 'intuitions' will only enshrine our irrationality.

Rawls is sensitive to this rather obvious point, and he tries to meet it by stipulating that a moral theory need not respect *every* intuitive judgement. Only 'considered judgements' need be taken into account:

we can discard those judgements made with hesitation, or in which we have little confidence. Similarly, those given when we are frightened, or when we stand to gain one way or the other can be left aside. All these judgements are likely to be erroneous . . .

Moreover, we may want to revise some of our judgements in the light of the theory, just as we may adjust the theory to accommodate some of the judgements. The process of give-and-take stops when the judgements and the theory are in a balance which Rawls calls 'reflective equilibrium'. Only then should we be satisfied with either.

These qualifications make the methodology very attractive. Indeed, it is easy to imagine the method of reflective equilibrium practised in a way that would satisfy even those who trust argument more than intuition. If all the arguments that challenge intuitions are incorporated into the theory, so that only intuitions supported by arguments remain when reflective equilibrium is reached, even the radicals must be satisfied. This, however, only conceals a real difference of approach among thinkers in the two camps. A fundamental objection to the method of reflective equilibrium remains: a false moral belief may be so deeply held that we assert it with confidence, even when we are calm and have nothing to gain, and we may be quite willing to modify our principles to accommodate it. The resulting theory would, in some sense, describe our intuitions, but it would not embody the truth about right and wrong. Our only ultimate protection against this is an approach to ethics that trusts argument more than intuition.

The Jack Palance Argument

We think that killing is worse than letting die because, to some extent, we overestimate how bad it is to kill. (The overestimation is largely responsible for our reluctance to accept active euthanasia.) But even more, we underestimate how bad it is to let people die. The following chain of reasoning is intended to show that letting people in foreign countries die of starvation is much worse than we commonly assume. It is designed to undermine confidence in the 'intuition' that we are less than murderers.

Suppose there were a starving child in the room where you are now—hollow eyed, belly bloated, and so on—and you have a sandwich at your elbow that you don't need. Of course you would be horrified; you would stop reading and give her the sandwich or, better, take her to a hospital. And you would not think this an act of supererogation: you would not expect any special praise for it, and you would expect criticism if you did not. Imagine what you would think of someone who simply ignored the child and continued reading, allowing her to die. Let us call the person who would do this Jack Palance, after the very nice man who plays such vile characters in the movies. Jack Palance indifferently watches the starving child die; he cannot be bothered even to hand her the sandwich. There is ample reason for judging him harshly; without putting too fine a point on it, he shows himself to be a moral monster.

When we allow people in far-away countries to die of starvation, we may think, as Foot puts it, that 'there is surely something wrong with us'. But we most emphatically do not consider ourselves moral monsters. We think this, in spite of striking similarities between Jack Palance's behaviour and our own. He could easily save the child; he does not; and the child dies. We could easily save some of those starving people; we do not; and they die. If he is a moral monster, and we are not, there must be some important difference between him and us. But what is it?

One obvious difference between Jack Palance's position and ours is that the person he lets die is in the same room with him, while the people we let die are mostly far away. Yet the spatial location of the dying people hardly seems a relevant consideration. It is absurd to suppose that being located at a certain map-coordinate entitles one to treatment which one would not merit if situated at a different longitude or latitude. Of course, if a dying person's location meant that we *could not* help, that would excuse us. But, since there are efficient famine-relief agencies willing to carry our aid to the far-away places, this excuse is not available. It would be almost as easy for us to send these agencies the price of the sandwich as for Palance to hand it to the child.

The location of the starving people does make a difference, psychologically, in how we feel. (Perhaps this is one source of the 'intuition' we are considering.) If there were a starving child in the same room with us, we could not avoid realizing, in a vivid and disturbing way, how it is suffering and how it is about to die. Faced with this realization our consciences probably would not allow us to ignore the child. But if the dying are far away, it is easy to think of them only abstractly, or to put them out of our thoughts altogether. This might explain why our conduct would be different if we were in Jack Palance's position, even though, from a moral point of view, the location of the dying is not relevant.

There is another way in which the location of the dying makes a difference to our feelings. The fact that they are scattered makes them easier not to notice. I noted above that according to UNICEF Director James Grant, 5,475,000 children die from malnutrition-related problems annually. There are only three cities in the United States with a population larger than that. Suppose all these people were dying in one huge city; it would be a front-page emergency. But because they are scattered, we don't seem to mind as much. (When they *are* concentrated in one place, as in the Ethiopian crisis of 1984, we respond. Strangely, when the same number of starving are scattered, it isn't perceived as a 'crisis'.)

There are other differences between Jack Palance and us, which may seem important, having to do with the sheer numbers of people, both affluent and starving, that surround us. In our fictitious example Jack Palance is one person confronted with the need of one other person. This makes his position relatively simple. In the real world our position is more complicated, in two ways: first, in that there are millions of people who need feeding, and none of us has the resources to care for all of them; and second, in that for any starving person we *could* help there are millions of other affluent people who could help as easily as we.

On the first point, not much needs to be said. We may feel, in a vague sort of way, that we are not monsters because no one of us could possibly save *all* the starving people—there are just too many of them, and none of us has the resources. This is fair enough, but all that follows is that, individually, none of us is responsible for saving everyone. We may still be responsible for saving someone, or as many as we can. This is so obvious that it hardly bears mentioning; yet it is easy to lose sight of, and philosophers have actually lost sight of it. Writing in *The Journal of Philosophy*, Richard Trammell says that one morally important difference between killing and letting die is 'dischargeability'. By this he means that, while each of us can discharge completely a duty not to kill anyone, no one among us can discharge completely a duty to save everyone who needs it. Again, fair enough; but all that follows is that, since we are bound to save only those we can, the group of people we have an obligation to save is smaller than the group we have an obligation not to kill. It does *not* follow that our duty with respect to those we can save is any less stringent. Suppose Jack Palance were to say,

'I needn't give this starving child the sandwich because, after all, I can't save everyone in the world who needs it.' If this excuse will not work for him, neither will it work for us with respect to the children we could save in India or Africa.

The second point about numbers was that, for any starving person we *could* help, there are millions of other affluent people who could help as easily as we. Some are in an even better position to help because they are richer. But by and large these people are doing nothing. This also helps to explain why we do not feel especially guilty for letting people starve. How guilty we feel about something depends, to some extent, on how we compare with those around us. If we were surrounded by people who regularly sacrificed to feed the starving, and we did not, we would probably feel ashamed. But because our neighbours do not do any better than we, we are not so ashamed.

But again, this does not mean that we should not feel more guilty or ashamed than we do. A psychological explanation of our feelings is not a moral justification of our conduct. Suppose Jack Palance was only one of twenty people who watched the child die; would that decrease his guilt? Curiously, many people seem to assume it would. They seem to feel that if twenty people do nothing to prevent a tragedy, each of them is only one-twentieth as guilty as he would have been if he had watched the tragedy alone. It is as though there is only a fixed amount of guilt, which divides. I suggest, rather, that guilt multiplies, so that each passive observer is fully guilty, if he could have prevented the tragedy but did not. Jack Palance watching the girl die alone would be a moral monster; but if he calls in a group of friends to watch with him, he does not diminish his guilt by dividing it among them. Instead, they are all moral monsters. Once the point is made explicit, it seems obvious.

The fact that most other affluent people do nothing to relieve hunger may very well have implications for one's own obligations. But the implication may be that one's own obligations increase rather than decrease. Suppose Palance and a friend were faced with two starving children, so that, if each did his 'fair share', Palance would only have to feed one of them. But the friend will do nothing. Because he is well off (he has two sandwiches at his elbow), Palance could feed both of them. Shouldn't he? What if he fed one and then watched the other die, announcing that he has done *his* duty and that the one who died was his friend's responsibility? This shows the fallacy of supposing that one's duty is only to do one's fair share, where this is determined by what would be sufficient *if* everyone else did likewise.

To summarize: Jack Palance, who refuses to hand a sandwich to a starving child, is a moral monster. But we feel intuitively that we are not so monstrous, even though we also let starving people die when we could feed them almost as easily. If this intuition is correct, there must be some important difference between him and us. But when we examine the most obvious differences between his conduct and ours—the location of the dying, the differences in numbers—we find no real basis for judging ourselves less harshly than we judge him. Perhaps there are some other grounds on which we might distinguish our moral position with respect to actual starving people, from Jack Palance's position with respect to the child in my story. But I cannot think of what they might be. Therefore, I conclude that if he is a monster, then so are we—or at least, so are we after our rationalizations and thoughtlessness have been exposed.

This last qualification is important. We judge people, at least in part, according to whether they can be expected to realize how well or how badly they behave. We judge Palance harshly because the consequences of his indifference are so immediately apparent. By contrast, it requires an unusual effort for us to realize the consequences of our indifference. It is normal behaviour for people in the affluent countries not to give for famine relief, or if they do give, to give very little. Decent people may go along with this normal behaviour pattern unthinkingly, without realizing, or without comprehending in a clear way, just what this means for the starving. Thus, even though those decent people may act monstrously, we do not judge them to be monsters. There is a curious sense, then, in which moral reflection can transform decent people into indecent ones: for if a person thinks things through, and realizes that he is, morally speaking, in Jack Palance's position, his continued indifference is more blameworthy than before.

The preceding is not intended to prove that letting people die of starvation is as bad as killing them. *This* argument does not prove the Equivalence Thesis is true, but it does provide strong evidence that letting die is much worse than we normally assume, and so that letting die is morally much *closer* to killing than we normally assume. These reflections also go some way towards showing just how fragile and unreliable our intuitions are in this area. They suggest that, if we want to discover the truth, we are better off looking at arguments than consulting intuitions.

The No Relevant Difference Argument

In Chapter 7 (pp. 111–14) I presented an argument—the 'Bare Difference Argument'—designed to show that the Equivalence Thesis is true. I believe that the Bare Difference Argument is sound; but it is, in a certain sense, superficial. It proves that killing and letting die are morally equivalent, but it provides no clue as to *why* they are equivalent. Even if it produces conviction it does not produce understanding. Now I want to present an argument that is deeper in this respect, an argument that exposes why the two are equivalent.

The first stage of the argument is concerned with some formal relations between moral judgements and the reasons that support them. It is a point of logic that moral judgement are true only if good reasons support them; for example, if there is no good reason why you ought to do some action, it cannot be true that you ought to do it. Moreover, when there is a choice to be made from among two or more possible actions, the preferable alternative is the one that is backed by the strongest reasons.

But when are the reasons for or against one act stronger than those for or against another act? A complete answer would have to include some normative theory explaining why some reasons are intrinsically weightier than others. Suppose you are in a situation in which you can save someone's life only by lying: the normative theory would explain why 'Doing A would save someone's life' is a stronger reason in favour of doing A than 'Doing B would be telling the truth' is in favour of doing B.

However, there are some purely formal principles that operate here. The simplest and least controversial formal principle is:

(1) If there are the *same* reasons for or against A as for or against B, then the reasons in favour of A are neither stronger nor weaker than the reasons in favour of B; and so A and B are morally equivalent—neither is preferable to the other.

This is a formal principle in that it implies nothing about the nature of the reasons that count for or against actions; it is a principle of logic in that it cannot be denied without self-contradiction. It is a principle that must be acknowledged by any consistent moral code, regardless of the content of that code.

Now, suppose we ask why killing is morally objectionable. We are concerned, of course, with killing as a *type* of action. There may be special reasons why particular killings are permissible or impermissible, but we are not concerned with those. We want to know why killing is, in general, wrong. In Chapters 2 and 3 I offered an account according to which killing is wrong because it puts an end to one's biographical life. You may prefer a different account. However, any reasonable account must acknowledge that the primary reason killing is wrong has to do with the fact that the victim ends up dead: he no longer has a good—his life—that he possessed before. Secondary reasons may have to do with harmful effects on the survivors. (Those who loved him may grieve; those who were depending on him will have to make other arrangements; and so forth.) *But notice that exactly the same can be said about letting someone die.* The primary reason it is morally objectionable to let someone die, when we could save him, is that he ends up dead; he no longer has a good—his life—that he possessed before. Secondary reasons may again have to do with harmful effects on those who survive. Thus, the explanation of why killing is wrong mentions features of killing that are also features of letting die, and vice versa. Since there are no comparably general reasons in favour of either, this suggests that

(2) There are the same reasons for and against letting die as for and against killing.

And if this is true, we get the conclusion:

(3) Therefore, killing and letting die are morally equivalent—neither is preferable to the other.

The central idea of the argument is that there is no morally relevant difference between killing and letting die, that is, no difference which may be cited to show that one is worse than the other. The argument therefore contains a premise—(2)—that is supported only inductively. The fact that the explanation of why killing is wrong applies equally well to letting die, and vice versa, provides compelling evidence that the generalization is true. Nevertheless, some doubt may remain: no matter how carefully we analyse the matter, it will always be possible that there is some subtle, morally relevant difference between the two that we have overlooked. In fact, philosophers who believe that killing is worse than letting die have sometimes tried to identify such differences. I believe that these attempts have failed. Here are three examples.

1. The first is one that I have already mentioned. Trammell urges that there is an important difference in the 'dischargeability' of duties not to kill and not to let die. We can completely discharge a duty not to kill anyone; but we cannot completely discharge a duty to save everyone who needs aid. This is obviously correct, but it does not show that the Equivalence Thesis is false, for two reasons. In the first place, the difference in dischargeability only shows that the class of people we have a duty to save is smaller than the class of people we have a duty not to kill. It does not show that our duty with respect to those we *can* save is any less stringent. In the second place, if we *cannot* save someone, and that person dies, then we do not let him die. It is not right to say that I let Josef Stalin die, for example, since there is no way I could have saved him. So if I cannot save everyone, then neither can I let everyone die.

2. It has also been urged that, in killing someone, we are *doing* something—namely, killing him—whereas, in letting someone die, we are not doing anything. In letting people die of starvation, for example, we only *fail* to do certain things, such as sending food. The difference is between action and inaction; and somehow this is supposed to make a moral difference.

There are also two difficulties with this suggestion. First, it is misleading to say, without further ado, that in letting someone die we do nothing. For there is one very important thing that we do: we let someone die. 'Letting someone die' is different, in some ways, from other sorts of actions, mainly in that it is an action we perform *by way of* not performing other actions. We may let someone die by not feeding him, just as we may insult someone by not shaking his hand. (If it is said, 'I didn't do anything: I simply refrained from taking his hand when he offered it,' it may be replied, 'You did do one thing—you insulted him.') The distinction between action and inaction is relative to a specification of *what* actions are or are not done. In insulting someone, we may *not* smile, speak, shake hands, and so on—but we *do* insult or snub the person. And in letting someone die, many things may not be done: we may not feed the person, or give medication, and so on. But there is one thing we do: we let someone die.

Second, even if letting die were only a case of inaction, why should any moral conclusion follow from *that* fact? It may seem that a significant conclusion follows if we assume that we are not responsible for inactions, or that we are not blameworthy for inactions, or something of the sort. However, there is no general correlation between the action/inaction distinction and any sort of moral assessment. We ought to do some things, and we ought not do others, and we can certainly be morally blameworthy for not doing things as well as for doing them—Jack Palance was blameworthy for not feeding the child. In many circumstances we are even legally liable for not doing things: tax fraud may involve only 'inaction'—failing to report certain things to the Department of Internal Revenue—but what of it? Moreover, failing to act can be subject to all the other kinds of moral assessment. Not doing something may, depending on the circumstances, be right, wrong, obligatory, wise, foolish, compassionate, sadistic, and so on. Since there is no general correlation between the action/inaction distinction and *any* of these matters, it is hard to see how anything could be made out of this distinction in the present context.

3. My final example is from Trammell again. He argues that 'optionality' is a morally relevant difference between killing and letting die. The point here is that if we fail to save someone, we leave open the option for someone else to save him; whereas if we kill, the victim is dead and that's that. This point, I think, has little significance. For one thing, while 'optionality' may mark a difference between killing and *failing to save*, it does not mark a comparable difference between killing and *letting die*. If X fails to save Y, it does not follow that Y dies; someone else may come along and save Y. But if X lets Y die, it does follow that Y dies; Y is dead and that's that. When Palance watches the child die, he does not merely fail to save the child; he lets her die. And when we fail to send food to the starving, and they die, we let them die—we do not merely fail to save them.

The importance of 'optionality' in any particular case depends on the actual chances of someone else's saving the person we do not save. Perhaps it is not so bad not to save someone if we know that someone else *will* save him. (Although even here we do not behave as we ought; for we ought not simply to leave what needs doing to others.) And perhaps it even gets us off the hook a little if there is the *strong chance* that someone else will step in. This thought probably motivates people who do not stop at auto accidents on busy highways—they think that surely someone else will stop. But in the case of the world's starving, we know very well that no person or group of persons is going to come along tomorrow and save all of them. So, as an excuse for not giving aid to the starving, the 'optionality' argument is clearly in bad faith. To say of any of those people, after they are dead, that someone else *might* have saved them, in the very weak sense in which that is true, does not excuse us at all. The others who might have saved them, but did not, are as guilty as we, but that does not diminish our guilt. Guilt multiplies, not divides.

I said that the No Relevant Difference Argument is deeper than the Bare Difference Argument, because it exposes why killing and letting die are morally the same. Let me explain. When we compare bad things, there are two ways they could turn out to be equally bad. One way is simply for them to be equally aversive: suppose I ask you which you would prefer, having your finger hit with a hammer (not *too* hard), or having to sit through a very bad movie? You might find these equally repellent, even though they are evils of very different types. The No Relevant Difference Argument shows that killing and letting die are equivalent in a second, stronger sense. Not only are they the same, they are the same because the underlying reasons why one is wrong are the very same reasons that explain why the other is wrong. Unlike the hurt thumb and the bad movie, they are evils of exactly the same type.

The radical nature of the Equivalence Thesis

In this essay I have several times disagreed with traditional Christian teachings. On the question of our duty towards starving people, however, the position I am defending is similar to the view attributed by St Matthew to Jesus. In the nineteenth chapter of St Matthew's gospel we find Jesus telling a young man who asks for guidance, 'Go and sell all that you have, and give it to the poor.' But, like most people—including most theologians—since then, the young man was not willing to accept such a radical ethic. St Matthew reports that 'When the young man heard that saying, he went away sorrowful, for he had great possessions.'

The Equivalence Thesis has radical implications for conduct. Not surprisingly, that fact has frequently been given as a reason for rejecting it not only as overly demanding but as false. Citing another biblical figure, Trammell complains that 'Denial of the distinction between negative and positive duties leads straight to an ethic so strenuous that it might give pause even to a philosophical John the Baptist.' Clearly, Trammell is right. Suppose someone is about to buy a gramophone record, purely for his own enjoyment, when he is reminded that with this eight dollars a starving person could be fed. On the view I am defending, he ought to give the money to feed the hungry person. This may not seem exceptional until we remember that the reasoning is reiterable. Having given the first eight dollars, he is not free to use another eight to buy the record. For the poor are always with him: there is always *another* starving person to be fed, and then another, and then another. 'The problem', as Trammell puts it, 'is that, even though fulfillment of one particular act of aid involves only minimal effort, it sets a precedent for millions of such efforts.' So we reach the peculiar conclusion that it is almost always immoral to buy gramophone records! And of course the same goes for fancy clothes, home computers, colour television sets, golf clubs, and cigars. Anyone who took the Equivalence Thesis seriously would have to abandon affluent living.

This sort of *reductio* argument is familiar in philosophy. Such arguments may be divided into three categories. The strongest sort shows that a theory entails a contradiction, and, since contradictions cannot be tolerated, the theory must be modified or rejected. Such arguments, when valid, are of course devastating. Second, an argument may show that a theory has a consequence which, while not inconsistent, is nevertheless demonstrably false— that is, independent evidence can be given that the offensive consequence is unacceptable. Arguments of this second type, while not quite so impressive as the first, can still be irresistible. The third type of *reductio* is markedly weaker than the others. Here it is merely urged that some consequence of the theory is counter-intuitive. The supposedly embarrassing consequence is perfectly consistent, and there is no independent proof that it is false; the complaint is only that it goes against what we have always believed. Now sometimes even this weak sort of argument can be persuasive, especially when we don't have much confidence in the theory, or when our confidence in the pre-theoretical belief is unaffected by the reasoning which supports the theory. However, it may happen that *the same reasoning which leads one to accept a theory also persuades one that the pre-theoretical beliefs were wrong*. If this did not happen, philosophy would always be in the service of what we already think; it could never challenge and change our beliefs. The present case, it seems to me, is an instance of this type. The same reasoning which leads to the view that we are as wicked as Jack Palance, and that killing is no worse than letting die, also persuades (me, at least) that the pre-reflective belief in the acceptability of our affluent way of living is mistaken.

So, I want to say about all this what H. P. Grice once said in a public discussion when someone objected that his theory of meaning had an unacceptable implication. Referring to the supposedly embarrassing consequence, Grice harumphed, 'See here, that's not an *objection* to my theory—*that's my theory.*' Grice not only accepted the implication; he embraced it as an integral part of what he wanted to say. Similarly, the realization that we are morally wrong to spend money on inessentials, when that money could go to feed the starving, is an integral part of the view that I am defending. It is not an embarrassing consequence of the view; it is (part of) the view itself.

What I have said so far goes against another familiar idea in moral philosophy—namely, that moral codes must not demand too much of people. The thought is that moral codes are practical guides for conduct, and that if they demand more than people are willing to give they are impractical and useless. If a moral code asks too much of people they will, like the young man in St Matthew's story, turn away from it. (This idea has often been used as a club against act-utilitarianism, which also implies that one should not indulge oneself while other people starve.) But I do not believe that this idea is correct, for what people are willing to accept does not necessarily match what is right. The question of truth in ethics is not the same as the question of what code has a chance of acceptance. However, there is *something* in the familiar idea. If we were to ask, 'What moral code is it best to promulgate in a society?' the fact that a code has no chance of acceptance might be a reason against trying to promulgate it. However, that would not in itself be a reason for thinking the code is not *true*.

There is another way in which the counter-intuitive nature of the Equivalence Thesis may be brought out. It follows from the Thesis that if the *only* difference between a pair of acts is that one is killing, while the other is letting die, those actions are equally good or bad—neither is preferable to the other. Defenders of the distinction have pointed out that in such cases our intuitions often tell us just the opposite: killing seems obviously worse. Here is an example produced by Daniel Dinello:

Jones and Smith are in a hospital. Jones cannot live longer than two hours unless he gets a heart transplant. Smith, who has had one kidney removed, is dying of an infection in the other kidney. If he does not get a kidney transplant, he will die in about four hours. When Jones dies, his one good kidney can be transplanted to Smith, or Smith could be killed and his heart transplanted to Jones . . . It seems clear that it would, in fact, be wrong to kill Smith and save Jones, rather than letting Jones die and saving Smith.

And another from Trammell:

If someone threatened to steal $1000 from a person if he did not take a gun and shoot a stranger between the eyes, it would be very wrong for him to kill the stranger to save his $1000. But if someone asked from that person $1000 to save a stranger, it would seem that his obligation to grant this request would not be as great as his obligation to refuse the first demand— even if he has good reason for believing that without his $1000 the stranger would certainly die . . . In this particular example, it seems plausible to say that a person has a greater obligation to refrain from killing someone, even though the effort required of him ($1000) and his motivation toward the stranger be assumed identical in both cases.

The conclusion we are invited to draw from these examples is that, contrary to what I have been arguing, the difference between killing and letting die *must* be morally significant.

Dinello's clever example contains a flaw, since the choice before the doctor is not, strictly speaking, a choice between killing and letting die. If the doctor kills Smith in order to transplant his heart to Jones, he will have killed Smith. But if he waits until Jones dies, and then transfers the kidney to Smith, he will *not* have 'let Jones die'. The reason is connected with the fact that not every case of not saving someone is a case of letting someone die. (Again, Josef Stalin died, and I did not save him, but I did not let him die.) Dinello himself points out that, in order for it to be true that X lets Y die, X must be 'in a position' to save Y, but not do so. (I was not in a position to save Stalin.) Now the doctor is in a position to save Jones only if there is a heart available for transplantation. But no such heart is available—Smith's heart, for example, is not available because Smith is still using it. Therefore, since the doctor is not in a position to save Jones, he does not let Jones die.

Trammell's example is not quite so easy to dismiss. Initially, I share the intuition that it would be worse to kill someone to prevent $1000 from being stolen than to refuse to pay $1000 to save someone. Yet on reflection I don't have much confidence in this feeling. What is at stake in the situation described is the person's $1000 and the stranger's life. But we end up with the *same* combination of lives and money, no matter which option the person chooses: if he shoots the stranger, the stranger dies and he keeps his $1000; and if he refuses to pay to save the stranger, the stranger dies and he keeps his $1000. It makes no difference, either to the person's interests or to the stranger's interests, which option is chosen. Why, then, do we have the curious intuition that there is a big difference here?

I conceded at the outset that most of us believe that in letting people die we are not behaving as badly as if we were to kill them. I think I have given good reasons for concluding that this belief is false. Yet giving reasons is often not good enough, even in philosophy. For if an intuition is strong enough, we may continue to rely on it and assume, as Nagel recommends, that *something* is wrong with the arguments opposing it, even though we are not sure exactly what is wrong. So in addition to the arguments, we need some account of why people have the allegedly mistaken intuition and why it is so persistent. Why do people believe so firmly that killing is so much worse than letting die, both in fictitious cases such as Trammell's, and in the famine cases in the real world? In some ways the explanation of this is best left to the psychologists; the distinctively philosophical job is accomplished when the intuition is shown to be false. Nevertheless, I shall hazard a hypothesis, since it shows how our intuitions can be explained without assuming that they are perceptions of the truth.

Human beings are to some degree altruistic, but they are also to a great degree selfish, and their attitudes on matters of conduct are largely determined by what is in their own interests, and what is in the interests of the few other people they especially care about. In terms of both the costs and the benefits, it is to their own advantage for people in the affluent countries to regard killing as worse than letting die. First, the *costs* of never killing anyone are not so great: we can live very well without ever killing. But the cost of not allowing people to die, when we could save them, would be very great. For any one of us to take seriously a duty to save the starving would require that we give up not only luxuries but things that we have come to consider 'necessities' for our nice lives. Money could no longer be spent on good things for ourselves while others starve. On the other side, we have much more to *gain* from a strict prohibition on killing than from a like prohibition on letting die. Because we are not in danger of starving, we will not suffer if people do not regard feeding the hungry as so important; but we would be threatened if people did not regard killing as very bad. So, both the costs and the benefits encourage us, selfishly, to view killing as worse than letting die. It is to our own advantage to believe this, and so we do.

A final word about intuitions

The idea that our intuitions are not to be trusted is central to the argument of this book. It is not surprising that our intuitions favour the traditional views I have been criticizing—after all, we have been raised and educated in a society formed by those views. But I have urged that our intuitions may be something other than perceptions of truth; they may embody errors produced by prejudice, selfishness, cultural conditioning, and the like. Rather than relying on them, I have said, we should look for guidance to argument and reasoning.

There is an obvious problem with this, and I must say something about it. The problem is that no moral view can escape reliance on intuition at some point. Hume, a philosopher I have quoted several times, saw this quite clearly. In the first appendix to his *Inquiry Concerning the Principles of Morals*, he wrote:

Ask a man *why he uses exercise*; he will answer, *because he desires to keep his health*. If you then inquire *why he desires health*, he will readily reply, *Because sickness is painful*. If you push your inquiries further and desire a reason *why he hates pain*, it is impossible he can ever give any. This is an ultimate end, and is never referred to any other object.

Perhaps to your second question, *why he desires health*, he may also reply that *it is necessary for the exercise of his calling*. If you ask *why he is anxious on that head*, he will answer, *because he desires to get money*. If you demand, *Why? It is the instrument of pleasure*, says he. And beyond this, it is an absurdity to ask for a reason. It is impossible there can be a progress *in infinitum*, and that one thing can always be a reason why another is desired. Something must be desirable on its own account, and because of its immediate accord or agreement with human sentiment and affection.

Arguments can take us only so far; at some point in our reasoning we will always come to some assumption that we must take for granted without argument. This is not merely a peculiar feature of *moral* argument. It is a fact about all arguments. In science and mathematics, just as in morals, chains of reasoning inevitably begin from assumptions or axioms taken as 'given'. How could it be otherwise? Reasoning cannot go on for ever, always referring back to some still more elementary premises. Reasoning must *start* somewhere. In morals, reasoning begins with assumptions about what is morally important.

Thus, a defender of traditional ethics, whose doctrines I have attacked, could reply '*Tu quoque.*' I reject his assumptions, saying that they express unreliable intuitions. But don't I ultimately have to depend on intuitions of my own? And if I do, how can I claim that my view is based on reason rather than intuition? It seems that we *both* have our intuitions and our arguments proceeding from them. So how can I claim any more than that?

The charge must, to some extent, be admitted. (J. L. Austin once remarked that, in philosophy, there is the part where you say it, and the part where you take it back.) Nevertheless, there is still a significant difference between a methodology that is ready to trust a large number of fairly specific intuitions, and one that seeks to avoid any reliance on intuition until it becomes absolutely necessary. (It is the difference, for example, between being willing to trust the feeling that merely being human is enough to give one's existence special value, or that killing is worse than letting die, and being willing, grudgingly, to rely on the feeling that suffering pain is a bad thing.) The idea cannot be to avoid reliance on unsupported 'sentiments' (to use Hume's word) altogether—that is impossible. The idea is always to be suspicious of them, and to rely on as few of them as possible, only after examining them critically, and only after pushing the arguments and explanations as far as they will go without them. Every concession to intuition is just that—a concession. The complaint about the intuitions underlying the traditional approach is, in the end, not that they are intuitions, but that they are intuitions trusted too easily.

9 THE MORALITY OF EUTHANASIA

An absolute rule?

The late Franz Ingelfinger, who was editor of the *New England Journal of Medicine*, observed that

> This is the heyday of the ethicist in medicine. He delineates the rights of patients, of experimental subjects, of fetuses, of mothers, of animals, and even of doctors. (And what a far cry it is from the days when medical 'ethics' consisted of condemning economic improprieties such as fee splitting and advertising!) With impeccable logic—once certain basic assumptions are granted—and with graceful prose, the ethicist develops his arguments . . . Yet his precepts are essentially the products of armchair exercise and remain abstract and idealistic until they have been tested in the laboratory of experience.

One problem with such armchair exercises, he complained, is that in spite of the impeccable logic and the graceful prose, the result is often an absolutist ethic that is unsatisfactory when applied to particular cases, and that is therefore of little use to the practising physician. Unlike some absolutist philosophers (and theologians), 'the practitioner appears to prefer the principles of individualism. As there are few atheists in fox holes, there tend to be few absolutists at the bedside.'

Dr Ingelfinger was right to be suspicious of absolute rules. However, despite his picture of the flexible physician, there are some rules that doctors do tend to regard as absolute. One such rule is the prohibition of mercy-killing. From the time of Hippocrates, whose oath has doctors pledge 'not to give a deadly drug', they have held firm to this absolute 'at the bedside' as well as in the seminar room. The 'principles of individualism' have made little headway against it.

Are the doctors right? The arguments I have already presented, especially those concerning the sanctity of life and the two senses of 'life', suggest that in fact euthanasia is morally acceptable, at least in some circumstances. As in the other matters, there is no need here to be an 'absolutist at the bedside'. But there are other arguments that demand attention before we can be confident of this conclusion.

In this chapter we will examine some other arguments that are commonly advanced for and against euthanasia. We will be concerned with the morality of killing in what we might call the 'standard case' of euthanasia—that is, the case of the suffering terminal patient who, while rational, requests to be killed as an alternative to a slow, lingering death. Moreover, we will be concerned with the morality of *individual acts* of killing in such cases: considered separately, are they morally wrong? This is slightly different from asking whether euthanasia ought to be illegal, in the way that questions of individual morality are often different from questions of social policy. In Chapter 10 we will look at a different set of arguments relating to the acceptability of euthanasia as social policy.

The argument from mercy

The most common argument in support of euthanasia is one that we may call 'the argument from mercy'. It is an exceptionally simple argument, at least in its main idea, which makes one uncomplicated point. Terminal patients sometimes suffer pain so horrible that it can hardly be comprehended by those who have not actually experienced it. Their suffering can be so terrible that we do not like even to read about it or think about it; we recoil even from its description. The argument from mercy says: euthanasia is justified because it puts an end to *that*.

The great Irish satirist Jonathan Swift took eight years to die while, in the words of Joseph Fletcher, 'His mind crumbled to pieces.' At times the pain in his blinded eyes was so intense he had to be restrained from tearing them out. Knives and other potential instruments of suicide were kept from him. For the last three years of his life, he could do nothing but drool; and when he finally died it was only after convulsions that lasted thirty-six hours.

Swift died in 1745. Since then, doctors have learned how to eliminate much of the pain that accompanies terminal illness, but the victory has been far from complete. Here is a more recent example.

Stewart Alsop was a respected journalist who died in 1975 of a rare form of cancer. Before he died, he wrote movingly of his experiences as a terminal patient. Although he had not thought much about euthanasia before, he came to approve of it after sharing a room briefly with someone he called Jack:

The third night that I roomed with Jack in our tiny double room in the solid-tumor ward of the cancer clinic of the National Institutes of Health in Bethesda, Md., a terrible thought occurred to me.

Jack had a melanoma in his belly, a malignant solid tumor that the doctors guessed was about the size of a softball. The cancer had started a few months before with a small tumor in his left shoulder, and there had been several operations since. The doctors planned to remove the softball-sized tumor, but they knew Jack would soon die. The cancer had metastasized—it had spread beyond control.

Jack was good-looking, about 28, and brave. He was in constant pain, and his doctor had prescribed an intravenous shot of a synthetic opiate—a pain-killer, or analgesic—every four hours. His wife spent many of the daylight hours with him, and she would sit or lie on his bed and pat him all over, as one pats a child, only more methodically, and this seemed to help control the pain. But at night, when his pretty wife had left (wives cannot stay overnight at the NIH clinic) and darkness fell, the pain would attack without pity.

At the prescribed hour, a nurse would give Jack a shot of the synthetic analgesic, and this would control the pain for perhaps two hours or a bit more. Then he would begin to moan, or whimper, very low, as though he didn't want to wake me. Then he would begin to howl, like a dog.

When this happened, either he or I would ring for a nurse, and ask for a pain-killer. She would give him some codeine or the like by mouth, but it never did any real good—it affected him no more than half an aspirin might affect a man who had just broken his arm. Always the nurse would explain as encouragingly as she could that there was not long to go before the next intravenous shot—'Only about 50 minutes now.' And always poor Jack's whimpers and howls would become more loud and frequent until at last the blessed relief came.

The third night of this routine, the terrible thought occurred to me. 'If Jack were a dog,' I thought, 'what would be done with him?' The answer was obvious: the pound, and chloroform. No human being with a spark of pity could let a living thing suffer so, to no good end.

I have discussed this case with some physicians who were indignant that Jack was not given larger doses of the pain-killing drug more often. They suggest that modern medicine can deal better with this type of pain. But it is worth noting that the NIH clinic is one of the best-equipped modern facilities we have; it is not as though Jack's suffering was caused by neglect in some backward rural hospital. Few of us could expect better care, were we in Jack's position. Moreover, the moral issue regarding euthanasia is not affected by whether more could have been done for Jack. The moral issue is whether mercy-killing is permissible *if* it is the only alternative to this kind of torment. We may readily grant that in any particular case where suffering can be eliminated, the argument for euthanasia will be weaker. But we will still need to know what is morally permissible in those cases in which, for whatever reason, suffering cannot, or will not, be eliminated.

I have quoted Alsop at length not for the sake of indulging in gory details but to give a clear idea of the kind of suffering we are talking about. We should not gloss over these facts with euphemistic language, or squeamishly avert our eyes from them. For only by keeping them firmly and vividly in mind can we appreciate the full force of the argument from mercy: if a person prefers—and even begs for—death as an alternative to lingering on *in this kind of torment*, only to die anyway after a while, then surely it is not immoral to help this person die sooner. As Alsop put it, 'No human being with a spark of pity could let a living thing suffer so, to no good end.'

Utilitarianism

The basic idea of the argument from mercy is clear enough; but how is it to be developed into a rigorous argument? Among philosophers, the utilitarians attempted to do this. They held that actions should be judged right or wrong according to whether they cause happiness or misery; and they argued that when judged by this standard, euthanasia turns out to be morally acceptable. The classic utilitarian version of the argument may be elaborated like this:

(1) Any action is morally right if it serves to increase the amount of happiness in the world or to decrease the amount of misery. Conversely, an action is morally wrong if it serves to decrease happiness or increase misery.

(2) Killing a hopelessly ill patient, who is suffering great pain, at his own request, would decrease the amount of misery in the world.

(3) Therefore, such an action would be morally right.

The first premise of this argument states the principle of utility, the basic utilitarian assumption. Today most philosophers think this principle is unacceptable, because they think the promotion of happiness and the avoidance of misery are not the *only* morally important things. To take one example: People *might* be happier if there were no freedom of religion; for, if everyone adhered to the same religious beliefs, there would be greater harmony among people. There would be no unhappiness caused by Jewish girls marrying Catholic boys; the religious element of conflicts such as in Northern Ireland would be removed; and so forth. Moreover, if people were brainwashed well enough, no one would mind not having freedom of choice. Thus happiness might be increased. But, the argument continues, even if happiness *could* be increased in this way, it would be wrong to do so, because people should be allowed to make their own choices. Therefore, the argument concludes, the principle of utility is unacceptable.

There is a related difficulty for utilitarianism, which connects more directly with euthanasia. Suppose a person is leading a miserable life—full of more unhappiness than happiness—but does not want to die. This person thinks a miserable life is better than none at all. Now I assume we would all agree that this person should not be killed; that would be plain, unjustifiable murder. Yet it *would* decrease the amount of misery in the world if we killed him—and so it is hard to see how, on strictly utilitarian grounds, it could be wrong. Again, the principle of utility seems to be an inadequate guide for determining right and wrong.

Such arguments have led many philosophers to reject this moral theory. Yet contemporary utilitarians have an easy answer. In the first place, in so far as euthanasia is concerned, the classical utilitarian argument retains considerable force, even if it is faulty. For even if the promotion of happiness and the avoidance of misery are not the *only* morally important things, they are still very important. So, when an action would decrease misery, that is *a* very strong reason in its favour. The utilitarian argument in favour of euthanasia might therefore be decisive, even if the general complaints about the principle of utility are sound.

Moreover, utilitarianism may also be defended against the general complaints. Classical utilitarianism, as set out by Bentham and Mill, is a combination of three ideas. The first is that actions are to be judged right or wrong entirely according to their *consequences*. Nothing else matters—actions are not good or bad 'in themselves', and moral 'rules' have no independent importance. Right actions are, simply, the ones that have the best results. The second idea is that good and evil are to be measured in terms of happiness and unhappiness—nothing else is ultimately valuable. Material goods, art and ideas, friendship, and so on, are good only *because* they contribute to happiness. Thus, right actions are said to be those that produce the most happiness, or prevent the most misery. Third, and finally, classical utilitarianism includes the idea of equality—each individual's happiness is counted as equally important.

The difficulties we noted for utilitarianism all may be traced to its narrow identification of good and evil with happiness and unhappiness. (This is, in fact, the same hedonistic conception of good and evil that we considered, and found wanting, in Chapter 3 above.) All that is necessary to save it, therefore, is to adopt a broader conception of individual welfare. The basic idea of the theory is that actions are right or wrong as they increase or decrease welfare. So, suppose we substitute a better conception of welfare: rather than speaking of maximizing *happiness*, let us speak of maximizing *interests*—let the principle of utility say that actions are right if they satisfy as many interests as possible. Such a broader principle will still be 'utilitarian' in that it still sees the rightness of actions as consisting in their effects on the welfare of the creatures affected by them. But the new principle avoids the problems that plagued the old one: if it is in a person's best interests to have freedom of choice in religion, or in choosing to remain alive, then the principle will not countenance taking away that freedom or that life. Armed with this better version of the principle of utility, we may then offer this improved argument concerning euthanasia:

(1) If an action promotes the best interests of everyone concerned, then that action is morally acceptable.

(2) In at least some cases, euthanasia promotes the best interests of everyone concerned.

(3) Therefore, in at least some cases euthanasia is morally acceptable.

It would have been in everyone's best interests if euthanasia had been employed in the case of Stewart Alsop's room-mate Jack. First, and most important, it would have been in Jack's own interests, since it would have provided him with an easier death, without additional pain. Moreover, it would have been best for his wife. Her misery, helplessly watching him suffer, was second only to his. Third, the hospital staff's interests would have been served, since if Jack's dying had not been prolonged, they could have turned their attention to other patients whom they could have helped. Fourth, other patients would have benefited since medical resources would no longer have been used in the sad, pointless maintenance of Jack's physical existence. Finally, if Jack himself requested to be killed, the act would not have violated his rights. Considering all this, how can euthanasia be wrong?

Two additional comments are necessary before we leave the argument from mercy. First, I have discussed the utilitarians in connection with this argument, but one does not have to accept a general utilitarian theory of ethics to find it persuasive. There are other possible theories that one might prefer. However, no matter what ethical theory one accepts, the consequences of one's actions—whether they do or do not promote people's interests, or cause happiness or misery—must be among the matters considered important. An ethical theory that did *not* have an important place for this would have no credibility at all. And, to the extent that these matters *are* seen as important, the argument from mercy will be compelling.

Second, it should be noted that the argument does *not* imply that euthanasia is justified *whenever* a patient says he can no longer endure pain. Suppose the doctor, or the family, knows that the painful condition can be cured, and that the patient's request to die is only a temporary irrational reaction, which he will later repudiate. It is entirely reasonable for them to take this into account, and to refuse the irrational request. The argument from mercy does not say otherwise; in such circumstances euthanasia would not promote his best interests, and would hardly be 'merciful' at all. This should not be taken to mean, however, that such requests are always irrational, or that pain always destroys a patient's ability to make sensible choices. Sadly, some requests to die, in circumstances such as those of Stewart Alsop's room-mate, are all too rational.

The argument from the Golden Rule

'Do unto others as you would have them do unto you' is one of the oldest and most familiar moral maxims. Stated in just that way, it is not a very good maxim: suppose a sexual pervert, with fantasies of being raped, started treating others as he would like to be treated. We might not be happy with the results. Nevertheless, the idea behind the Golden Rule is a good one. Moral rules apply to everyone alike. You cannot say that you are justified in treating someone else in a certain way unless you are willing to admit that that person would be justified in treating *you* in that way if your positions were reversed.

Kant's moral philosophy is usually regarded as the major historical alternative to utilitarianism. Like the utilitarians, Kant sought to express all of morality in a single principle. Kant's principle may be viewed as a sophisticated version of the Golden Rule. He argued that we should act only on rules that we are willing to have applied universally; that is, we should behave as we would be willing to have *everyone* behave. Thus, the one supreme principle of morality, which he called the 'Categorical Imperative', says:

Act only according to that maxim which you can at the same time will to become a universal law.

What does this mean? When we are trying to decide whether to do a certain action, we must first ask what general rule we would be following if we did it. Then, we ask whether we would be willing for everyone to follow that rule, in similar circumstances. (This determines whether 'the maxim of the act'—the rule we would be following—can be 'willed' to be a 'universal law'.) If we would not be willing for the rule to be followed universally, then we should not follow it ourselves. Thus, if we are not willing for others to apply the rule to *us*, we ought not apply it to *them*.

In the eighteenth chapter of St Matthew's gospel there is a story that perfectly illustrates this point. A man is owed money by another, who cannot pay, and so he has the debtor thrown into prison. But he himself owes money to the King and begs that *his* debt be forgiven. At first the King forgives the debt. However, when the King hears how this man has treated the one who owed him, he changes his mind and 'delivers him unto the tormentors' until he can pay. The moral is clear: If you do not think that others should apply the rule 'Don't forgive debts!' to *you*, then you should not apply it to others.

The application of this to the question of euthanasia is fairly obvious. Each of us is going to die some day, although most of us do not know when or how, and will probably have little choice in the matter. But suppose you were given a choice: suppose you were told that you would die in one of two ways, and were asked to choose between them. First, you could die quietly, and without pain, at the age of eighty, from a fatal injection. Or second, you could choose to die at the age of eighty-plus-a-few-days of an afflic-tion so painful that for those few days before death you would be reduced to howling like a dog, with your family standing helplessly by. It is hard to believe that anyone would choose to have a rule applied that would force upon him or her the second option—if, that is, they were making a choice based upon *their own preferences*. And if we would not want such a rule, which excludes euthanasia, applied to us, then we should not apply such a rule to others.

The contemporary British philosopher R. M. Hare has made the same point in a slightly different way. Hare tells the following (true) story:

The driver of a petrol lorry was caught in an accident in which his tanker overturned and immediately caught fire. He himself was trapped in the cab and could not be freed. He therefore besought the bystanders to kill him by hitting him on the head, so that he would not roast to death. I think that somebody did this, but I do not know what happened in the courts afterwards.

Now will you please all ask yourselves, as I have many times asked myself, what you wish that men should do to you if you were in the situation of that driver. I cannot believe that anybody who considered the matter seriously, as if he himself were going to be in that situation and had now to give instructions as to what rule the bystanders should follow, would say that the rule should be one ruling out euthanasia absolutely.

There is a considerable irony here. Kant was personally opposed to mercy-killing; he thought it contrary to reason. Yet his own Categorical Imperative seems to sanction it. The larger irony, however, is for those in the Christian Church who have for centuries opposed euthanasia. The article written by Professor Hare, from which the story of the lorry driver is taken, has the title 'Euthanasia: A Christian View'. According to the New Testament accounts, Jesus himself promulgated the Golden Rule as the supreme moral principle—'This is the Law and the Prophets,' he said. But, as Hare points out, if this is the supreme principle of morality, then how can euthanasia be absolutely wrong? This seems to be another one of those instances in which the historical Church has strayed from the principles laid down by its founder.

We have looked at two arguments that tend to show that euthanasia is morally acceptable. Now let us turn to some arguments that support the opposite view. The most common argument against euthanasia is simply that it is a violation of the prohibition against killing—or, against the taking of innocent human life. Since I have already discussed this contention at some length, I will concentrate here on different arguments.

Religious arguments

Social observers are fond of remarking that we live in a secular age, and there is surely something in this. The power of religious conceptions was due, in some considerable measure, to their usefulness in explaining things. In earlier times, religious ideas were used to explain everything from the origins of the universe to the nature of human beings. So long as we had no other way of understanding the world, the hold of religion on us was powerful indeed. Now, however, these explanatory functions have largely been taken over by the sciences: physics, chemistry, and their allies explain physical nature, while evolutionary biology and psychology combine to tell us about ourselves. As there is less and less work for religious hypotheses to do, the grip of religious ideas on us weakens, and appeals to theological conceptions are heard only on Sunday mornings. Hence, the 'secular age'.

However, most people continue to hold religious beliefs, and they especially appeal to those beliefs when morality is at issue. Any discussion of mercy-killing quickly leads to objections based on theological grounds, and 'secular' arguments for euthanasia are rejected because they leave out the crucial element of God's directions on the matter.

Considering the traditional religious opposition to euthanasia, it is tempting to say: if one is not a Christian (or if one does not have some similar religious orientation) then perhaps euthanasia is an option; but for people who do have such a religious orientation, euthanasia cannot be acceptable. And the discussion might be ended there. But this is too quick a conclusion; for it is possible that the religious arguments against euthanasia are not valid *even for religious people*. Perhaps a religious perspective, even a conventional Christian one, does *not* lead automatically to the rejection of mercy-killing. With this possibility in mind, let us examine three variations of the religious objection.

What God commands

It is sometimes said that euthanasia is not permissible simply because God forbids it, and we know that God forbids it by the authority of either scripture or Church tradition. Thus, one eighteenth-century minister, Humphrey Primatt, wrote ironically that, in the case of aged and infirm animals,

God, the Father of Mercies, hath ordained Beasts and Birds of Prey to do that distressed creature the kindness to relieve him his misery, by putting him to death. A kindness which *We* dare not show to our own species. If thy father, thy brother, or thy child should suffer the utmost pains of a long and agonizing sickness, though his groans should pierce through thy heart, and with strong crying and tears he should beg thy relief, yet thou must be deaf unto him; he must wait his appointed time till his charge cometh, till he sinks and is crushed with the weight of his own misery.

When this argument is advanced, it is usually advanced with great confidence, as though it were *obvious* what God requires. Yet we may well wonder whether such confidence is justified. The sixth commandment does not say, literally, 'Thou shalt not *kill*'—that is a bad translation. A better translation is 'Thou shalt not commit *murder*,' which is different, and which does not obviously prohibit mercy-killing. Murder is by definition *wrongful* killing; so, if you do not think that a given kind of killing is wrong, you will not call it murder. That is why the sixth commandment is not normally taken to forbid killing in a just war; since such killing is (allegedly) justified, it is not called murder. Similarly, if euthanasia is justified, it is not murder, and so it is not prohibited by the commandment. At the very least, it is clear that we cannot infer that euthanasia is wrong *because* it is prohibited by the commandment.

If we look elsewhere in the Christian Bible for a condemnation of euthanasia, we cannot find it. These scriptures are silent on the question. We do find numerous affirmations of the sanctity of human life and the fatherhood of God, and some theologians have tried to infer a prohibition on euthanasia from these general precepts. (The persistence of the attempts, in the face of logical difficulties, is a reminder that people insist on reading their moral prejudices *into* religious texts much more often than they derive their moral views *from* the texts.) But we also find exhortations to kindness and mercy, and the Golden Rule proclaimed as the sum of all morality; and these principles, as we have seen, support euthanasia rather than condemn it.

We *do* find a clear condemnation of euthanasia in Church tradition. Regardless of whether there is scriptural authority for it, the Church has historically opposed mercy-killing. It should be emphasized, however, that this is a matter of history. Today, many religious leaders favour euthanasia and think the historical position of the Church has been mistaken. It was an Episcopal minister, Joseph Fletcher, who in his book *Morals and Medicine* formulated the classic modern defence of euthanasia. Fletcher does not stand alone among his fellow churchmen. The Euthanasia Society of America, which he heads, includes many other religious leaders; and the recent 'Plea for Beneficent Euthanasia', sponsored by the American Humanist Association, was signed by more religious leaders than people in any other category. So it certainly cannot be claimed that *contemporary* religious forces stand uniformly opposed to euthanasia.

It is noteworthy that even Roman Catholic thinkers are today reassessing the Church's traditional ban on mercy-killing. The Catholic philosopher Daniel Maguire has written one of the best books on the subject, *Death By Choice*. Maguire maintains that 'it may be moral and should be legal to accelerate the death process by taking direct action, such as overdosing with morphine or injecting potassium'; and moreover, he proposes to demonstrate that this view is '*compatible with historical Catholic ethical theory*', contrary to what most opponents of euthanasia assume. Historical Catholic ethical theory, he says, grants individuals permission to act on views that are supported by 'good and serious reasons', even when a different view is supported by a majority of authorities. Since the morality of euthanasia *is* supported by 'good and serious reasons', Maguire concludes that Catholics are permitted to accept that morality and act on it.

Thus, the positions of both scripture and Church authorities are (at least) ambiguous enough so that the believer is not bound, on these grounds, to reject mercy-killing. The argument from 'what God commands' should be inconclusive, even for the staunchest believer.

The idea of God's dominion

Our second theological argument starts from the principle that 'The life of man is solely under the dominion of God.' It is for God alone to decide when a person shall live and when he shall die; we have no right to 'play God' and arrogate this decision unto ourselves. So euthanasia is forbidden.

This is perhaps the most familiar of all the theological objections to euthanasia; one hears it constantly when the matter is discussed. However, it is remarkable that people still advance this argument today, considering that it was decisively refuted over 200 years ago, when Hume made the simple but devastating point that *if it is for God alone to decide when we shall live and when we shall die, then we 'play God' just as much when we cure people as when we kill them.* Suppose a person is sick and we have the means to cure him or her. If we do so, then we are interfering with God's 'right to decide' how long the life shall last! Hume put it this way:

Were the disposal of human life so much reserved as the peculiar providence of the Almighty that it were an encroachment on his right, for men to dispose of their own lives; it would be equally criminal to act for the preservation of life as for its destruction. If I turn aside a stone which is falling upon my head, I disturb this course of nature, and I invade the peculiar providence of the Almighty by lengthening out my life beyond the period which by the general laws of matter and motion he had assigned it.

We alter the length of a person's life when we save it just as much as when we take it. Therefore, if the taking of life is to be forbidden on the grounds that only God has the right to determine how long a person shall live, then the saving of life should be prohibited on the same grounds. We would then have to abolish the practice of medicine. But everyone (except, perhaps, Christian Scientists) concedes that this would be absurd. Therefore, we may *not* prohibit euthanasia on the grounds that only God has the right to determine how long a life shall last. This seems to be a complete refutation of this argument, and if refuted arguments were decently discarded, as they should be, we would hear no more of it.

Suffering and God's plan

The last religious argument we shall consider is based on the idea that suffering is a part of God's plan for us. God has ordained that people should suffer; he never intended that life should be continally pleasurable. (If he had intended this, presumably he would have created a very different world.) Therefore, if we were to kill people to 'put them out of their misery', we would be interfering with God's plan. Bishop Joseph Sullivan, a prominent Catholic opponent of euthanasia, expresses the argument in a passage from his essay 'The Immorality of Euthanasia':

If the suffering patient is of sound mind and capable of making an act of divine resignation, then his sufferings become a great means of merit whereby he can gain reward for himself and also win great favors for the souls in Purgatory, perhaps even release them from their suffering. Likewise the sufferer may give good example to his family and friends and teach them how to bear a heavy cross in a Christlike manner.

As regard those that must live in the same house with the incurable sufferer, they have a great opportunity to practice Christian charity. They can learn to see Christ in the sufferer and win the reward promised in the Beatitudes. This opportunity for charity would hold true even when the incurable sufferer is deprived of the use of reason. It may well be that the incurable sufferer in a particular case may be of greater value to society than when he was of some material value to himself and his community.

This argument may strike some readers as simply grotesque. Can we imagine this being said, seriously, in the presence of suffering such as that experienced by Stewart Alsop's room-mate? 'We know it hurts, Jack, and that your wife is being torn apart just having to watch it, but think what a good opportunity this is for you to set an example. You can give us a lesson in how to bear it.' In addition, some might think that euthanasia is exactly what *is* required by the 'charity' that bystanders have the opportunity to practise.

But, these reactions aside, there is a more fundamental difficulty with the argument. For if the argument were sound, it would lead not only to the condemnation of euthanasia but of *any* measures to reduce suffering. If God decrees that we suffer, why aren't we obstructing God's plan when we give drugs to relieve pain? A girl breaks her arm; if only God knows how much pain is right for her, who are we to mend it? The point is similar to Hume's refutation of the previous argument. This argument, like the previous one, cannot be right because it leads to consequences that no one, not even the most conservative religious thinker, is willing to accept.

We have now looked at three arguments that depend on religious assumptions. They are all unsound, but I have *not* criticized them simply by rejecting their religious presuppositions. Instead, I have criticized them on their own terms, showing that these arguments should not be accepted even by religious people. As Daniel Maguire emphasizes, the ethics of theists, like the ethics of all responsible people, should be determined by 'good and serious reasons', and these arguments are not good no matter what worldview one has.

The upshot is that religious people are in the same position as everyone else. There is nothing in religious belief in general, or in Christian belief in particular, to preclude the acceptance of mercy-killing as a humane response to some awful situations. So, as far as these arguments are concerned, it appears that Christians may be free, after all, to accept the Golden Rule.

The possibility of unexpected cures

Euthanasia may also be opposed on the grounds that we cannot really tell when a patient's condition is hopeless. There are cases in which patients have recovered even after doctors have given up hope; if those patients had been killed, it would have been tragic, for they would have been deprived of many additional years of life. According to this argument, euthanasia is unacceptable because we never know for certain that a patient's situation is hopeless. *Any* so-called hopeless patient might defy the odds and recover.

The argument has two sources: first, it draws some plausibility from the fact that doctors have sometimes made mistakes; and second, it trades on a naive view of the possibilities of medical research.

It must be admitted, of course, that doctors have sometimes made mistakes in labelling cases 'hopeless', and so we should be cautious in any given instance before saying there is no chance of recovery. But it does not follow from the fact that physicians have *sometimes* been mistaken that they can *never* know for sure that a case is hopeless. That would be like saying that since some people have confused a Rolls-Royce with a Mercedes, no one can ever be certain which is which. In fact, doctors do sometimes know for sure that a patient cannot recover. There may be spontaneous remissions of cancer, for example, at a relatively early stage of the disease. But after the cancer has spread throughout the body and reached an advanced stage of development, there may truly be no hope whatever. Although there may be some doubt about some cases—and where there is doubt, perhaps euthanasia should not be considered—no one with the slightest medical knowledge could have had any doubt about Jack. He was going to die of that cancer, and that is all there is to it. No one has ever recovered from *that* condition, and doctors can explain exactly why this is so.

The argument from the possibility of unexpected cures sometimes takes a slightly different form, and appeals to a naive view of medical research. According to this view, researchers are continually exploring new possibilities of treating disease; and we never know when a new 'miracle cure' for a previously untreatable disease might be discovered. Thus, if we grant a dying patient's request for euthanasia, we run the risk that the next day a cure for his condition might be discovered—'If only we had waited, he could have been saved,' it may be said.

This argument will have little appeal to those more familiar with the realities of medical research. Progress in treating disease comes, not with the sudden and unexpected discovery of magical remedies, but from slow and painstaking investigation. Whether it is reasonable to hope for a 'cure' depends on the particular case in question. In the case of some diseases, investigators may have promising results from some lines of inquiry; here, it may be reasonable to hold out some hope for a dying patient, *if* death can be postponed long enough. In other cases, we may be dealing with a disease that is getting very little attention from researchers, or the researchers investigating it may obviously be very far from achieving any impressive results. Here, it may be simply dishonest to tell a patient with only a short time to live that there is hope. Or again, it may be that even if a cure is found, it will do a particular patient no good because in him the disease is so far advanced that the 'cure' would not help *him* even if it were found.

What, then, are we to conclude? We may certainly conclude that extreme care should be taken so as to avoid declaring a patient 'hopeless' when there really is a chance of recovery; and we may perhaps conclude that in any case where there is the slightest doubt, euthanasia should not be considered. However, we may *not* conclude that doctors *never* know that a case is hopeless. Nor may we always hold out the hope of a 'miracle cure'. Sadly, we know that in some cases there is no hope, and in those cases the possibility of an unexpected cure cannot be offered as an objection to euthanasia.

10 LEGALIZING EUTHANASIA

Morality and law

Should mercy-killing be against the law? This is a question of social policy, and it is different from the question of whether individual acts are morally defensible. Because they are different questions, various combinations of views are possible.

For example, those who believe that euthanasia is immoral may nevertheless hold that it should not be illegal. They may reason that, if a person *wants* to die, that is strictly a personal affair, regardless of how foolish or immoral the desire may be. They may think that, in this respect, euthanasia is like sexual promiscuity: both are matters for private, individual decision, and not government coercion. These may be areas where genuine moral issues are at stake, but they are not areas where the government should intrude.

On the other hand, some thinkers have argued for an exactly opposite view of the matter. They hold that individual acts of mercy-killing are morally acceptable; none the less, they say, such acts should not be made legal, because they fear the consequences of legalization might be so bad. They argue that legalized euthanasia might lead to a breakdown in respect for life that would eventually make all our lives less secure.

Thus, it is important to keep the issues separate. In the last chapter, we looked at arguments concerning the morality of the matter; now we turn to the question of social policy.

How mercy-killers are treated in court

In 1967 Robert Weskin's mother was dying of leukaemia in a Chicago hospital, in terrible pain, and he took a gun into the hospital and shot her three times. Weskin made no attempt to hide what he had done, saying 'She's out of her misery now. I shot her.' He was charged with murder, but the jury found him not guilty.

From a legal point of view, the jury's verdict was incorrect. American law makes no distinction between euthanasia and murder; and so, legally, this was an open-and-shut case. But, when juries are faced with cases like this one, they often refuse to convict.

Sometimes it is the judge, rather than the jury, who uses his discretionary powers to soften the law's impact. When Irene Eldridge, a 71-year-old retired school teacher, helped her sister commit suicide, the Philadelphia judge simply dismissed the charges. In other cases, unusually light sentences may be imposed. William Jones, a Detroit man, was indicted for murder after he admitted that he had electrocuted his wife. An amputee and diabetic who was in constant pain, she had asked to be killed; her husband, who did this, maintained throughout the trial that his act was an act of love. He was convicted, but the judge, who was said to have wept as he pronounced sentence, sentenced him only to a year and a day.

The situation is very much the same in Great Britain, where mercy-killing is also illegal. In 1971, James Price drowned his six-year-old son, whom he described as 'just a living cabbage', and then drove to a police station to turn himself in. Six hundred people in Mr Price's Birmingham neighbourhood petitioned the court, asking for clemency, and the judge placed him on probation. Probation was also given in the 1974 case of Elizabeth Wise, who killed her nine-month-old daughter after doctors told her the child had no hope of living. (The child was blind, deaf, and unable to swallow, because three-fourths of its brain had been destroyed by disease.) Mrs Wise pleaded guilty to having given the child barbiturates crushed in its milk. The judge placed her on probation, and like Mr Price she never went to jail.

But the courts are not always so lenient; what the judges and juries are willing to do depends very much on the details of the particular case. In one case from the 1950s, for example, the defendant killed an infant that was not nearly so disabled as the others we have mentioned, and then tried to lie his way out:

a lawyer killed his six-month-old mongoloid son by wrapping an uninsulated electrical cord around his wet diaper and putting the baby on a silver platter to insure good contact before plugging the cord into the wall. At the trial he claimed that the child's death was an accident, and he was convicted of first-degree murder and sentenced to electrocution himself, although the sentence was later commuted to life.

All these cases involved laypeople; cases involving *physicians* are much rarer than one might expect. In fact, there have been only two occasions on which doctors have been tried for mercy-killing in the United States. In New Hampshire in 1950, Dr Herman Sander gave a patient four intravenous injections of air and then noted on the patient's chart that he had done so. The patient, who had terminal cancer, had asked to be put out of her misery. At the trial, the defence claimed that the patient was already dead at the time of the injections—which was a bit strange, since if the woman was already dead why were the injections given? At any rate, the jury acquitted Dr Sander.

The next such trial of a physician, and the only other one in the United States to date, occurred twenty-four years later in New York. Dr Vincent Montemareno was charged with giving a lethal injection of potassium chloride to a patient with terminal cancer. At first the prosecutor told the Press that the case would be tried as a case of mercy-killing; Dr Montemareno, he said, had killed the patient to put her out of misery. But by the time the trial began, the prosecutor had changed his mind and claimed that the doctor had murdered her for his own convenience, so that he would not have to return to the hospital later in the evening. At the conclusion of the trial the jury voted promptly to acquit.

There is, therefore, a considerable gap between the official position of the law—euthanasia is murder—and what actually happens in courts of law. Some commentators think this is as it should be: the law must not condone mercy-killing, they say; but at the same time, it is appropriate for judges and juries to treat defendants in these cases compassionately. However, it is at least *prima facie* undesirable for there to be such a wide gap here, for if we deem a type of behaviour not fit for punishment, why should we continue to stigmatize that behaviour as criminal? What is gained by putting the defendants through the ordeal? The most common answer offered by those who oppose legalization is that, by maintaining the legal prohibition, we safeguard the important principle of respect for life that would otherwise be eroded.

The slippery-slope argument

The basic idea of this argument is that if euthanasia were legally permitted, it would lead to a general decline in respect for human life. Suppose, in the beginning, we allowed mercy-killing only for those in extreme agony who requested death. Our motives would be honourable, and the results might be good. However, once we had started cold-bloodedly killing people, where would it stop? Where would we draw the line? The point is that once we accept killing in some cases, we have stepped on to a 'slippery slope', down which we will inevitably slide, and in the end all life will be held cheap. Sometimes a different analogy—the 'wedge'—is used; then it is said that once we admit the thin edge of the wedge, we are on the way to abandoning our traditional view of the importance of human life.

Bishop Sullivan, whom we met in the previous chapter, puts the argument this way:

> to permit in a single instance the direct killing of an innocent person would be to admit a most dangerous wedge that might eventually put all life in a precarious condition. Once a man is permitted on his own authority to kill an innocent person directly, there is no way of stopping the advancement of that wedge. There exists no longer any rational grounds for saying that the wedge can advance so far and no further. Once the exception has been made it is too late; hence the grave reason why no exception may be allowed. That is why euthanasia under any circumstances must be condemned.

And, filling in the details, Sullivan says:

> If voluntary euthanasia were legalized, there is good reason to believe that at a later date another bill for compulsory euthanasia would be legalized. Once the respect for human life is so low that an innocent person may be killed directly even at his own request, compulsory euthanasia will necessarily be very near. This could lead easily to killing all incurable charity patients, the aged who are a public care, wounded soldiers, all deformed children, the mentally afflicted, and so on. Before long the danger would be at the door of every citizen.

Although Sullivan is an official of the Catholic Church, it is clear that this argument is not a religious one. It requires no religious assumptions of any kind; and in fact, many non-Catholics have also used it. Unlike Sullivan, Philippa Foot thinks that in some individual cases, euthanasia is *morally* all right. However, she thinks it should not be legalized, because of 'the really serious problem of abuse':

Many people want, and want very badly, to be rid of their elderly relatives and even of their ailing husbands or wives. Would any safeguards ever be able to stop them describing as euthanasia what was really for their own benefit? And would it be possible to prevent the occurrence of acts which were genuinely acts of euthanasia but morally impermissible because infringing the rights of a patient who wished to live? . . . The possibility of active voluntary euthanasia might change the social scene in ways that would be very bad. As things are, people do, by and large, expect to be looked after if they are old or ill. This is one of the good things that we have, but we might lose it, and be much worse off without it. It might come to be expected that someone likely to need a lot of looking after should call for the doctor and demand his own death. Something comparable could be good in an extremely poverty-stricken community where the children genuinely suffered from lack of food; but in rich societies such as ours it would surely be a spiritual disaster.

The conclusion of the argument is that no matter what view you take of individual instances of mercy-killing, as a matter of social policy we ought to enforce a rigorous rule against it. Otherwise, we are courting disaster.

How are we to assess this argument? In the first place, we should notice that it contains a crucial ambiguity, so that it is really two arguments, not one. We may call these the *logical* version of the slippery slope, and the *psychological* version.

The 'logical' version of the argument

The logical form of the argument goes like this. Once a certain practice is accepted, from a logical point of view we are committed to accepting certain other practices as well, since there are no good reasons for not going on to accept the additional practices once we have taken the all-important first step. But, the argument continues, the additional practices are plainly unacceptable; therefore, the first step had better not be taken.

Interpreted in this way, the slippery-slope argument makes a point about *what you are logically committed to* once certain practices are accepted. It says that once you allow euthanasia for the patient in terrible agony, *you are logically committed* to approving of euthanasia in other cases as well. Bishop Sullivan, in the passage previously quoted, apparently intends this, for he says that 'Once a man is permitted on his own authority to kill an innocent person directly . . . *there exists no longer any rational grounds* for saying that the wedge can advance so far and no further.'

But this is surely false. There *are* rational grounds for distinguishing between the man in agony who wants to die and other cases, such as that of an old infirm person who does not want to die. It is easy to say what the rational ground is. It is simply that in the first case the person requests death, while in the second case the person does not request it. Moreover, in the first case, the person is suffering terribly, and in the second case the person is not. These are morally relevant differences to which we can appeal in order to distinguish the cases; therefore, we are *not* logically committed to accepting 'euthanasia' in the second case merely because we approve it in the first. The principle on which we support euthanasia in the first case does not commit us to euthanasia in the second case.

Thus, the logical form of the slippery-slope argument does not work in the case of euthanasia; and so it does not provide good grounds for thinking that euthanasia ought to be legally prohibited.

The 'psychological' version of the argument

This form of the argument is very different. It claims that once certain practices are accepted, *people shall in fact* go on to accept other, more questionable practices. This is simply a claim about what people will do and not a claim about what they are logically committed to. Thus, this form of the argument says that if we start off by killing people to put them out of extreme agony, we shall *in fact* end up killing them for other reasons, regardless of logic and nice distinctions. Therefore, if we want to avoid the latter, we had better avoid the former. This is the point Foot is making, and it is a much stronger argument than the 'logical' version of the slippery slope.

How strong is the psychological version of the argument? Does it show that euthanasia ought to be illegal? The crucial question is whether legalizing euthanasia would in fact lead to terrible consequences. This is an empirical question—a question of fact—about which philosophers have no special inside information. But then, neither does anyone else; there is no definitive 'scientific' answer to this question. Each of us is left to form his or her own best estimate concerning what would happen in our society if euthanasia came to be accepted.

But this does not mean that we are free to believe anything we wish, tailoring our estimates to our prejudices. Some estimates are more reasonable than others, and if we are interested in the truth we will try to be as reasonable as possible. There are several reasons for thinking that the acceptance of euthanasia would *not* lead to any sort of general breakdown in respect for life.

First, we have a good bit of historical and anthropological evidence that approval of killing in one context does not necessarily lead to killing in different circumstances. As has been previously mentioned, in ancient Greece people killed defective infants without any feeling of shame or guilt—but this did not lead to the easy approval of other types of killing. Many other instances of this kind could be cited. In Eskimo societies, the sacrifice of infants and feeble old people was widely accepted as a measure to avoid starvation; but among the East Greenland Eskimos murder was virtually unheard of. Such evidence suggests that people are able to distinguish between various types of cases, and keep them separated very well.

Second, in our own society killing has been, and still is, accepted in many circumstances. For example, we allow killing in self-defence. But what if it were argued that we should not allow this, on the grounds that acceptance of killing in self-defence would inevitably lead to a breakdown in respect for life? Of course, we know that this is not true, because we know that acceptance of killing in self-defence *has not* led to any such consequences. But why hasn't it? Because, first, it is rather unusual for anyone to kill in self-defence—most of us will never face such a situation—and second, we are not so stupid that we are unable to distinguish this case, in which killing is justified, from other cases in which it is not justified. Exactly the same seems to be true of killing terminal patients who ask to be put out of misery. Such cases are fairly rare—most of us know of such cases only by reading of them—and we can distinguish them from other, very different cases easily. (While actual killing in self-defence is rare, we might note that there are *many* cases in which people *would be* justified in killing in self-defence, if only they were able to do so—namely, all the helpless victims of brutal murders. If we included these cases in our tabulation, there would probably be many more cases of justifiable self-defence than cases of justifiable euthanasia.)

Third, Professor Foot suggests that 'It might come to be expected that someone likely to need a lot of looking after should call for the doctor and demand his own death.' But this situation would become possible only if it were legal for doctors to kill *anyone* who requests it. It would not be possible under a legal arrangement that authorized doctors to administer euthanasia only to terminal patients in special circumstances. (Later in this chapter, under the heading 'How to legalize euthanasia', I will have more to say that is relevant to this point.)

Finally, it must be admitted that if euthanasia were legalized, there might be *some* abuses, just as there are abuses of virtually every social practice. There is no absolute guarantee against that. But we do not normally think that a social practice should be precluded simply because it might sometimes be abused. The crucial issue is whether the evil of the abuses would be so great as to outweigh the benefit of the practice. In the case of euthanasia, the question is whether the abuses, or the bad consequences generally, would be so numerous as to outweigh the advantages of legalization. The choice is not between a present policy that is benign and an alternative that is potentially dangerous. The present policy has its evils, too; and for patients such as Stewart Alsop's roommate Jack those evils are very real: we must not forget that these evils have to be weighed against any feared disadvantages of the alternative.

For these reasons, my own conclusion is that the psychological version of the slippery-slope argument does not provide a decisive reason why euthanasia should remain illegal. The possibility of bad consequences should perhaps make us proceed cautiously in this area; but it need not stop us from proceeding at all.

The Nazi analogy

Opponents of legalized euthanasia often argue that there has been one conspicuous instance in which the acceptance of mercy-killing *did* lead to great horrors—this happened, they say, in Germany between 1933 and 1945. Comparisons with the Nazis turn up frequently in discussions of our subject. Before we leave the slippery-slope argument we need, therefore, to take a brief look at this analogy.

It is well known that, under Hitler, some doctors committed, or helped to commit, atrocities. They helped to devise efficient ways of murdering millions of sick and retarded people, Jews, Gypsies, homosexuals, and other 'undesirables'; and they conducted grotesque medical 'experiments' in which concentration-camp inmates were subjected to unspeakable tortures. After the war fifteen Nazi physicians were convicted of these crimes at Nuremberg. Seven of them were sentenced to death.

Telford Taylor, who was the chief prosecutor at the war-crimes trials, has written that it was something of an accident that this trial ever took place:

the whole structure of the Nazi state had collapsed, leaving enormous deposits of documents and a wide range of people who could have contributed evidence. The volume was so great that neither during the first trial nor indeed for two or three years was there any general mastery of this great mass of captured evidence. The selection of people to be tried was largely determined by the evidence in hand at the moment.

What actually happened, Taylor says, is that while compiling evidence against Hermann Goering, documents turned up linking him to the infamous 'high altitude experiments', in which concentration-camp inmates were placed in low-pressure chambers purportedly for the purpose of determining the limits of human endurance at high altitudes. 'One thing led to another', Taylor remarks, and soon there was a collection of evidence regarding the medical horrors:

it seemed that this was an area which had a certain unity, where there was a collection of important material, where there was a subject of interest not only to criminal lawyers, but which would also in a sense probe more than some other subjects why things happened the way they did in Nazi Germany. And also, between the British and ourselves, we had a pretty good collection of individual doctors who were implicated by these documents. We then decided to have such a trial.

So the trial took place, and the behaviour of the Nazi doctors soon became one of the most widely publicized aspects of the Third Reich.

Soon after the trial, while this publicity was at its peak, it occurred to an American doctor named Leo Alexander that the Nazi atrocities might be used to discredit proposals for euthanasia. He formulated a view of history according to which the Nazis began by endorsing euthanasia for the incurably ill, and then, having taken this first step, went on to the rest. He presented this version of events in the *New England Journal of Medicine* in 1949:

Whatever proportions [Nazi] crimes finally assumed, it became evident to all who investigated them that they had started from small beginnings. The beginnings at first were merely a subtle shift in emphasis in the basic attitude of the physicians. It started with the acceptance of the attitude, basic in the euthanasia movement, that there is such a thing as life not worthy to be lived. This attitude in its early stages concerned itself merely with the severely and chronically sick. Gradually the sphere of those to be included in this category was enlarged to encompass the socially un-productive, the ideologically unwanted, the racially unwanted and finally all non-Germans. But it is important to realize that the infinitely small wedged-in lever from which this entire trend of mind received its impetus was the attitude toward the nonrehabilitable sick.

Thus was the Nazi analogy introduced into the debate about euthanasia. Ever since, proponents of legalized euthanasia have had to defend themselves from the charge that they want to start us down the path taken by the Nazis.

On its face, the charge is not at all plausible. Are we to believe that Hitler and his followers were at first an ordinary group of people who permitted mercy-killing from a sense of compassion? And that this led them, in less than a decade, to be transformed into the monsters of the concentration camps? Of course this is not what happened. What, then, did happen?

When doing something that the world will condemn, one way of masking the nature of one's actions is by misusing words. Thus the word 'euthanasia' was used by Hitler as a euphemism for some of his murderous policies—euthanasia, after all, had been advocated by numerous humanitarians, and so, if he could have that word applied to his policies, it might seem that he was up to something more benign. But as Lucy Dawidowicz, the distinguished historian of the Nazi era, points out, 'when we apply these terms to the Nazi experience, we should see them in quotation marks, for they do not have our meaning'.

The meaning of Nazi 'euthanasia' can be understood only in the context of their especially virulent kind of racism. The Nazis accepted a quasi-mystical theory about the ultimate value of the purity of the *Volk*—the German people, who, they thought, were destined to rule the world. It was the task of the German State to safeguard this racial purity. Thus, they set out to 'strengthen' the race by increasing the numbers of racially pure Aryans and decreasing the numbers of others. The increase was to be accomplished by encouraging the right kind of breeding. The decrease was accomplished, at first, by enforced sterilization, and later, by mass exterminations.

Hitler had already formulated this idea of racial purity, and the means to achieve it, before coming to power. In 1924 he wrote that the State *'must declare unfit for propagation all who are in any way visibly sick, all who have inherited a disease and can therefore pass it on'* (italics in the original). He did, as Alexander noted, accept the idea that 'there is such a thing as life not worthy to be lived'. But this was not, in Hitler's mind, at all the same idea as that espoused by contemporary proponents of euthanasia. The unworthy life, for the Nazis, was the life that could not form part of the *Volk*.

Contemporary proponents of euthanasia advocate mercy-killing in response to the patient's request. Among the Nazis, there was never any thought of killing as a compassionate act for the benefit of suffering terminal patients; indeed, this was not even used as a false excuse when they would lie about what they were doing. Families were informed that their sick or mentally retarded kin had died from such maladies as pneumonia or appendicitis. Nor was there ever any thought of securing the permission of the victims. The sterilizations as well as the killings were completely involuntary. Where, then, is the analogy with the real euthanasia movement?

Dawidowicz concludes her investigation of the Nazi horrors by saying 'I do not think we can usefully apply the Nazi experience to gain insight or clarity to help us resolve our problems and dilemmas . . . It's historically irrelevant to the contemporary debate [about euthanasia].' It is irrelevant because the Nazis never *had* a policy of euthanasia in our sense—they never even considered having one. Thus, they could not have been caused to slide down any slippery slope by it. They did not, in fact, slide down any kind of slope at all, because their whole racist ideology was firmly in place from the beginning.

The grain of truth in the slippery-slope argument

Proponents of the slippery-slope argument do, however, have at least one legitimate point. Advocates of legalized euthanasia always frame their proposals so that they apply only to a very narrow range of cases—typically, the bills submitted for legislative consideration permit euthanasia only for dying patients suffering severe pain who, while of sound mind, request death. Then, in reply to conservative worries, the advocates insist that legalizing euthanasia in *this* sense would not necessarily lead to any wider practice of killing. Yet, it can be argued, there is surely something dishonest going on here, for advocates of euthanasia almost always approve of killing in a wider range of cases than this.

Consider, for example, the views propounded in this book. I have argued or implied that killing (or deliberately allowing to die, which on my view is morally the same thing) would not be wrong in a variety of cases: the case of Hans Florian's wife, the case of Repouille's son, the case of Baby Jane Doe, and the case of persons in irreversible coma. None of these are examples of patients who request death. Obviously, though, I would favour removing legal penalties for killing in these cases. So isn't there something a little devious in arguing for legalized *voluntary* euthanasia, and then insisting that this need not lead to approval of any further types of killings?

The charge must be admitted: I, for one, would favour removing legal penalties in all these types of cases, and I suspect that most other defenders of euthanasia would agree. Where a person's biographical life is over, or where there is no prospect of a biographical life, there is no point to insisting that biological life be preserved. That principle leads to acceptance of non-voluntary as well as voluntary euthanasia. Nevertheless, this is not a damaging concession. Non-voluntary euthanasia—where the person is unable to form a rational desire—is not the truly objectionable case. In fact, many people have less difficulty accepting this (as in the case of irreversible coma) than accepting voluntary euthanasia. It is *involuntary* euthanasia—killing people who wish *not* to die— that is morally odious. And nothing in my principle, or in the other pro-euthanasia arguments we have considered, would lead to that.

Let me put the point in a slightly different way. The slippery-slope argument could be formulated to say, 'If voluntary euthanasia is accepted, then we will inevitably be pushed to accepting (some forms of) non-voluntary euthanasia as well.' This is probably true; and it is what we might call the grain of truth in the argument. But, for all the reasons we have considered, there is nothing wrong with accepting (some forms of) non-voluntary euthanasia, and so the concession is not damaging. If, on the other hand, the argument is construed as asserting *more* than that—if the argument is construed as warning we will be pushed to accepting *involuntary* euthanasia—it is not convincing.

The argument from liberty

The debate over the legalization of euthanasia is, in one sense, a simple debate. The slippery-slope argument is *the* outstanding argument against legalized euthanasia; if it fails, it is hard to see where opponents can turn for support. Those who favour legalization also have one principal argument. I will call it the 'argument from liberty'. According to this argument, each dying patient should be free to choose euthanasia, or reject it, as a matter of personal liberty. No one, including the government, has the right to tell another what choice to make. If a dying patient wants euthanasia, that is a private affair; after all, the life belongs to the individual, and so the individual should be the one to decide.

This argument starts from the principle that people should be free to live their own lives as they see fit. But of course the right to liberty is not completely unrestricted. We are not free to murder or rape or steal. It is an interesting theoretical problem to explain why *those* restrictions should be placed on our freedom, while many other restrictions are unacceptable. The classical solution to this problem was provided by Bentham, who observed that in murder, rape, and theft, *we are doing harm to other people*. That, he reasoned, is what makes the difference. So he suggested this principle: People's freedom may be restricted only to prevent them from doing harm to others. Bentham's disciple John Stuart Mill gave this principle its most elegant expression when he wrote:

the sole end for which mankind are warranted, individually or collectively, in interfering with the liberty of action of any of their number, is self-protection. The only purpose for which power can be rightfully exercised over any member of a civilized community, against his will, is to prevent harm to others. His own good, physical or moral, is not a sufficient warrant . . . Over himself, over his own body and mind, the individual is sovereign.

With apologies to Bentham, I will call this 'Mill's Principle'.

There are two general classes of interferences that Mill's Principle would prohibit. First, we cannot force a person to conform to our ideas of right and wrong so long as that person is not harming others. Take sexual promiscuity, for example. Many people think that sexually promiscuous behaviour is immoral. The implication of Mill's Principle is that, even if it were immoral, we have no business trying to force people to stop behaving that way; for so long as they harm no one, it is no one else's business what they do in private. It is important to notice that this argument does *not* depend on the assumption that promiscuity is 'really' all right. It simply does not matter, so far as this argument is concerned, whether it is moral or immoral. All that matters is whether harm is done to other people.

Second, if Mill's Principle is correct, then we may not interfere with a person's actions 'for his own good'. We may think people are behaving foolishly, for example, if they invest their money in a highly speculative stock. And suppose they are. The point is that, if it is *their* money and only they will be hurt by it, then it is their business and we have no right to interfere. We might have the right to *advise* them against the investment, and urge them not to make it, but in the end it is their decision and not ours. The same goes for other, similar cases. If someone is feeling poorly, we may advise or urge a visit to a doctor, but we have no right to force this on a person, even 'for his own good'. It is one's own health, and, as Mill put it, 'Over himself, over his own mind and body, the individual is sovereign.' (Mill excluded children and mental incompetents from the scope of this rule on the grounds that they are incapable of making rational choices concerning their own interests.)

If Mill's Principle is correct, a terminal patient who wishes to end his or her life rather than continue suffering has the right to do so. We may not prohibit it, either on the grounds that we think it immoral, or on the grounds that we are acting for the patient's own good. We may advise and urge the patient against it, but that is all.

However, this only establishes a right to *suicide* in such cases. A further, additional step is required to reach the conclusion that a third party may kill the patient. It is, however, easy to provide the extra step in the argument. Mill's Principle is intended to cover not only the behaviour of individuals acting alone but of groups of individuals who voluntarily agree to act together. Sexual alliances, for example, do not involve individuals acting alone but groups of two or more. The relevant question is: Does their conduct affect anyone other than themselves, the 'consenting adults' who are involved in the affair? If not, others have no right to interfere. An act of euthanasia, in which the patient requests a lethal drug and the doctor provides it, is a 'private affair' in this sense; those participating are 'consenting adults', and no one else's interests need be involved. Therefore, if we are to respect the right to liberty of dying patients, we must respect their right to enter into euthanasia agreements with their doctors, or with any other competent adults willing to help them.

The same argument can be made to apply to patients in irreversible coma, or to patients who have become permanently incompetent, in the following way. Of course patients in irreversible coma are not able to request that they be killed or allowed to die. Nevertheless, they may leave instructions beforehand that if their condition becomes hopeless, they are to be killed or allowed to die. A number of agencies, including medical societies, have encouraged patients to leave such instructions and have designed forms for this purpose. For example, since 1973 the Connecticut State Medical Society has endorsed a 'background statement' to be signed by patients, which includes a sentence binding doctors not to postpone death when matters have become hopeless: 'I value life and the dignity of life, so that I am not asking that my life be taken, but that my life not be unreasonably prolonged or the dignity of life destroyed.' Many other medical groups have adopted such guidelines, and in some States the law has taken favourable notice of them. Following Mill's Principle, we could say that the right of patients to leave such instructions is just one implication of their right to control their own affairs, regardless of whether other people think their decisions are right or wrong or wise or foolish.

How to legalize euthanasia

Opposition to the legalization of euthanasia comes from those who believe it is immoral, from those who fear the consequences of legalization, and from those who believe that, although it may be a fine idea in theory, in practice it is impossible to devise any workable laws to accommodate euthanasia. This last point is important. If we wanted to legalize euthanasia, exactly how could we go about doing it? It is not enough that one defend legalization 'in theory'; there must be some *specific* legal procedure that one supports.

When we look at the proposals championed by the leading pro-euthanasia organizations, what we find is not encouraging. The British Euthanasia Society, for example, once suggested this procedure: The patient, who must be over twenty-one and 'suffering from a disease involving severe pain and of an incurable and fatal character', must submit an application, accompanied by two medical certificates signed by doctors, to a special 'Euthanasia Referee' who will then conduct an interview with the patient. If the Referee is satisfied with the results of the interview, he issues a euthanasia permit and the patient may be killed seven days after receipt of the permit in the presence of an official witness.

The Euthanasia Society of America proposed an even more cumbersome procedure. The patient, 'suffering from severe physical pain caused by a disease for which no remedy affording lasting relief or recovery is at the time known to medical science', must petition for euthanasia in the presence of two witnesses, and file the petition, along with a doctor's certificate, with the court. The court will then appoint a committee of three people, including at least two physicians, who will investigate the case and then report back to the court. Then, if the court is satisfied, it will grant the request, which must then be carried out in the presence of at least two members of the committee.

The problem with these proposals is, obviously, that they are so elaborate, and take so much time, that they are hardly conducive to the 'quick and easy death' that is the whole point of euthanasia. Think of Stewart Alsop's room-mate Jack trying to invoke these procedures—while he was probably capable of making a rational request for death, going through all this would have been a terrible ordeal. And anyway, by the time he could go through it all, he might already be dead. As the American lawyer Yale Kamisar remarks, 'the legal machinery is so drawn-out, so complex, so formal and so tedious as to offer the patient far too little solace'. On the other hand, if the procedures are simplified, the danger is that too few safeguards will be provided against unnecessary killings. Thus, opponents of legalization such as Kamisar argue that proponents are pursuing an impossible goal; we cannot devise procedures which *both* (1) provide sufficient protection against abuse and mistake, and (2) provide a quick and easy death.

I wish to make a suggestion concerning how euthanasia might be legalized that is very different from the above proposals, and which may avoid these problems. However, before I can make this suggestion, I need to outline some elementary points about Anglo-Saxon law.

Individuals charged with a crime have no obligation to prove their innocence. The burden of proof is on the prosecution, and the defence may consist entirely in pointing out that the prosecution has not decisively proven guilt. If the prosecution has not discharged its obligation to prove guilt, the jury's duty is to acquit the defendant.

However, if the prosecution does establish a strong case, a more active defence is required. Then there are two options available. The defendant may deny having done the criminal act in question, and offer evidence that he did not do it. Or, while admitting to the act, the defendant may nevertheless argue that he should not be punished for it.

There are two legally accepted ways of arguing that a person should not be punished for an act even while admitting that the act is prohibited by law and that the person did it. First, an *excuse* may be offered, such as insanity, coercion, ignorance of fact, unavoidable accident, and so on. If it can be shown that the defendant was insane when the crime was committed or that he was coerced into doing it or that it was an unavoidable accident, then the defendant may be acquitted. Second, a *justification* may be offered. A plea of self-defence against a charge of murder is an example of a justification. The technical difference between excuses and justifications need not concern us here.

(I am also ignoring, as irrelevant to present purposes, the following complication: a defence may be offered 'in the alternative', that is, the defendant may offer an excuse or justification without admitting he did the act. This is sometimes jokingly referred to by lawyers as the defence 'I didn't do it, but anyway it was an accident.' The point seems to be that a defendant should be able to use one defence without forfeiting another.)

Here is an example to illustrate these points. Suppose you are charged with murdering a man, and the prosecution can make a strong case that you did in fact kill the victim. You might respond by trying to show that you did *not* kill him—you might present evidence that you were in another city when the crime took place, for example. Or you might admit that you killed him, and then have your lawyers argue that you were insane or that the killing was a tragic accident for which you are blameless or that you had to kill him in self-defence. If any of these claims can be made out, then you should be off the hook.

When such a defence is offered, the burden may be on the defence, and not the prosecution, to adduce evidence that the facts alleged are true. (Initially, the prosecution does not have to prove that the killing was *not* in self-defence; instead the defence must offer reasons to show that it *was*. The prosecution will then try to rebut the defence's evidence.) Thus it is not quite accurate to say that in our legal system the burden of proof is always on the prosecution. When an excuse or justification is offered, *some* of the burden will shift to the defence.

Now, my suggestion for legalizing euthanasia is that a plea of mercy-killing be acceptable as a defence against a charge of homicide in much the same way that a plea of self-defence is acceptable. When people plead self-defence, it is up to them to offer evidence that their own lives were threatened and that the only way of fending off the threat was by killing the attacker first. Under my proposal, someone charged with homicide, in any of the varieties this charge may take, could plead mercy-killing; and then, if it could be shown that the victim while competent requested death, and that the victim was suffering from a painful terminal illness, the defendant would also be acquitted.

Under this proposal no one would be 'authorized' to decide when a patient should be killed any more than people are 'authorized' to decide when someone may be killed in self-defence. There are no committees to be established within which people cast votes for which they are ultimately not legally accountable; people who choose to mercy-kill bear full legal responsibility, as individuals, for their actions. In practice, this would mean that anyone contemplating mercy-killing would have to be very sure that there is independent evidence to confirm the patient's condition and desire to die; for otherwise one might not be able to make out a defence in a court of law—if it should come to that—and one would be legally liable for homicide. This evidence would most naturally take the form of independent medical testimony that the patient was dying painfully, testimony from neutral parties that the patient did make a serious and reasonable request for death, and so on. It should not be thought that this sort of evidence is impossibly difficult to obtain or assess: in fact, it *is* available in many of the actual cases cited in this book, and actual judges and juries have been persuaded by it to go easy on actual defendants.

The proposals of the British and American euthanasia societies were unworkably cumbersome because they attempted to specify procedures such that, if they were followed, no one involved would be legally liable for the killing. Thus the procedures had to be sufficiently detailed to ensure against carelessness and abuse. My proposal avoids the cumbersome and time-consuming aspects of the earlier proposals by not attempting to do this. The safeguard against careless mistake and abuse is simply that the one who kills is accountable for his act. This may be thought unacceptable by some advocates of euthanasia on the grounds that it is self-defeating—the fear of prosecution would deter people from engaging in euthanasia, and thus make it impossible for the dying to obtain relief. There is something to this, but not enough to render my proposal pointless. After all, numerous instances of mercy-killing already take place—I have mentioned some of them—in a legal climate that provides *no* official defence for the act. If euthanasia were recognized as a defence, there would be no fewer, and surely more, such cases. And I see no better means of legalization.

If this proposal were adopted, it would *not* mean that every time euthanasia was performed a court trial would follow. In clear cases of self-defence, prosecutors do not bring charges. Why should they? It would be a pointless waste of time; and, moreover, it would constitute harassment of the accused, for which they could be disciplined by the court. Similarly, in clear cases of mercy-killing, where there is no doubt about the patient's hopeless condition or desire to die, charges would not be brought for the same reasons. It is possible, of course, that 'right-to-life' groups might bring pressure for prosecutions, as they now bring pressure for legal action in other sorts of cases, and this might increase the number of charges brought. Even so, we could still expect that the number of actual prosecutions would be well below the number of possible prosecutions.

Thus, under this proposal, the need to write complicated legislation permitting euthanasia is bypassed. The problems of devising procedures do not arise. We would rely on the good sense of judges and juries to separate the cases of justifiable euthanasia from the cases of unjustifiable murder, just as we already rely on them to separate the cases of insanity and self-defence and coercion. In fact, what would happen in court under this proposal is very much like what often happens now. Many juries are already functioning as though mercy-killing *were* an acceptable defence: when faced with genuine mercy-killers, they refuse to convict. The main consequence of my proposal would be to sanction officially what these juries already do.

NOTES ON SOURCES

Footnotes and references clutter a text, often making it ugly and unpleasant to read. The style common in scientific work—references like '[Adams, Brown, Callahan, and Dippitty 1972, II, 361]' scattered through otherwise readable paragraphs—is especially distracting, and as printing has become more expensive this kind of ugly but cheap device has been tried even in the humanities. Popular writing avoids such intrusions, with good reason. But in scholarly books they seem necessary, both to keep the writer honest and to allow readers to find additional information. I say only that they 'seem' necessary because, at least in a book like this, it is rare for a reader actually to track down a reference.

Here I have tried to have it both ways. The text itself contains no footnotes and no references other than names and titles that seemed natural to mention as part of the narrative. Honesty and the reader's curiosity are served, however, by the following account of my sources. I believe this is a satisfactory substitute for the usual scholarly apparatus, and it has the advantage of not disfiguring the text.

General Acknowledgments

I am grateful to Nicola Bion of Oxford University Press for her patient and helpful editorial work. In addition I would like to acknowledge three other general debts that are especially important.

When I first began to think about the question of why killing people is wrong, I assumed, as most people do, that there is nothing wrong with killing non-human animals. So I thought that an adequate theory would explain both why killing people is wrong *and* why killing non-humans is all right. This assumption proved to be a discouraging barrier to progress, for every plausible account I could discover had the unwelcome consequence that killing (at least some) non-humans *was* morally objectionable. Reading the works of Peter Singer jarred me loose from this assumption, and convinced me that it is a mere prejudice. What I say about non-humans owes a lot to him, even if he does not agree with the details of the view I defend. Singer also read, and made several helpful comments on, the penultimate draft of this book.

My account of why it is bad to die differs in some important ways from Thomas Nagel's account in his essay 'Death', in *Mortal Questions*

(Cambridge, 1979). Nevertheless, I have learned a great deal from this short paper, which I consider to be one of the best works of moral philosophy to have appeared in recent years.

Finally, my deepest debt is to William Ruddick, a former colleague at New York University. I have learned so much from him, in conversations over a period of years, that I am often uncertain which ideas are mine and which are his. He convinced me that it might be worth while to investigate the distinction between being alive and having a life. There must be many pages where I am just elaborating things he said.

None of the chapters in this book is a straight reprint of anything I have published before. However, I have felt free to incorporate arguments and examples that have appeared in various essays I have written during the past decade. Therefore, the reader will find scattered throughout the book bits and pieces of the following previously published papers: 'Euthanasia, Killing, and Letting Die', *Ethical Issues Relating to Life and Death*, edited by John Ladd (Oxford, 1979); 'Killing and Starving to Death', *Philosophy*, Vol. 54 (1979); 'Euthanasia', *Matters of Life and Death*, edited by Tom Regan (New York, 1980); 'When Does a Person Die?', *Alabama Journal of Medical Sciences*, Vol. 17 (1980); 'More Impertinent Distinctions', *Biomedical Ethics*, edited by Thomas Mappes and Jane Zembaty (New York, 1981); 'Reasoning about Killing and Letting Die', *Southern Journal of Philosophy*, Vol. 19 (1981); 'Barney Clark's Key', *Hastings Center Report* (April 1983); 'Do Animals Have a Right to Life?', *Ethics and Animals*, edited by Harlan B. Miller and William H. Williams (Clifton, NJ, 1983); 'The Sanctity of Life', *Bioethics Reviews 1983*, edited by James Humber and Robert Almeder (Clifton, NJ, 1983); and 'Euthanasia and the Physician's Professional Commitments', *Southern Journal of Philosophy*, Vol. 22 (1984).

Introduction

1 The quotation from Herodotus is from his *History*, translated by George Rawlinson and excerpted in John Ladd, ed., *Ethical Relativism* (Belmont, Ca., 1973), p. 12.

1 The Western tradition

7-19 For information on the history of Western attitudes towards killing, see Edward Westermarck, *The Origin and Development of the Moral Ideas*, 2 vols (London, 1906–1908), and W. E. H. Lecky, *History of European Morals*, 2 vols (New York, 1919). My own thoughts about the relevance of this history were first prompted by some remarks towards the end of Peter Singer's essay 'Unsanctifying Human Life', in John Ladd, ed., *Ethical Issues Relating to Life and Death* (Oxford, 1979).

8-9 The quotations from Seneca are from *De Ira* i, 15, and the 58th Letter to Lucilius. The 'smoky room' passage from Epictetus is found in his *Dissertations*, I. IX, 16.

10, 13 The biblical passages quoted are from Matthew 5:39 and 43–4, and Genesis 1:26.

10 The quotation from Tertullian is from *De Corona*, 11. The quotation from Westermarck's *Christianity and Morals* (1939) may be found on p. 239.

12–14 All the quotations from St Thomas Aquinas are from two sources: *Summa Theologica*, II, II, Q. 64, Art. 6; and *Summa Contra Gentiles*, III, II, 112.

13–14 Kant's remarks about animals are in his *Lectures on Ethics*, translated by Louis Infield (New York, 1963), pp. 239–40.

17 The quotation from Maimonides is from *Mishneh Torah: The Book of Judges*, 'Law of Mourning', 4:5.

17 The historical survey of non-Western attitudes to euthanasia is Raanan Gillon, 'Suicide and Voluntary Euthanasia: Historical Perspective', in A. B. Downing, ed., *Euthanasia and the Right to Death* (Los Angeles, 1969).

18 The quotation from Thomas More is from his *Utopia*, Book II (1516); the one from Francis Bacon is from his *New Atlantis* (1626).

2 The sanctity of life

20 The quotation about the Jain monks is from Ninian Smart, *The Religious Experience of Mankind* (London, 1971), p. 106. For a Buddhist statement concerning plant life, see *The Buddha's Philosophy of Man: Early Indian Buddhist Dialogues*, edited by Trevor King (London, 1981), pp. 8–33.

21–2 Albert Schweitzer's reflections on 'reverence for life' are nicely summarized in his *Civilization and Ethics*, translated by John Naish and conveniently excerpted in *Animal Rights and Human Obligations*, edited by Tom Regan and Peter Singer (Englewood Cliffs, NJ, 1976).

22 The 8-volume *Encyclopedia of Philosophy*, a marvellous reference work, was edited by Paul Edwards and published in 1967. Schweitzer's name does not appear in the index.

23 The quotation from St Augustine is from *The Catholic and Manichaean Ways of Life*, translated by D. A. Gallagher and I. J. Gallagher (Boston, 1966), p. 102.

27–8 The discussion of the 'point' of moral rules, with the example of the novice driver, owes much to R. M. Hare's discussion in Chapter 4 of *The Language of Morals* (Oxford, 1952).

28–30 An excerpt from the federal courts' consideration of the case of Repouille, including some interesting judicial reflections on mercy-killing, may be found in *Morality and the Law*, edited by Richard Wasserstrom (Belmont, Ca., 1971).

31–2 The two articles about letting defective infants die are: Anthony

Shaw, 'Dilemmas of "Informed Consent" in Children', *New England Journal of Medicine*, Vol. 289 (1973), pp. 885–90; and Raymond S. Duff and A. G. M. Campbell, 'Moral and Ethical Dilemmas in the Special-Care Nursery', same issue of same journal, pp. 890–4.

32–3 The case of Matthew Donnelly is reported in Robert M. Veatch, *Case Studies in Medical Ethics* (Cambridge, Mass., 1977), p. 238.

33 The estimate of rhesus monkey intelligence is from H. F. and M. K. Harlow, *Lessons from Animal Behaviour for the Clinician* (London, 1962), Ch. 5.

34 The quotation about hypothermia and the mammalian diving response is from *Newsweek*, 6 February 1984, p. 76.

34–5 The report concerning baboons in the London Zoo is from Floyd L. Ruch and Philip G. Zimbado, *Psychology in Life*, 8th edition (Glenview, Ill., 1967), p. 539.

37–8 On the relation of Christian teaching to reason in ethics, see St Thomas Aquinas, *Summa Theologica*, Ia–2ae, xix, 6, and Daniel C. Maguire, 'A Catholic View of Mercy Killing', in *Beneficent Euthanasia*, edited by Marvin Kohl (Buffalo, NY, 1975).

3 Death and evil

40, 44 The quotation from Epicurus are from his *Letter to Menoecus*, Whitney J. Oates, ed., *The Stoic and Epicurean Philosophers* (New York, 1940), pp. 30–1. In the same volume compare Lucretius, 'On the Nature of Things', pp. 870ff. and 898ff. Montaigne's version of the argument is given in his essay 'That to Philosophize is to Learn How to Die', *The Complete Essays of Montaigne*, translated by Donald Frame (Stanford, 1948), pp. 56–67.

41–3 On the relations between the concepts of death, dying, and being dead, see Ninian Smart, 'Philosophical Concepts of Death', in Arnold Toynbee, *et al.*, *Man's Concern with Death* (New York, 1968).

45–8 On the implications of hedonism for the morality of killing, see Richard G. Henson, 'Utilitarianism and the Wrongness of Killing', *Philosophical Review*, Vol. 81 (1971), pp. 320–37.

46–7 Dr Wonmug was, in the comics, the scientist who invented the time machine that brought Alley Oop to the twentieth century. His name is derived, by translation and partial homonym, from 'Einstein'.

52–3 The case of Jimmie R. is presented in Oliver Sacks, 'The Lost Mariner', *New York Review of Books*, 16 February 1984, pp. 14 ff.

54 For the Texas burn case, see 'A Demand to Die', *Hastings Center Report*, June 1975, and 'Whatever Happened to Donald C.?', *Medical Humanities Report* (Michigan State University), Spring 1982.

56–7 Aristotle discusses the question of whether a person can be harmed after death at 1100a–1101a of the *Nicomachean Ethics*. Foot's remarks about Nietzsche are from her article 'Immoralist', *New York Review of Books*, 17 February 1966, p. 8.

57 Edward Johnson's discussion of whether mental complexity matters is in his paper 'Life, Death, and Animals', in *Ethics and Animals*, edited by Harlan B. Miller and William H. Williams (Clifton, NJ, 1983).

4 'Innocent Humans'

For additional information about the case of Baby Jane Doe, including excerpts from Dr Koop's testimony, see Peter Singer and Helga Kuhse, 'The Future of Baby Doe', *New York Review of Books*, 1 March 1984, pp. 17 ff; and *Should the Baby Live? The Problem of Handicapped Infants* by the same authors (Oxford, 1985).

63 The quotation from Patrick Buchanan is from the *Birmingham News*, 16 November 1983, p. 11a.

69 The quotations from Kelly and Sullivan are from Gerald Kelly, SJ, 'The Duty of Using Artificial Means of Preserving Life', *Theological Studies* ll (1950); and Joseph V. Sullivan, 'The Immorality of Euthanasia', in Marvin Kohl, ed., *Beneficient Euthanasia* (Buffalo, NY, 1975).

73 The *locus classicus* of the animal-rights discussion is Peter Singer, *Animal Liberation* (New York, 1975). Tom Regan's *The Case for Animal Rights* (Berkeley, 1983) is the fullest and most recent treatment. On the question of whether extraterrestrials might have equal rights, see Eando Binder, 'The Teacher From Mars', in *My Best Science Fiction Story*, edited by Leo Marguiles and Oscar J. Friend (New York, 1949).

74–6 Nozick's views about the importance of being human are expounded in his 'About Mammals and People', *New York Times Book Review*, 27 November 1983.

5 Suicide and euthanasia

79, 84 The quotations from Barney Clark's doctors are taken from Associated Press reports widely carried in newspapers, for example in the Memphis, Tennessee *Commercial Appeal*, 5 December 1982, p. c2.

81 Beauchamp's definition of suicide is taken from his essay 'Suicide', in *Matters of Life and Death*, edited by Tom Regan (New York, 1980), p. 77.

81 The case of Captain Oates is discussed by R. F. Holland in 'Suicide', *Talk of God: Royal Institute of Philosophy Lectures Volume II* (London, 1969). The quotation from Scott is from *Scott's Last Expedition* (London, 1935), Vol. i, p. 462; quoted by Holland. Holland is an example of a philosopher who takes the second of the two approaches to explaining what suicide is.

6 Debunking irrelevant distinctions

88, 90–1 The 1973 American Medical Association policy statement, 'The

Physician and the Dying Patient', was distributed by the AMA in a reproduced typescript, available upon request from their central office. The 1982 statement, 'Principles of Medical Ethics', was published by them in *Current Opinions of the Judicial Council of the American Medical Association* (1982).

92 Anthony Kenny's 'The History of Intention in Ethics', included in his book *The Anatomy of the Soul* (Oxford, 1973), is an excellent treatment of the subject to which I am indebted.

92 The quotations from Pascal is from the *Provincial Letters*, No. 7; quoted in Kenny, *The Anatomy of the Soul*, p. 140.

93 The quotation from Thomas D. Sullivan is from 'Active and Passive Euthanasia: An Impertinent Distinction?', *Human Life Review*, Vol. 3 (1977).

95–7 The quotations from Paul Ramsey are from *The Patient as Person* (New Haven, Conn., 1970), pp. 115–16.

98 Kelly's definitions of ordinary and extraordinary means are in his *Medico-Moral Problems* (Catholic Hospital Association, 1958), p. 129. Ramsey, in *The Patient as Person*, p. 122, refers to this with approval as 'the standard definition'.

100–2 For the details of the Quinlan case, see Joseph and Julia Quinlan, *Karen Ann: The Quinlans Tell Their Story* (New York, 1977). The Catholic scholar who made the angry remark about the nuns was Andrew Greely, in his review of this book in the *New York Times Book Review*, 9 October 1977, pp. 10–11.

102–3 On the Herbert and Conroy cases, see 'Nonfeeding: Lawful killing in CA, Homicide in NJ', by George J. Annas, *Hastings Center Report*, Vol. 13 (December 1983). This article includes the citations for the court opinions quoted in the text.

7 Active and passive euthanasia

106 Socrates' remark about letting patients die is from Plato's *Republic*, III, 407e.

109 Dr Shaw's description of what happens when an infant is allowed to starve is from his article 'Doctor, Do We Have a Choice?', *New York Times Magazine*, 30 January 1972, pp. 44–54.

115 Ramsey endorses the argument that, in passive euthanasia, one is not the cause of death, on p. 151 of *The Patient as Person*.

115 The quotation from Dr Elkinton is from 'The Dying Patient, the Doctor, and the Law', *Villanova Law Review*, Vol. 13 (1968) p. 743.

120 Roger Rigterink's discussion of the relation between the physician's professional commitments and the active/passive distinction is in his essay 'On Why Doctors Need to Practice Passive Rather than Active Euthanasia', *Southern Journal of Philosophy*, Vol. 22 (1984).

122 Thomson's objection to the Bare Difference Argument is from her 'Killing, Letting Die, and the Trolley Problem', *Monist*, Vol. 59 (1976), p. 204.

127 Philippa Foot's remarks, which I construe as defending a version of the Compromise View, are from her 'Active Euthanasia with Parental Consent: Commentary', *Hastings Center Report*, Vol. 9 (1979), pp. 20–1.

8 Further reflections on killing and letting die

129 For an account of the difficulties of getting reliable information about world hunger—a little out of date now, but still quite helpful—see Nick Eberstadt, 'Myths of the Food Crisis', *New York Review of Books*, 19 February 1976, pp. 32–7.

130 The quotation from Philippa Foot about letting people in India and Africa starve is from her 'The Problem of Abortion and the Doctrine of the Double Effect', *Oxford Review*, No. 5 (1967).

130–1 Nagel's remarks about intuitions and arguments are from the Preface to his *Mortal Questions*.

131 Moore's defence of common sense against the absurd conclusions of the metaphysicians may be found in his *Philosophical Papers* (London, 1959).

132 Ross's *The Right and the Good* was published in Oxford in 1930.

132 J. J. C. Smart's *Outline of a System of Utilitarian Ethics*, originally published as a separate book, is included in *Utilitarianism: For and Against* by Smart and Bernard Williams (Cambridge, 1973).

133 The quotations from Rawls are from his *A Theory of Justice* (Cambridge, Mass., 1971), Ch. I, section 9. An earlier version of his thoughts on this matter are to be found in his 'Outline of a Decision Procedure for Ethics', *Philosophical Review*, Vol. 60 (1951).

134–9 At several points in the Jack Palance argument, I am indebted to Peter Singer's 'Famine, Affluence, and Morality', *Philosophy and Public Affairs*, Vol. 1 (1972)—especially for what he says about the irrelevance of the location of the dying.

136 All quotations from Richard Trammell are from his 'Saving Life and Taking Life', *Journal of Philosophy*, Vol. 72 (1975).

141–2 On p. 151 of *The Patient as Person* Paul Ramsey suggests that the morally important difference between killing and letting die is that, in the latter, one 'does nothing'—thus he suggests the second of the three counter-arguments considered on p. 141–2.

146 Dinello's example is from his essay 'On Killing and Letting Die', *Analysis*, Vol. 31 (1971), pp. 85–6.

148–9 The quotation from Hume is from the first appendix to *An Inquiry Concerning the Principles of Morals*, first published in 1751.

9 The morality of euthanasia

151 The first quotation is from Franz J. Ingelfinger, 'Bedside Ethics for the Hopeless Case', *New England Journal of Medicine*, Vol. 289 (1973), p. 914.

152 Joseph Fletcher's comments about the death of Jonathan Swift may be found in Fletcher's book *Morals and Medicine* (Boston, 1960), p. 174.

153 The quotation about Jack is from Stewart Alsop, 'The Right to Die With Dignity', *Good Housekeeping*, August 1974, pp. 69, 130.

158 Kant's presentation of the 'Categorical Imperative' may be found in his *Foundations of the Metaphysics of Morals* (1785); the best translation is the Liberal Arts Press version by Lewis White Beck (Indianapolis, 1959).

159 The example of the lorry driver is from R. M. Hare, 'Euthanasia: A Christian View', *Philosophic Exchange* (Brockport, NY) II:I (1975), p. 45.

161 Humphrey Primatt's words are from his *A Dissertation on the Duty of Mercy and the Sin of Cruelty to Brute Animals* (London, 1776), p. 65.

162 The American Humanist Association's 'Plea for Beneficent Euthanasia' is in the *Humanist* for July/August 1974.

162-3 Daniel Maguire's views are given in his book *Death by Choice* (New York, 1975) and in an article, 'A Catholic View of Mercy Killing', in *Beneficent Euthanasia*, edited by Marvin Kohl, (Buffalo, NY, 1975). The quotation in the text is from p. 36 of the latter work.

163 Hume's demolition of the argument that only God may decide the length of a life is in his essay 'Of Suicide', first published posthumously in 1784. It is conveniently reprinted in Alasdair MacIntyre, ed., *Hume's Ethical Writings* (New York, 1965).

164 Bishop Sullivan's words about the opportunities provided by suffering are contained in his essay 'The Immorality of Euthanasia', in Kohl, ed., *Beneficent Euthanasia*, p. 14.

10 Legalizing euthanasia

169 Information about some of the court cases is taken from Press reports: *Miami News*, 3 July 1973, p. 3-A (Weskin, Jones, Eldridge); *New York Times*, 26 December 1971, p. 47 (Price); *Miami Herald*, 26 October 1974, p. 11-A (Wise).

169 The quotation concerning the lawyer who electrocuted his six-month-old son is from Yale Kamisar, 'Some Non-Religious Views Against Proposed Mercy-Killing Legislation', *Minnesota Law Review*, Vol. 6 (1958), p. 1022.

171-2 Sullivan's version of the slippery-slope argument is from 'The Immorality of Euthanasia', as previously cited, p. 24. The quotation from Philippa Foot on the same subject is from her essay 'Euthanasia', *Philosophy and Public Affairs*, Vol. 6 (1977), pp. 111-12.

175-8 The quotations from Telford Taylor and Lucy Dawidowicz about the Nazis are from their contributions to a Special Supplement of the *Hastings Center Report*, Vol. 6 (1976), 'Biomedical Ethics and the Shadow of Nazism'. I am generally indebted to Dawidowicz for much that I say on this subject. Leo Alexander's article 'Medical Science Under Dictatorship' appeared in the *New England Journal of Medicine*, Vol. 241 (1949), pp. 39–47.

178-80 On the question of whether proponents of legalization are really after more than just legalized *voluntary* euthanasia, see the article by Yale Kamisar cited above.

180 The quotation from John Stuart Mill setting out the principle of liberty is from Mill's *On Liberty* (1859), Ch. 1.

183 The quotation from Yale Kamisar is from 'Euthanasia Legislation: Some Non-Religious Objections', in *Euthanasia and the Right to Death*, edited by A. B. Downing (London, 1969), p. 89.

INDEX

OXFORD

MORE OXFORD PAPERBACKS

Details of a selection of other books follow. A complete list of Oxford Paperbacks, including The World's Classics, Twentieth-Century Classics, OPUS, Past Masters, Oxford Authors, Oxford Shakespeare, and Oxford Paperback Reference, is available in the UK from the General Publicity Department, Oxford University Press (JH), Walton Street, Oxford OX2 6DP.

In the USA, complete lists are available from the Paperbacks Marketing Manager, Oxford University Press, 200 Madison Avenue, New York, NY 10016.

Oxford Paperbacks are available from all good bookshops. In case of difficulty, customers in the UK can order direct from Oxford University Press Bookshop, 116 High Street, Oxford, Freepost, OX1 4BR, enclosing full payment. Please add 10 per cent of published price for postage and packing.

MORAL DILEMMAS IN MODERN MEDICINE

Edited by Michael Lockwood

Test-tube babies, surrogate mothers, the prescribing of contraceptive pills to girls under sixteen—these are some of the moral dilemmas in medicine that have recently hit the headlines, and will continue to do so for some time. Mary Warnock, Bernard Williams, and R. M. Hare are among those who tackle the ethical problems in modern medical practice from the standpoints of philosophy, medicine, and the law. Other contributors are: Michael Lockwood, Ian Kennedy, J. A. Muir Gray, Raanan Gillon, and Roger Higgs.

SHOULD THE BABY LIVE?

The Problem of Handicapped Infants

Helga Kuhse and Peter Singer

This book concerns itself with both the practical and philosophical issues of allowing certain handicapped babies to die. The authors' conclusions are not absolutist in any direction: rather they believe that careful rational examination of the admittedly complex issues—which they present clearly and by way of actual examples—can lead to responsible decisions of different kinds in different cases. *Studies in Bioethics*

THE REPRODUCTION REVOLUTION

New Ways of Making Babies

Peter Singer and Deane Wells

'it is a delight to welcome *The Reproduction Revolution* a lucid, sensitive, up-do-date account of just what has been achieved, what has *not* been achieved, and what might be achieved in applying bioscience to human procreation . . . the book is far and away the clearest guide yet published to the techniques of artificial fertilisation, surrogate motherhood and sex selection; futuristic possibilities such as cloning and genetic manipulation; and the ethical issues which are with us today or likely to arise in the future . . . this must be one of the best buys of the year'   *New Society*

'more valuable than hordes of specialist committees are books like this which discuss the issues, opening them up for the interested but ethically inexpert'   *Hospital Doctor*

LAW AND MORALS

Warnock, Gillick, and Beyond

Simon Lee

This highly topical book examines the relationship between law and morals, and relates its findings to such issues of current debate as discrimination, abortion, contraception for teenagers, experiments on embryos, and surrogate motherhood. It exposes popular misconceptions, and asks us to go beyond outdated ethical arguments to a new realization that by separating our moral from our factual disagreements, society may yet come to a consensus on some of its most intractable questions.

'The outstanding virtue of this book is the brevity with which it deals with such a substantial list of subjects. Nobody can pretend to find it too long or too difficult, though it does make demands and stimulate questions. Even for those who disagree with its conclusions, it is important.'
Catholic Herald

'a marvellous book' *New Society*

'This is an excellent and thought-provoking book.' *Universe*

THE MORAL STATUS OF ANIMALS

Stephen R. L. Clark

Most of us exploit animals for our own purposes. The Moral status of animals has long been a subject of heated debate. According to the great philosophers, morality has nothing to say about our relations with non-humans. Modern liberals, though have allowed that animals should at least be spared unnecessary pain.

In his lively and controversial book Stephen Clark argues that this liberal principle is powerful enough in itself to require most of us to be vegetarian. He discusses the arguments and rationalizations offered in defence of our behaviour in farms, laboratories, and at home, and reveals their roots in neurotic fantasy.

'an erudite, intriguing, provocative, disturbing book which deserves close attention' *Month*

FREEDOM AND REASON

R. M. Hare

'What I think about morals is up to me.' 'You can't think just what you like about moral questions.' Mr. Hare's aim is to resolve this antinomy by showing how, when thinking morally, a man can be both free and rational.

Topics touched on include: 'ought' and 'can' and the problem of moral weakness; the place of imagination in moral thinking; ideals, moral and aesthetic; and the rational basis of toleration. The book ends with a more detailed practical illustration of moral reasoning, drawn from arguments about our attitude to racial conflicts.

THE LANGUAGE OF MORALS

R. M. Hare

'It is indeed the accuracy, the thoroughness of this analysis that makes *The Language of Morals* by far the best introduction to moral philosophy to appear for many years.' *New Statesman*

'This then is a book upon which all serious students of moral philosophy—dons as well as undergraduates—will have to ponder.' *Mind*

'It is a perceptive contribution toward the solution of many fundamental problems of ethics.' *Philosophical Review*

MORAL PHILOSOPHY

D. D. Raphael

Do moral philosophers have anything to say which is useful, let alone comprehensible, to people with more down-to-earth concerns? Professor Raphael would answer 'Yes' on both counts. Unlike most 'introductions' to moral philosophy, this book is written expressly for the beginner. Also, it is not confined to the theory of ethics in any narrow sense, but makes a point of showing the connections between abstract ethics and practical problems.

'It would be difficult to find a clearer introduction to modern moral philosophy.' *Tablet*

An OPUS book

ETHICS SINCE 1900

Mary Warnock

'In this lively and fascinating book Mrs Warnock tells with admirable clarity the story of the development of English moral philosophy in the twentieth century . . . most attractively written, spontaneous, forthright and unfuzzy.' *Times Literary Supplement*

'The book is a classic among handbooks: unpretentious, but very individual, with a vigour and clarity which make it as attractive to read as it is instructive.' *Christian World*

MAN AND MOUSE

Animals in Medical Research

William Paton

Sir William Paton has had more than forty years' experience in medical research. He now presents for the first time for the layman the case for *responsible* animal experiment—a case which rests on the enormous benefits gained for mankind.

'Sir William Paton has written this timely and very readable book to explain why experiments on animals have been done and why they remain essential. Using measured arguments, clearly presented with forceful logic, he discusses their ethical justification, their scientific value and the enormous benefits obtained from them. The opposed views are critically dissected and their misunderstandings and errors explored. His analysis extends from the needs of the community to the care and humanity required of everyone involved in scientific experiments on animals. Britain has a notable history of discoveries in biology and medicine that have depended on studies with animals. This book is a strong and well written defence of the responsibilit of the scientist to help man and other animals by careful experimentation, guided by knowledge and compassion.' *Journal of Royal Society of Medicine*

WHY ARE WE WAITING

An Analysis of Hospital Waiting-lists

John Yates

This book sets out to challenge the British complacency about hospital waiting-lists, and rejects the assumption that a large proportion of British citizens must inevitably have to wait long periods of time for simple surgical procedures.

The book is aimed at two audiences—those within and those outside the NHS. For those outside the NHS it reveals the most enormous variations in the provision and use of resources between the hundreds of health authorities throughout the length and breadth of Britain. For those who work in the Health Service it may not be a popular message because it expresses openly some of the inefficiencies of the current system. In so doing it runs the risk of bringing some criticism to the large number of surgeons and managers who are devoting a lot of time and attention to improving the situation.

UNEMPLOYMENT AND HEALTH

Richard Smith

It is 15 years since unemployment rose above one million in Britain, and yet most health workers and health authorities are only just awakening to the tremendous implications for health. Richard Smith, a doctor and journalist, draws together for the first time in this book the wide range of evidence that shows how unemployment harms health. The evidence comes from a wide range of sources—historical, medical, psychological, political, sociological, statistical, journalistic, and literary. Dr Smith also discusses how we can respond to the implications for health of unemployment and tackles the issue of what the disappearance of employment as we know it may mean for health.

THE PHILOSOPHIES OF SCIENCE:

An Introductory Survey

Second Edition

Rom Harré

The new edition of this survey of scientific thought contains a new chapter in which Dr Harré examines science as a social activity, analysing such problems as funding, and experiments on live animals.

'Harré's *The Philosophies of Science* offers a respectably cool, hard look at scientific throught and its relationship with the great historical schools of philosophy . . . both scholarly and lucid . . . and as good an introduction to the subject as could be wished for.' *Times Literary Supplement*

An OPUS Book

A HISTORICAL INTRODUCTION TO THE PHILOSOPHY OF SCIENCE

Second Edition

John Losee

Since the time of Plato and Aristotle, scientists and philosophers have raised questions about the proper evaluation of scientific interpretations. A *Historical Introduction to the Philosophy of Science* is an exposition of positions that have been held on issues such as the distinction between scientific inquiry and other types of interpretation; the relationship between theories and observation reports; the evaluation of competing theories; and the nature of progress in science. The book makes the philosophy of science accessible to readers who do not have extensive knowledge of formal logic or the history of the sciences.

CORONARY HEART DISEASE:

The Facts

J. P. Shillingford

'For patients and their families this is an excellent, readable book and it has few competitors. Professor Shillingford has produced a book which most doctors would like to have written, and which GPs and hospital doctors can recommend to patients and their families without hesitation. It would not do any harm if doctors read it as well; they might improve their ability to pass on clear advice and information to patients and their families.' *British Book News*

'Nurses should have no hesitation in recommending it to patients. It will reassure those who have suffered heart attacks and play a part in health education.' *Nursing Mirror*

'I recommend this book both to the patient and everyone in contact with him. It is easy to read, full of common sense and simple in its approach to the facts of coronary heart disease.' *Physiotherapy*

ARTHRITIS AND RHEUMATISM

The Facts

J. T. Scott

Introduction by Dorothy Eden

The words 'arthritis' and 'rheumatism' are general terms for a large number of diseases which collectively exact an enormous toll on society, in terms of both individual suffering and economic cost.

This book describes the individual disorders that occur in adults and children in simple but comprehensive terms, together with what is known of their causes and treatment. Rheumatoid arthritis receives special emphasis. The author stresses the measures which the patient him- or herself can take in order to continue functioning and to prevent deformity. An introduction by novelist Dorothy Eden gives the patient's point of view.

'A good introduction to the subject . . . In simplification this book has lost nothing because the material has been so well chosen by a humane specialist.' *Nursing Times*

THE LIMITS OF SCIENCE

Peter Medawar

'[Peter Medawar's] latest and, in my view, most wonderful book . . . (is) so much fun to read that you may fail to recognize, until later, that he is writing seriously on serious matters, doing his best to protect scientific endeavour against damage by people (and governments) who have an insufficient grasp of the importance of the enterprise. He takes up important matters, honestly and in high courage. His book should be read and welcomed by scientists, especially young scientists just starting out, and by a non-scientist public wanting a better understanding of how a scientific mind works in high gear. In short, by just about everyone I can think of.' Lewis Thomas in *Nature*

ARISTOTLE TO ZOOS

A Philosophical Dictionary of Biology

Peter & Jean Medawar

In this book Peter and Jean Medawar have compiled their personal A–Z of the life sciences. In some two hundred short essays on a wide variety of biological topics of general interest they offer both an introduction for the layman and a source of new insight for the specialist. The book provides a blend of fact, literary allusion, historical anecdote, mythical and folk tradition.

'One of the most delightful, and delightfully eccentric, dictionaries I have ever encountered.' *New York Times Book Review*

'beautifully written . . . a thoroughly incisive and level-headed treatment of how practising biological scientists think and what they think about' *Times Higher Education Supplement*

PLUTO'S REPUBLIC

Incorporating The Art of the Soluble and Induction and
Intuition in Scientific Thought

Sir Peter Medawar

What *is* science? What sort of person is a scientist? What kind
of reasoning leads to scientific discovery? These are the central
questions to which Sir Peter constantly returns in these wide-
ranging studies. The answers are often surprising.

'The 1960 winner of the Nobel Prize for Medicine sheds light
on popular misconceptions and *idées fixes* in the field of scientific thought. Valuable explanations of topics we assume we
understand but would be hard pressed to clarify.' *Sunday
Telegraph*

'A definitive edition of Medawar's essays.' Bernad Dixon, *New
Scientist*

MAN AGAINST DISEASE

Preventive Medicine

J. A. Muir Gray

Do governments spend enough time and money in the most
efficient manner on the prevention of sickness? Does the individual devote enough attention to his own good health? Dr.
Muir Gray considers the scope for preventing disease and pre-
mature death in both developed and underdeveloped countries,
from the promotion of child health to the problems of old age.

'This is an excellent book.' *Lancet*

'There can be few people, lay or professional, who would not
derive pleasure and profit from reading it.' *British Book News*